Suffering-Focused Ethics

Defense and Implications

Magnus Vinding

Ratio Ethica

Ratio Ethica, Copenhagen.
Copyright © 2020 Magnus Vinding
Parts of this book have previously been published elsewhere by the author.
ISBN: 9798624910911

Contents

Introduction.. 1

Part I: The Case for Suffering-Focused Ethics

1: Asymmetries Between Happiness and Suffering 13
2: Happiness as the Absence of Suffering 39
3: Creating Happiness at the Price of Suffering Is Wrong 52
4: The Principle of Sympathy for Intense Suffering................ 60
5: A Moral Realist Case for Minimizing Extreme Suffering 75
6: Other Arguments for Focusing on Suffering................... 93
7: Biases Against Focusing on Suffering 111
8: Objections Against Focusing on Suffering 141

Part II: How Can We Best Reduce Suffering?

9: Uncertainty Is Big 185
10: We Should Be Cooperative............................. 205
11: Non-Human Animals and Expansion of the Moral Circle 214
12: Promoting Concern for Suffering........................ 228
13. The Abolitionist Project 239
14: Reducing S-Risks 247
15: Donating to Reduce Suffering 256
16: Researching the Question.............................. 261
17: The Importance of Self-Investment 266
18: What You Can Do 273
Recommended Websites.................................. 277
Acknowledgments 278
Bibliography... 280

Introduction

The problem of suffering is the greatest problem of all. This is my conviction, and why I have set out to write this book, in which I will explore the why and how of reducing suffering.

The core motivation that animates this book derives from a set of related questions widely considered among the deepest, most profound questions we can ask ourselves:

What matters?
What is most valuable in the world?
What is the highest purpose we can pursue?

I have long been obsessed with these questions, and contemplated the many answers people have provided, including the pursuit of happiness, meaning, knowledge, and love. Virtually all such common answers resonate deeply with me, as I suspect they do with most people. Yet ultimately, after a long and resistant process of examination, I have come to view one answer as standing high above all others: the reduction of extreme suffering.

This was very much not the answer I wanted. Yet it is, most sincerely, what I have found. And I suspect most people would in fact, if not agree, then at least strongly sympathize with this view when confronted with real-world cases of extreme suffering. For we can indeed easily fall into the trap of approaching questions concerning value and purpose from a position of abstract philosophizing, quite detached from the reality of extreme suffering. Yet, as philosopher David Pearce notes: "An adequate theory of value should be as true in the gas chambers of Auschwitz as in the philosopher's study."[1] And when we make an effort to consider what it

---

1   Pearce, 2015.

would in fact be like to encounter extreme suffering, it becomes difficult to deny its immense significance and urgency.

If, for instance, we found ourselves walking past a house in which a person is enduring torturous suffering, and if we were in a position to alleviate this suffering at no risk to ourselves, would we not then be hard-pressed to consider anything else more important? Indeed, would saving this person from torment not likely be among the most important things we could ever do? To choose to walk by and pursue other aims instead would seem as ethically wrong as could be. And if we then further imagine a similar situation where we ourselves happen to be the one in a state of extreme suffering, the case for considering the alleviation of such suffering an overriding ethical priority seems even more compelling.

Yet, in our best attempt to derive a rational theory of value and ethics, should it really matter who is enduring the suffering, or how close to us the suffering occurs? Should suffering not be equally worth preventing no matter who is experiencing it and where? If the reduction of extreme suffering is of supreme importance sometimes, such as when we are confronted with it directly, then why not always? After all, we live in a world in which there are always countless beings experiencing unbearable suffering, and in which we can always do much to alleviate such suffering.

0.1 A Demanding Obligation Obscured by Omission Bias?

Pointing to something that can justify creating a world with more rather than less extreme suffering is indeed not easy. For this very reason, it is also not easy to defend not making a considerable effort to reduce such suffering. Imagine, for instance, if we were offered some gain — a hundred dollars, say — at the price that a person will be tortured in the worst imaginable ways for a full hour. Few of us would consider it defensible to accept this deal. Next, imagine a similar case, except now we are asked to *give away* a hundred dollars to prevent a full hour of torture that would otherwise happen.

Intuitively, the latter case seems fundamentally different, and yet the possible outcomes in these two cases are practically identical. Either we are a hundred dollars richer at the price of allowing more extreme suffering in the world, or we are a hundred dollars poorer for the gain of creating a world with less extreme suffering. So if we cannot defend receiving goods to make extreme suffering happen, how can we defend not giving up goods to reduce it when the outcome is virtually the same?[2]

This tendency to view harms caused by acts of omission much more leniently than harms caused by acts of commission has been referred to as the "omission bias".[3] And to the extent we care about creating the best outcomes possible, we should be quite wary of this bias. After all, the suffering caused by an act of omission would be just as bad for the victim as if it were caused by an act of commission. It only seems different *to us*, probably in large part because we can expect to be punished and judged more harshly for acts of commission than for acts of omission. Yet if our primary aim is to create ethically optimal outcomes rather than to gain approval from our peers,[4] we should not view the two anywhere near as differently as we do.[5]

One may, of course, object that it is not realistic to think that we could prevent so much suffering by giving away a mere hundred dollars. Two things can be said in response. First, the main point here is not about the exact amount of extreme suffering prevented, but rather that there is a deep asymmetry in how we view acts of omission and commission respectively. This asymmetry suggests that we are intuitively underestimating how

---

2   A similar thought experiment is found in Moor, 2013.
3   Ritov & Baron, 1990; Spranca et al., 1991. For elaborate arguments against a strong moral distinction between inflicting and failing to prevent harm, see Kagan, 1989, chaps. 3-4; Bennett, 1995.
4   And we are probably self deceived about the degree to which we care about these respective objectives, as argued in Simler & Hanson, 2018.
5   It may be objected that there is a relevant difference in the example above in that money, as well as most other goods, have diminishing marginal value, and hence not giving up some amount of money is not the same as refusing to receive the same amount. While this is true, diminishing marginal value is not a plausible explanation for why we view the two acts in this thought experiment so differently. If it were, we would consider it acceptable to receive the money if only we happened to have a hundred dollars less. Yet we do not, and least of all in the case of a person of average wealth in an affluent country of today. The difference in our evaluation in this thought experiment is probably better explained by the so-called endowment effect: our tendency to ascribe greater value to things because we already own them. Yet while this tendency may help *explain* the difference in our evaluation, it does not help justify it.

important it is to take action to reduce extreme suffering, and by extension, that we underestimate our obligation to do so. Second, while it is not clear how much extreme suffering a hundred dollars can be expected to reduce if spent optimally, it is by no means unthinkable that such a donation could reduce far *more* than a single hour of torturous suffering.[6] This is a deeply humbling proposition.

0.2 The Stakes Are Astronomical

We appear to be living in a unique time in the history of Earth-originating sentient life — the last moments in which such life is bound to a single planet. Provided that technological progress continues at roughly the rate we have seen over the last couple of centuries, human civilization is bound to move into the rest of the solar system within a few centuries.[7] Consequently, the future could contain an astronomical number of sentient beings.

Philosopher Nick Bostrom puts the "lower bound of the number of biological human life-years [that can be sustained] in the future accessible universe" at 10^{34}, and given that human consciousness can be emulated in different substrates, he estimates that the future accessible universe could sustain 10^{60} such life-years.[8] These astronomical numbers are almost impossible to appreciate. The scale of events that have hitherto only taken place on Earth — including extreme suffering — could soon be multiplied by many orders of magnitude.

This renders it critical that we start considering which future outcomes are worth steering toward. For example, can creating extremely happy lives for, say, 99.999999 percent of a population of 10^{32} people justify the creation of lives full of extreme suffering for the rest, i.e. 10^{24} people?

As this question hints, the potentially vast size of a future cosmic population implies that even if we require what may seem a very large amount of happiness to "outweigh" a given amount of extreme suffering, such a high happiness-to-suffering ratio could still justify the creation of

---

6   Some support for this claim is found in the next section and in chapter 15.
7   Vinding, 2017c.
8   Bostrom, 2013, p. 18; 2014a, p. 103.

extreme suffering on a scale far greater than what is physically possible on our planet — torture chambers and Holocausts on a scale many orders of magnitude larger than what Earth could sustain even if it were covered in such horrors. We have to ask ourselves: Can *anything* justify the creation of extreme suffering on such an enormous scale?

If we think so, we would seem to face the problem of evil 2.0. Where the original problem of evil asked why a benevolent being would create so much suffering on Earth, the problem of evil 2.0 would be to answer why a benevolent agent, or set of agents, would allow the creation of *so much more* suffering (in absolute terms). A problem we should contemplate deeply now, before we create such a future.

The importance of thinking these things through is further highlighted by arguments that suggest that space expansion outcomes as happy as the one described above, with a vast majority of beings living very happy lives, are most likely overoptimistic. Political scientist Daniel Deudney and author Phil Torres have argued that such a cosmic population is likely to end up in a state of continual cosmic war.[9] As Phil Torres sums up his analysis:

> [C]olonizing our solar system, galaxy, and beyond will engender a Hobbesian predicament in which all actors are perpetually in fear of being destroyed—that is, when they aren't engaged in devastating wars with their neighbors.[10]

Thus, the prospect of a very bad future is not a mere thought experiment, but may in fact be a likely outcome.

If we return to the hundred dollars mentioned above, and the question of how much extreme suffering this money might reduce if spent well, we see that it would only have to prevent a tiny fraction of extreme suffering in a vast future cosmic population — perhaps a mere one in 10^{24} — to prevent not just a full hour of extreme suffering but a full human lifetime of it. Whether a hundred dollars spent optimally could accomplish this much is unclear yet not far-fetched. What *is* clear is that a lot is at stake, as

---

9   Deudney, 2020; Torres, 2018a; 2018b.
10 Torres, 2018a, p. 74.

small differences today could make an enormous difference in the future. Indeed, we are currently confronted with the possibility to reduce extreme suffering more than ever, to an extent we cannot comprehend. And yet almost no one is talking about this, let alone examining the implications. It is urgent that we start doing so.

0.3 Outline of the Book

"Suffering-focused ethics" is an umbrella term for ethical views that grant special priority to the reduction of suffering.[11] This is a useful term: it highlights a crucial point of agreement among a wide range of ethical views, and thereby enables us to work out practical implications that have broad support. The point of the term "suffering-focused ethics" is thus not to be a novel or impressive contribution to ethical theorizing, but instead to serve as a pragmatic concept that can unite as effective a coalition as possible toward the shared aim of making a real-world difference — to reduce suffering for sentient beings. That is what this book is all about.

The book is divided into two parts. The aim of the first part is to argue for suffering-focused ethics. Here I present a wide range of arguments in favor of the view that we should grant the reduction of suffering a foremost priority. This entails, among other things, that reducing suffering should take precedence over increasing happiness (for the untroubled). Beyond that, I also present arguments for a set of more specific views according to which we should minimize *extreme* suffering in particular.[12] However, one need not accept all the arguments and views I explore in the first part of the book in order to accept the core practical claim they all support: that we should grant the reduction of suffering particular importance.

This then leads to the topic I explore in the second part: how can we best reduce suffering in practice? This is a difficult question about which there is bound to be much uncertainty. However, there does in fact exist a

---
11 Gloor & Mannino, 2016. The term was coined by Brian Tomasik.
12 These stronger, suffering-minimizing views imply my core claim: that we should grant the reduction of suffering a foremost priority in practice. Yet the reverse does not hold — my core claim does not imply a strict suffering-minimizing view.

wealth of sophisticated ideas and research about how to best reduce suffering, often highly counterintuitive. My aim in the second part is to present and discuss these ideas.

0.4 What I Am Not Saying

When defending an ethic focused on the reduction of suffering, one is often accused of being animated by depression, and of underestimating the good things in life, such as happiness and meaning. Indeed, one is sometimes even accused of being misanthropic and in favor of violence, at least implicitly.[13] It is therefore worth making clear from the outset that none of that is the case here. The moral focus on suffering I defend in this book is not animated by depression, but by reasoned arguments. (And for the record, most people who know me consider me a happy and exuberant person, as do I myself.)[14] Nor is the case for suffering-focused ethics predicated on the notion that the good things in life are not intrinsically great and worth pursuing — one can think they are while still not believing that they justify increasing the total amount of extreme suffering in the world.

Misanthropic sentiments do not motivate my case either. On the contrary, my case for prioritizing the reduction of suffering is motivated primarily by a firm commitment to reason.[15] It stems from a commitment to do what is best for sentient beings. And, as we shall see, misanthropic sentiments are most unlikely to be conducive to this aim. The same is true of violence (indeed, successfully reducing suffering all but surely requires a firm commitment to non-aggression and non-violence).[16] A much better strategy is to engage respectfully in a cooperative and measured conversation about why and how we should reduce suffering. I hope this book will help inspire such a conversation.

---

13 See e.g. Ord, 2013; Peterson & Benatar, 2018.
14 To be sure, such personal notes *should* not be of great relevance, yet they probably are nonetheless, lest people write off everything I say here with an *ad hominem* fallacy resting on a false premise: he is depressed, and hence wrong about value and ethics.
15 Vinding, 2018d.
16 I shall say more on this in chapter 10. Non-violence should not be confused with a pure pacifism that permits no defense against aggressors.

0.5 An Opportunity for Reflection

I realize that the views and arguments I present in this book may challenge some of the reader's deepest, most cherished convictions. Yet rather than seeing the arguments I present as a threat or as something unwelcome, I hope the reader will see them as an invitation and an opportunity to reflect on their priorities. I hope the reader will agree that it is vitally important to get our priorities right, and that we should let our ethics be guided by open-ended reflection that remains charitable and fair even to views that seem disagreeable at first sight.

I too used to hold a very different view from the one I hold now. I used to be a classical utilitarian (that is, I used to believe that happiness and suffering are morally symmetric, and that we should maximize the sum of happiness minus suffering). I used to focus mostly on happiness, and to reject suffering-focused arguments out of hand.[17] I partly rejected such arguments because I had never found them stated in a way that could override my optimistic and wishful mind's insistence on a good story. Yet the main reason for my rejection of suffering-focused views was simply that I would shy away from the issue.[18] In particular, I gave virtually no thought to just how bad suffering can get — as in, how bad it can *really* get.[19]

The endeavor of moral reflection is too important for it to be hostage to such self-imposed ignorance and evasion. If we want to get our priorities right, we must insist on searching for the best arguments and the most plausible views, however unpleasant they may be. This includes

---

17 For instance, classical utilitarianism would, in theory, say that we should torture a person if it resulted in "correspondingly greater" happiness for others (see section 3.1). I used to simply shrug this off with the reply that such an act would never be optimal in practice according to classical utilitarianism. Yet this reply is a cop-out, as it does not address the issue that imposing torture for joy would be right *in theory*. Beyond that, with a small modification to the thought experiment, my cop-out reply is not even true at the practical level, since classical utilitarianism, at least as many people construe it, indeed often would demand that we prioritize increasing future happiness rather than reducing future torment, in effect producing happiness at the price of torturous suffering that could have been prevented. As a classical utilitarian, I just never gave much thought to this.
18 See section 7.2 and Cohen, 2001.
19 See section 4.3. Another significant oversight was that I overlooked the extent to which my focus on increasing happiness was really about reducing suffering; more on this in the second chapter.

squarely facing the daunting and horrifying phenomenon that is suffering, and doing our best to appraise it honestly. Otherwise, we risk missing our precious opportunity to form a truly well-considered view of what our priorities should be.

Part I

The Case for Suffering-Focused Ethics

1

Asymmetries Between Happiness and Suffering

In this chapter, I shall present arguments for the existence of various asymmetries between happiness and suffering. Let me therefore begin by clarifying what I mean by these terms. By suffering and happiness I refer to an overall state of feeling in a given moment, with suffering being an overall bad feeling, or state of consciousness, and happiness being an overall good feeling.[1] The bad and good parts in these respective definitions are unsurprising, yet it is worth taking note of the "overall feeling" part. For it is in fact possible, and even quite common, for an experience to contain an aversive component without the experience being bad overall. For example, one's experience may contain a component of pain or bittersweet sorrow, but if this component does not render the overall experience negative or disagreeable, then this experience does not constitute suffering on the definition employed here. Indeed, I suspect this is one of the reasons we often underestimate suffering: we tend to conflate a merely local, aversive aspect of experience contained within an overall agreeable feeling with suffering

---

[1] I here follow Jamie Mayerfeld, who defines suffering and happiness in a similar way, Mayerfeld, 1999, pp. 14-15. One cannot, I submit, define suffering in more precise or reductive terms than this. For just as one cannot ultimately define the experience of, say, phenomenal redness in any other way than by pointing to it, one cannot define a bad overall feeling, i.e. suffering, in any other way than by pointing to the aspect of consciousness it refers to.

proper — a truly negative and nasty overall state of consciousness. This is an egregious conflation.

Having clarified the meaning of happiness and suffering, let us proceed to review some arguments in favor of asymmetries between the two, specifically asymmetries that suggest we should prioritize reducing suffering over increasing happiness.

1.1 Asymmetries in Population Ethics

A widely shared such asymmetrical view is the Asymmetry in population ethics, according to which we have a strong moral[2] reason to not bring miserable lives into existence, yet no strong moral reason to bring happy lives into existence. This view has been defended by a number of philosophers, including Jan Narveson, who wrote: "We are in favor of making people happy, but neutral about making happy people."[3]

Such a moral asymmetry between suffering and happiness in the context of creating new lives appears especially plausible upon considering the unpalatable implications that would follow from rejecting it. For example, as philosopher Simon Knutsson writes:

> When spending resources on increasing the number of beings instead of preventing extreme suffering, one is essentially saying to the victims: "I could have helped you, but I didn't, because I think it's more important that individuals are brought into existence. Sorry."[4]

In a similar vein, philosophers Lukas Gloor and Adriano Mannino ask us to consider the following thought experiment:

---

[2] I use the terms "moral" and "ethical" synonymously.
[3] Narveson, 1973.
[4] Knutsson, 2016f.

> *Imagine two planets, one empty and one inhabited by 1,000 beings suffering a miserable existence. Flying to the empty planet, you could bring 1,000,000 beings into existence that will live a happy life. Flying to the inhabited planet instead, you could help the 1,000 miserable beings and give them the means to live happily. If there is time to do both, where would you go first? If there is only time to fly to one planet, which one should it be?*

Even though one could bring about 1,000 times as many happy beings as there are existing unhappy ones, many people's moral intuition would have us help the unhappy beings instead. To those holding this intuition, taking care of suffering appears to be of greater moral importance than creating new, happy beings.[5]

Yet, in contrast, most people would probably consider it better that a thousand existing lives went from being happy to being miserable than that we add a million miserable lives to the world. In other words, we do not seem to consider the prevention of miserable lives less important than securing the happiness of existing people, which, Gloor and Mannino argue, "suggests that we care about reducing suffering for existing and potential beings equally, whereas we prioritize the promotion of happiness in actual beings over the happiness in their merely potential peers."[6]

A similar view that supports the Asymmetry is the antifrustrationist position defended by philosopher Christoph Fehige, according to which "we have obligations to make preferrers satisfied, but no obligations to make satisfied preferrers."[7] This asymmetry reflects Fehige's view that:

> We don't do any good by creating satisfied extra preferences. What matters about preferences is not that they have a satisfied existence, but that they don't have a frustrated existence.[8]

---
5 Gloor & Mannino, 2016.
6 Ibid. For many of us, a similar asymmetry exists with respect to the forfeit of potential future pleasures versus the prospect of future pains (for ourselves). As Jamie Mayerfeld notes: "The prospect of future pain disturbs us more than the forfeit of future pleasure." Mayerfeld, 1999, p. 133.
7 Fehige, 1998, p. 518.
8 Ibid.

This, according to Fehige, implies that "*maximizers of preference satisfaction* should instead call themselves *minimizers of preference frustration.*"[9] Philosopher Peter Singer expressed a similar view in the past:

> The creation of preferences which we then satisfy gains us nothing. We can think of the creation of the unsatisfied preferences as putting a debit in the moral ledger which satisfying them merely cancels out. … Preference Utilitarians have grounds for seeking to satisfy their wishes, but they cannot say that the universe would have been a worse place if we had never come into existence at all.[10]

These asymmetrical views in population ethics are all related to the intuition that the state of non-existence is entirely unproblematic — some would even say perfect — for those who have never been born, a view associated with traditions such as Buddhism and Epicureanism.[11]

Another view that shares this intuition is the antinatalist position defended by philosopher David Benatar, among others.[12] The antinatalist view not only holds that we have a stronger reason not to create a miserable life than to create a happy life, but indeed maintains that the creation of life is *always* bad for the being who is created. Therefore, according to antinatalism, it would always have been better for any being never to have come into existence. Benatar writes that the basic insight behind his antinatalist position is that:

---

9   Ibid. One may object that this view does not pertain to happiness and suffering as I have defined them here, yet this is not the case. For even as there are differences, it is not plausible to claim that happiness and suffering, as I have defined them, are not at least closely related to preference satisfaction and frustration respectively, *cf.* Aydede, 2014.
10   Singer, 1980. It should be noted, however, that Singer now defends hedonistic utilitarianism rather than preference utilitarianism, Lazari-Radek & Singer, 2014.
11   I say more on this view in the following chapter. Epicurus is furthermore associated with an argument that says that, since non-existence is unproblematic, death is not bad. Yet this view of death need not follow from the view that non-existence is unproblematic (for those never born). For example, philosopher David Benatar, whom we shall visit next, shares the view that non-existence is not bad, and indeed that it is always better never to have been, yet he also holds that death is very bad. One argument in support of this view is that death "differs fundamentally from never having been born, in that it is typically preceded and accompanied by suffering and/or frustrated preferences." Gloor & Mannino, 2016.
12   Other thinkers associated with antinatalism include 11th-century philosopher and poet Abu al-ʿAlaʾ al-Maʿarri, philosopher Peter Wessel Zapffe, and philosopher Julio Cabrera, Cabrera, 1996; 2019.

Although the good things in one's life make it go better than it otherwise would have gone, one could not have been deprived by their absence if one had not existed.[13]

More specifically, Benatar's argument rests on the asymmetry that seems to exist between the importance of reducing suffering for potential beings versus the (un)importance of increasing the happiness of such beings:

> [T]here is a crucial difference between harms (such as pains) and benefits (such as pleasures) which entails that existence has no advantage over, but does have disadvantages relative to, non-existence. Consider pains and pleasures as exemplars of harms and benefits. It is uncontroversial to say that
> (1) the presence of pain is bad, and that
> (2) the presence of pleasure is good.
> However, such a symmetrical evaluation does not seem to apply to the *absence* of pain and pleasure, for it strikes me as true that
> (3) the absence of pain is good, even if that good is not enjoyed by anyone, whereas
> (4) the absence of pleasure is not bad unless there is somebody for whom this absence is a deprivation.[14]

In other words, since the absence of suffering is good while the absence of pleasure is not bad, the state of non-existence is, according to Benatar, good (good + not bad = good). By contrast, the presence of suffering and pleasure is bad and good respectively, and hence, according to Benatar, this is worse than the non-existence of both.[15]

An objection to this view may be that if no life is worth starting, then no life can be worth continuing, and hence we are all better off dying. Yet Benatar argues against this view by pointing out that different standards

---

13 Benatar, 2006, p. 1. Benatar's view also rests on many other arguments, however, including many of the other asymmetries we will review in this chapter. (I should note that I disagree with Benatar's focus on human procreation, Vinding, forthcoming.)
14 Benatar, 2006, p. 30.
15 Ibid., chap. 2.

apply in these two cases: "We require stronger justification for ending a life than for not starting one."[16] For example, debilitating pain or missing limbs count as a much more plausible reason not to start a life than they do to end a life.

In response to the objection that it would be wrong to not create more beings in order for them to experience happiness, and that we indeed are obliged to make more happy people, Benatar writes:

> [I]t is not the case that people are valuable because they add extra happiness. Instead extra happiness is valuable because it is good for people—because it makes people's lives go better. To think otherwise is to think that people are mere means to the production of happiness. Or, to use another famous image, it is to treat persons as mere vessels of happiness.[17]

One need not, however, accept the antinatalist position to accept the much more general claim that we should grant particular importance to the reduction of suffering. Merely accepting some version of the underlying asymmetry we have seen arguments for here — i.e. an asymmetry between the importance of preventing suffering versus creating happiness for potential beings — can provide a strong reason to prioritize the reduction of suffering in practice, not least given the vast number of beings who might exist in the future.[18]

---

16   Ibid., p. 23. And again, there is the point that ending a life is fundamentally different from not bringing a life into the world, since ending a life "is typically preceded and accompanied by suffering and/or frustrated preferences." Gloor & Mannino, 2016.
17   Benatar, 2006, p. 37. Clark Wolf makes a similar point: "The value of well-being is a function of its value for persons, not vice versa ..." Wolf, 1997, VII.
18   Indeed, even if one holds the reduction of suffering to be equally important to the promotion of happiness for existing beings, and even if one gives the suffering of future beings significantly less weight than the reduction of suffering for existing beings, the acceptance of an asymmetry in the importance of reducing suffering versus increasing happiness in potential beings would still plausibly imply that one should primarily work to reduce suffering for future beings, since the number of beings who are likely to exist in the future is so vast. A consideration with similar implications is reviewed in section 6.2.

1.2 Asymmetries in Quantity

Another asymmetry, quite different from the one reviewed in the previous section, is an asymmetry found in the *quantity* of happiness and suffering, both in the realm of potential and actual states. At the level of potential states, we can observe that, as philosopher Jamie Mayerfeld notes, it is a "sense shared by many people that the intensity of happiness can expand very little in comparison with the intensity of suffering."[19] In other words, the range of possible positive experiences does not seem to reach remotely as high as the range of possible negative experiences reaches deep.[20] Here is Adam Smith hinting at this asymmetry:

> What can be added to the happiness of the man who is in health, who is out of debt, and has a clear conscience? ... Though little can be added to this state, much may be taken from it. Though between this condition and the highest pitch of human prosperity, the interval is but a trifle; between it and the lowest depth of misery the distance is immense and prodigious.[21]

Psychological evidence supports the existence of such an asymmetry at the level of potential states, not just between happiness and suffering, but between bad and good states in general. For instance, a systematic review by psychologist Roy Baumeister et al. titled "Bad Is Stronger Than Good" found that:

---

19 Mayerfeld, 1999, p. 67. See also Mathison, 2018, chap. 2.
20 And even if one thinks the best states of happiness can, in one sense, be as intense as the worst states of suffering, this does not imply that such states of happiness can outweigh similarly intense states of suffering in any evaluative sense, much less a moral one, cf. section 6.1.
21 As quoted in Mayerfeld, 1999, p. 67. Smith also wrote that "Pain ... whether of mind or body, is a more pungent [forceful] sensation than pleasure ..." Smith, 1759, p. 44. David Hume made a similar point: "All the goods of life united would not make a very happy man; but all the ills united would make a wretch indeed ..." Hume, 1779, part 10, Demea speaking. He also wrote that pain is "infinitely more violent and durable [than pleasure]." Ibid., Philo speaking (in response to the more optimistic Cleanthes).

> The greater power of bad events over good ones is found in everyday events, major life events (e.g., trauma), close relationship outcomes, social network patterns, interpersonal interactions, and learning processes. Bad emotions, bad parents, and bad feedback have more impact than good ones, and bad information is processed more thoroughly than good. The self is more motivated to avoid bad self-definitions than to pursue good ones. ... Hardly any exceptions (indicating greater power of good) can be found. Taken together, these findings suggest that bad is stronger than good, as a general principle across a broad range of psychological phenomena.[22]

To get a clearer sense of the scope of the asymmetry in potential between happiness and suffering, we can imagine a situation in which we are offered ten years of maximal bliss at the price that we must experience some duration of the very worst states of suffering. How much such suffering would we be willing to endure in order to attain this happiness if the alternative were to experience a neutral and untroubled state of consciousness?

Many of us would reject such an offer completely.[23] Some, however, will be willing to accept the offer (at least while they are in a position

---

22 Baumeister et al., 2001.
23 One can argue that this preference would in fact obtain for everyone, at least *while* experiencing these very worst states of suffering, since the experience of extreme suffering has often elicited a clear judgment that no amount of positive goods could ever outweigh the suffering (see section 4.3). And if an experience of suffering does not feel like it can justify this sentiment in the moment of the experience — as it clearly has in some states of suffering for some people — then it can reasonably be argued that this state of suffering does not qualify as being among the worst states possible. After all, one's evaluative attitude with respect to one's experience is itself an integral part of that experience, and indeed a significant determinant of how good or bad it feels. In other words, a state of suffering that feels redeemable by a positive good is, almost by definition, quite far indeed from the very worst states of suffering, and hence an idealized torturer imposing the worst of suffering on someone would also alter the victim's mind-brain so that the victim sincerely deems its suffering unbearable and irredeemable in the moment. And if the very worst states of suffering entail the judgment that no positive good can ever outweigh them in the moment they are experienced, the crucial question we must ask ourselves is how it can be justified to say something else — i.e. that they *can* be outweighed — from another vantage point. How can we justify imposing such suffering on other, unwilling consciousness-moments, whether we deem them "us" or not? (I shall delve deeper into this matter in the fourth and fifth chapters.)

where they have not yet experienced these very worst of states). Yet how big a sacrifice would such people be willing to make? Would they be willing, from the outset, to endure a full hour of the most extreme suffering? Perhaps even an entire day? Some might go as far as saying an entire day, yet very few, if any, would be willing to push the scale to anywhere near 50/50. That is, it seems safe to say that a great majority of people would firmly reject ten years of the most extreme suffering in order to attain ten years of the most sublime happiness.

Those who would be willing, from the outset, to endure a full day of the most extreme suffering in order to enjoy ten years of the most extreme happiness are, I think, among those who are willing to push it the furthest to attain such happiness. Yet notice how far they are from 50/50 (i.e. symmetry) in terms of the "days of happiness to days of suffering" ratio they are willing to accept. We are not talking 80/20 or even 99/1 here, but rather 3,650/1. And that is for those who are willing to push it. Even an iceberg, for metaphorical comparison, has more of its relative mass above the surface than this — 300 times more, in fact.

So not only is there no symmetry here, but the disvalue of the worst suffering is, even in this relatively suffering-permissive tradeoff, orders of magnitude greater than the value of the greatest happiness, which lends strong support to the view that the prevention of suffering should take priority over the promotion of happiness in practice. For even on a view according to which we are willing to really push it and endure what is, arguably by most accounts, an unreasonable amount of suffering in order to gain happiness, the disvalue of suffering still strongly dominates the value of happiness.

A short moment of the very worst forms of suffering[24] can make an entire happy life seem of little value in comparison. Yet the same thing cannot be said in reverse — a short moment of the greatest happiness cannot make an entire miserable life seem of comparatively slight disvalue. Indeed, it seems *a priori* plausible, and will be defended at length in later chapters, that some states are so bad that no amount of positive goods could ever outweigh just a single instance of them.[25] In contrast, it seems

---
24 To get a vague sense of what I am talking about here, see section 4.3.
25 See the fourth and fifth chapters, as well as sections 8.10, 8.11, and 8.12.

highly *implausible* that there exists any positive good that can never be outweighed by any amount of suffering.

Upon conceding the existence of a significant value asymmetry at the level of potential states of happiness and suffering, it does not seem all that far-fetched to expect that such an asymmetry is also found at the level of *actual* states. That is: that the quantity of suffering also strongly prevails over the quantity of happiness in the actual world.[26] At the same time, however, we should also strongly *not* expect to be able to find such an asymmetry, since we tend to be biased against negative conclusions.[27] Indeed, most of us will be quite resistant to the conclusion that suffering prevails in the actual world, even if we agree that there is a strong asymmetry at the level of potential states.

This instinctive resistance notwithstanding, the view that the quantity of suffering predominates[28] in the world has been held and expressed by quite a number of people, especially in the East. According to Buddhist scholar Jayarava: "Buddhists, and most Indians, believe that we live in a world in which suffering is predominant …"[29] And the view has also been held by many thinkers in the West.[30] Here is Johann Wolfgang von Goethe:

---

26 By "prevails", I mean it prevails in evaluative terms, i.e. that the disvalue of all the suffering in the world is greater than the value of all its happiness — not that it necessarily prevails in terms of, say, there being more moments of suffering than happiness (a measure that fails to take differences in intensity into account).

27 See Cohen, 2001. We shall delve deeper into this matter in the seventh chapter.

28 One can reasonably question what it means to say that suffering predominates, *cf.* Knutsson, 2016b. By what standard is it measured? I do not here assume an objective definition. In this context, I would roughly define it as "predominates according to what individual people find plausible given their outside view" — a standard that will, of course, vary from person to person.

29 Jayarava, 2012.

30 The thinkers whose writings and ideas are strongly in line with this view include most of the philosophers in the pessimist tradition, such as Hegesias of Cyrene, Baltasar Gracián, Voltaire, Giacomo Leopardi, Arthur Schopenhauer, Philipp Mainländer, Peter Wessel Zapffe, Emil Cioran, and Thomas Ligotti (Ligotti, 2011).

> In all times and in all countries things have been miserable. Men have always been in fear and trouble, they have pained and tortured one other; what little life they had, they made sour one to the other. ... Most people, after having played the game of life for a time, preferred to depart rather than to begin anew. That which perhaps gave or gives them some degree of attachment to life was and is the fear of death. Thus life is; thus it always was; thus it will always remain.[31]

George Orwell was more terse: "Most people get a fair amount of fun out of their lives, but on balance life is suffering, and only the very young or the very foolish imagine otherwise."[32]

This claim of Orwell's — "on balance life is suffering" — can be interpreted in various ways, and it is important not to conflate these different interpretations. For instance, one may take it to mean that most moments in people's lives are moments of suffering. Yet it is not necessary to believe this (rather strong) empirical statement in order to believe another interpretation: that the disvalue of the totality of suffering in the world is greater than the value of the totality of happiness.

For example, even if one believes that happiness is preponderant in most people's lives, it still seems plausible to think that the value of such happiness is not preponderant over the disvalue of all the suffering caused by atrocities such as the Holocaust, the Rwandan genocide, the Cambodian genocide, the Armenian genocide, and the bombings of Hiroshima and Nagasaki (to pick but a few of the atrocities committed by humanity in the latest century); or the suffering caused by such diseases as smallpox (estimated to have caused suffering and death for more than 300 million

---

31 As quoted in Neiman, 2002, pp. 209-210. David Hume expressed similarly pessimistic sentiments in Hume, 1779, part 10. For example: "Were a stranger to drop on a sudden into this world, I would show him, as a specimen of its ills, a hospital full of diseases, a prison crowded with malefactors and debtors, a field of battle strewed with carcasses, a fleet foundering in the ocean, a nation languishing under tyranny, famine, or pestilence. To turn the gay side of life to him, and give him a notion of its pleasures; whither should I conduct him? to a ball, to an opera, to court? He might justly think, that I was only showing him a diversity of distress and sorrow." (Demea speaking.)

32 Orwell, 1947. The following tragicomic quote attributed to Woody Allen hints at the same idea: "Life is full of misery, loneliness, and suffering — and it's all over much too soon."

people in the 20th century alone),[33] the Spanish flu (estimated to have infected 500 million and killed at least 50 million people),[34] and HIV/AIDS (estimated to have infected more than 70 million and killed roughly half that number);[35] or the suffering caused by natural disasters such as the 2004 Indian Ocean tsunami and the 2010 Haitian earthquake. And, of course, these sources of suffering are just a tiny selection of all those that could be mentioned.

Indeed, Goethe and Orwell's quotes, as well as the examples of suffering given above, pertain only to the experiences of humans, who constitute but a small minority of sentient beings on Earth.[36] If we include the experiences of non-human animals, the view that suffering prevails becomes even more compelling. This is true for various reasons.[37]

First, the vast majority of non-human animals come into existence in a circumstance where they are doomed to live short lives full of frustrated desires, since thousands of beings are born where only a few can survive. For if a reproducing pair has thousands of offspring, as the most numerous animals do, then, on average, if the population is roughly stable, only two of them can survive long enough to reproduce. And most wild animals in fact die much sooner, due to starvation, disease, and predation, among other agonizing causes.[38]

Predation alone is a compelling reason to think that suffering prevails in nature, not least because it is ubiquitous. For example, a study on a population of white-footed mice found that 93 percent were killed by predators, which is probably not an unusual percentage.[39] And the suffering predation causes is frequently extreme and protracted (resources that show the agony entailed by predation are found in the following note).[40]

---

33 Saint Louis University, 2008.
34 Johnson & Mueller, 2002.
35 UNAIDS, 2019.
36 Tomasik, 2009d.
37 For arguments for the view that suffering prevails in the lives of most non-human animals, see Horta, 2010a; 2010b; 2015; 2017a; 2017b; Iglesias, 2018.
38 Iglesias, 2018.
39 Collins & Kays, 2014.
40 [This footnote contains disturbing content; its purpose is to enlighten skeptics about the badness of predation.]
It is worth noting that we are strongly biased to not appreciate the true horror of preda-

Predation was also the example Arthur Schopenhauer cited to demonstrate the preponderance of suffering in the world:

> A quick test of the assertion that enjoyment outweighs pain in this world, or that they are at any rate balanced, would be to compare the feelings of an animal engaged in eating another with those of the animal being eaten.[41]

Another reason to believe that suffering prevails, and to believe the sum of human happiness to be relatively insignificant in the bigger picture, is humanity's practice of exploiting and killing non-human animals. Each year, humans exploit and kill more than 60 billion land animals. Most of these beings live out their lives under the horrific conditions of factory farming, confined to tiny spaces and often with body parts removed — birds "debeaked" and pigs "tail-docked", almost always without anesthetic — so as to reduce the degree to which they molest each other out of frustration. These are lives of unspeakable misery and pain.

The ways in which we end these lives are no better. Chicks are routinely ground up alive, pigs are painfully asphyxiated with carbon dioxide (a supposedly "humane" method of slaughter), chickens are frequently boiled alive,[42] and throat-slitting is still a common method for killing land animals in most parts of the world. The story gets even worse when we also include the ways in which we exploit and kill aquatic animals, as

---

tion, since most victims of predation are non-human animals, and most of us do not feel remotely the same when seeing a non-human animal get eaten alive compared to when we see the same fate befall a human, even if the suffering is the same, or indeed greater, in the non-human case. Thus, to appreciate the true horror of predation, it may be necessary to see a human get eaten alive by predators, and then try to generalize the resulting feelings of horror to the non-human victims of predation (and it should be noted that human deaths due to predation are not, in fact, a rarity; for example, tigers alone are estimated to have killed more than 373,000 people between 1800 and 2009, Nyhus et al., 2010, pp. 132-135). The following video shows a man who gets eaten alive by lions: abolitionist.com/reprogramming/maneaters.html
The following video shows a baby giraffe who gets eaten alive by lions: youtube.com/watch?v=xhQRorfuEgs ["Baby Giraffe eaten alive by 3 Lion Cubs"]
The following video shows Komodo dragons eating a deer alive: youtube.com/watch?v=fmwC9HzcWbQ ["Komodo dragons attack and eat alive deer"]
41   Schopenhauer, 1851, p. 42.
42   Dockterman, 2013.

we each year exploit more than a hundred billion fish on similarly horrific aquatic factory farms,[43] and kill more than a trillion fish in total, from farms and the wild.[44] These deaths probably involve extreme suffering more often than not, as we drag them out of the ocean with hooks and nets; allow them to endure painful suffocation above the surface, often for an unbearably protracted while; and then cut off their heads, almost always without any stunning to reduce the pain. To put things in perspective, we kill more than twenty times as many sentient beings in this way *every day* than the number of humans killed in wars in the entire 20th century.[45] This is indeed a bleak story of extreme suffering on an incomprehensible scale.

The reasons we have seen above for thinking that the quantity of suffering predominates greatly, both at the level of potential and actual states, lend strong support to the view that we should prioritize reducing suffering over increasing happiness.

1.3 Asymmetries in Ease of Realization

Beyond the asymmetry in quantity, there is also a strong asymmetry in the ease of realizing states of happiness and suffering respectively.[46] This is true at various levels and for various reasons.[47] One level at which it holds true is that it is much easier to bring about states of extreme suffering than to bring about states of extreme happiness. A single event can result in intense pain and suffering that last a lifetime. For example, a single fall can result in two broken legs and chronic pain; a single car accident can cause a lifetime of pain, physical disability, and PTSD; a single push of a button can result in millions of lives tormented in fire and nuclear

---

43 Mood & Brooke, 2012.
44 Mood & Brooke, 2010. In relation to the idea that fish do not feel pain, see Braithwaite, 2010; Brown, 2015; Balcombe, 2016; Jabr, 2018.
45 For an estimate of the latter number, see White, 2010.
46 One can, of course, argue that this asymmetry is not strictly independent of the asymmetry in quantity. In particular, one may argue that the asymmetry in ease of realization, along with the asymmetry in quantity at the level of potential states, in large part explain the asymmetry in quantity at the level of actual states.
47 Similar points to the one I make in this section are also made in Mathison, 2018, 1.1.6.

radiation. Yet not a single example can be given of the reverse. No single event can guarantee intense, long-lasting pleasure.[48]

This ties into another relevant asymmetry, namely that we build up tolerance toward pleasure but not toward pain and suffering (or at least not to remotely the same extent). This is especially true of extreme suffering. In the words of Jamie Mayerfeld: "As marathon torture sessions wear on, the victims do not grow accustomed or indifferent to their pain."[49] This asymmetry in tolerance also helps explain why pain tends to last much longer than pleasure, and why there is such a thing as chronic pain, yet no such thing as chronic pleasure.[50]

Another reason suffering is easier to bring about comes down to a much more general fact about the world — failure is generally much easier than success. For example, there are many more ways not to solve a Rubik's Cube than to solve it. More saliently, there are many more ways for our bodies and minds to be harmed and dysfunctional than healthy and functional. The former merely requires us to be blighted by one of the many severe afflictions that can taint our lives — depression, anxiety, frustration, chronic pain, infection, trauma, etc. — whereas the latter, being free from harm and dysfunction, requires us to stay clear of *all* such afflictions. And sadly, as Baumeister et al. report in their review article, bad

---

[48] It may be objected that we likely could create a single thing, e.g. a mental health pill, that makes us permanently happy. Yet even if we grant that this is possible, it remains true that it is much easier to bring about great suffering, such as via a fall, than to create such a pill. Moreover, a single, severely bad event will tend to affect many areas of life, physical and psychological, whereas this hypothetical pill presumably only protects against (some forms of) psychological suffering — it does not guard against physical harm.

[49] Mayerfeld, 1999, p. 39. David Hume made a similar observation: "Pleasure, scarcely in one instance, is ever able to reach ecstasy and rapture; and in no one instance can it continue for any time at its highest pitch and altitude. … But pain often, good God, how often! rises to torture and agony; and the longer it continues, it becomes still more genuine agony and torture." Hume, 1779, part 10, Philo speaking.

[50] David Benatar has made a similar point: "[P]ains tend to last longer than pleasures. Compare the fleeting nature of gustatory and sexual pleasures with the enduring character of much pain. There are chronic pains, of the lower back or joints for example, but there is no such thing as chronic pleasure (An enduring sense of satisfaction is possible, but so is an enduring sense of dissatisfaction, and thus this comparison does not favour the preponderance of the good.)" Benatar, 2017b.

health strongly affects our quality of life in a negative direction, whereas "variations in good health have small or negligible effects."[51]

It is virtually impossible for a sentient being to avoid suffering, as it is readily induced by injury, illness, and loss. The attainment of happiness, by contrast, is quite avoidable, as evidenced by reports from sufferers of chronic depression.[52] And since the unharmed sentient state requires so many things to be just right, the harmed state also tends to be far more stable.[53]

The insight that there are many more ways for things to be bad than good is called the "Anna Karenina principle", after the famous quote from Tolstoy's *Anna Karenina*: "Happy families are all alike; every unhappy family is unhappy in its own way." Aristotle also emphasized this principle in the *Nicomachean Ethics*:

> Again, it is possible to fail in many ways (for evil belongs to the class of the unlimited, … and good to that of the limited), while to succeed is possible only in one way (for which reason also one is easy and the other difficult — to miss the mark easy, to hit it difficult) …[54]

Another reason it is much easier to bring about suffering than happiness is that suffering is, in a sense, the default state that creeps in on us if we do not make an effort to avoid it. For instance, if we do not make an effort to eat well and exercise, poor health and misery will ensue. As David Benatar writes:

---

51 Baumeister et al., 2001, p. 354.
52 A similar point has been made by Bruno Contestabile: "Suffering is unavoidable because of accidents, defeats, illnesses and aging. Happiness is avoidable …" Contestabile, 2005.
53 The same point is made in Contestabile, 2005 and Baumeister et al., 2001. The latter also gives many empirical examples of how bad states are more readily attainable than good ones.
54 Aristotle, 350 BC, Book 2. Aristotle's point seems to relate most directly to the difficulty of living a virtuous life versus the ease of living an unvirtuous life. Yet it should be noted that he did not draw a strong distinction between the virtuous life and the happy life, and, by extension, the unvirtuous life and the unhappy life.

> [L]ife is a state of continual striving. We have to expend effort to ward off unpleasantness — for example, to prevent pain, assuage thirst, and minimise frustration. In the absence of our strivings, the unpleasantness comes all too easily, for that is the default.[55]

Our condition is rather like walking up a steep staircase, in that there are many more ways to fall down than there are to move upward, and most falls we can make are much easier to perform, and are much longer, than any step upward. And even if we refuse to take any steps, and instead choose to make no effort whatsoever, we will still gradually move down toward misery. We are not just on a staircase, but on a steep escalator moving downward. (Biological beings have, of course, evolved abilities to tackle these tough conditions quite competently, at least while they are in their prime, yet it must be remembered that these abilities are themselves the product of an enormous amount of failure and suffering that has occurred, and continues to occur, in each successive generation.)

That great happiness is difficult to attain and promote, whereas it is comparatively feasible to reduce extreme suffering, also provides a strong reason to devote our marginal resources toward preventing suffering rather than promoting happiness.[56] In other words, there seem to be strongly diminishing returns in trying to increase happiness (for those who are untroubled) compared to reducing and preventing suffering, implying that we should prioritize the latter.[57]

---

[55] Benatar, 2017b.
[56] The same point is made in Singer, 2018, about 9 minutes in. As Toby Ord notes: "[T]he decision procedure (or rule of thumb) of focusing on eliminating suffering seems to lead to more Classical Utilitarian value than addressing suffering and happiness in equal measure. As another example, adding happiness to those who are already happy seems to typically lead to less Utilitarian value than using the same resources to alleviate suffering." Ord, 2013. Similarly, Mayerfeld notes that "most utilitarians agree we accomplish more by trying to prevent suffering than by trying to increase happiness …" Mayerfeld, 1999, p. 149. Yet Mayerfeld argues against the claim that asymmetries of this kind (e.g. that it is generally cheaper to reduce suffering) alone can account for the common-sense view that we should give greater priority to the reduction of suffering, ibid., pp. 146-148; Mayerfeld, 1996, pp. 325-328.
[57] This claim about diminishing returns can be defended in at least two independent ways. One is based on the asymmetry in potential ranges we saw in the previous section. As Adam Smith noted, little can be added to the happiness of someone who is already doing okay, while much can be taken away from it, implying that there are diminish-

1.4 Asymmetries in Quality

An altogether different asymmetry between happiness and suffering, which has nothing to do with their respective quantities or accessibility, is the fundamental *qualitative* difference between them. Suffering is inherently a cry for betterment. It carries, as philosopher Thomas Metzinger puts it, a unique "urgency of change".[58] The experience of happiness, on the other hand, as well as neutral states absent of happiness, carry no urgent call for betterment whatsoever, and hence increasing the happiness of those who are not suffering has no urgency in the least.[59]

This asymmetry has been highlighted by many thinkers. Here, for instance, is a famous quote from philosopher Karl Popper:

> I believe that there is, from the ethical point of view, no symmetry between suffering and happiness, or between pain and pleasure. … In my opinion human suffering makes a direct moral appeal, namely, the appeal for help, while there is no similar call to increase the happiness of a man who is doing well anyway. A further criticism of the Utilitarian formula "Maximize pleasure" is that it assumes a continuous pleasure-pain scale which allows us to treat degrees of pain as negative degrees of pleasure. But, from the moral point of view, pain cannot be outweighed by pleasure, and especially not one man's pain by another man's pleasure. Instead of the greatest happiness for the greatest number, one should demand, more modestly, the least amount of avoidable suffering for all …[60]

---

ing returns in helping someone who is already okay. Another way to defend it is via the argument presented in this section: even assuming equal ranges of positive and negative experiences, creating great happiness just happens, empirically, to be much more difficult than reducing great suffering — especially for future beings, since creating great happiness for them requires many things to be just right, whereas preventing great suffering for them merely requires not creating them. If one then combines these two independent arguments, the diminishing returns thesis that implies we should focus on reducing suffering becomes doubly compelling.

58 Metzinger, 2016, "Option 4: eliminating the NV-condition".
59 And to the extent seemingly positive states do contain an "urgency of change", one may argue that they are in fact negative, *cf.* Gloor, 2017; Knutsson, 2019d.
60 Popper, 1945, chap. 9, note 2. To be sure, Popper is here making a claim about the moral (dis)value of suffering versus happiness, yet it is clear that his claim rests, at least in

David Pearce, who defends negative utilitarianism (the view that an action is morally right if and only if it minimizes suffering), describes his view in a similar way:

> [N]egative utilitarianism ... challenges the moral symmetry of pleasure and pain. It doesn't question the value of enhancing the happiness of the already happy. Yet it attaches value in a distinctively *moral* sense of the term only to actions which tend to minimise or eliminate suffering. This is what matters above all else.[61]

A third thinker defending a qualitative asymmetry of this kind is psychologist and philosopher Richard Ryder. Specifically, Ryder argues for a position called "painism", which holds that one individual's pleasure can never morally outweigh the pain of another, and that our overriding moral objective is to reduce pain (defined broadly so as to cover all forms of suffering).[62]

Note that none of the views outlined above imply that there is no value in happiness. What they do imply, however, is that the value there may be in creating happiness is not comparable to the moral value of reducing suffering. Thus, increasing the happiness of the already happy can be quite fine on these views, yet it does not carry value in a strong moral sense, since it, in Popper's words, answers no moral appeal for help. Reducing suffering, on the other hand, *does* answer such an appeal.

A similar way to conceive of the qualitative difference between suffering and happiness is in terms of a "problem versus non-problem" dichotomy: suffering is inherently problematic, the neutral absence of happiness is not. Indeed, it takes an outside observer to say that a neutral state absent of happiness is problematic — such a judgment must be imposed from outside — whereas the problematic nature of a state of suffering is exposed directly from the inside.[63] Thus, as Adriano Mannino notes:

---

part, on this underlying qualitative asymmetry between them: suffering is intrinsically urgent and problematic — "an appeal for help" — while happiness and the neutral absence of happiness are not. The same point applies to the views of Pearce and Ryder mentioned below.
61   Pearce, 1995, chap. 2.
62   Ryder, 2009b, p. 402. See also Ryder, 2001; 2011.
63   This point was made by David Pearce, personal communication.

> The non-creation of happiness is not problematic, for it never results in a problem for anyone (i.e. any consciousness-moment), and so there's never a problem you can point to in the world; the non-prevention of suffering, on the other hand, results in a problem.[64]

The view that we should prioritize the reduction and prevention of suffering over the creation of happiness can then be said to derive from an intuitive "understanding of ethics as being about solving the world's problems: We confront spacetime, see wherever there is or will be a problem, i.e. a struggling being, and we solve it."[65]

Explaining the qualitative asymmetry in terms of such a "problem versus non-problem" dichotomy may be considered equivalent to explaining it in terms of "urgent versus not urgent" — or at any rate *strictly less urgent* — as we did above, and as Karl Popper has also done: "[T]he promotion of happiness is in any case much less urgent than the rendering of help to those who suffer, and the attempt to prevent suffering."[66]

This asymmetry in urgency is well in line with common sense. For example, we would rightly rush to send an ambulance to help someone who is enduring extreme suffering, yet not to boost the happiness of someone who is already doing well, no matter how much we may be able to boost it. Indeed, even if we could only reduce the afflicted person's intense suffering by a modest amount, this would still be more urgent than increasing the happiness of a completely untroubled person to maximal heights. Similarly, if we were in the possession of pills that could raise the happiness of those who are already happy to the greatest heights possible, there would be no urgency in distributing these pills, whereas if a single person fell to the ground in unbearable agony right before us, there would indeed be an urgency to help.[67] Increasing the happiness of the already happy is, unlike the alleviation of extreme suffering, not an emergency.

---

64 Quoted from a Facebook conversation from 2013. (And in the case of extreme suffering, it can be argued that the word "problem" grossly understates the reality in question.)
65 Gloor & Mannino, 2016.
66 Popper, 1945, chap. 5, note 6.
67 A similar thought experiment is found in Mayerfeld, 1999, p. 133.

Another thought experiment that lends support to this qualitative asymmetry is to consider a hypothetical endeavor that leads to the abolition of suffering in all sentient life.[68] Would it be reasonable to maintain that our moral obligations remain exactly the same after the completion of this endeavor as before? After we abolished suffering, would we have equally strong obligations to lift sentient beings to new heights of happiness? Or would we instead have discharged our prime moral obligation, and thus have reason to lower our shoulders and breathe a deep and justified sigh of moral relief?[69] It seems plausible to say the latter. As Jamie Mayerfeld writes about a world without suffering: "We could go on improving the world in a variety of ways, but it would be less clear that this was, in most cases, morally required."[70]

An additional argument that can be made in favor of a qualitative asymmetry is that the absence of extreme happiness is not bad in remotely the same way as the presence of extreme suffering is bad. For example, if a person is in a state of dreamless sleep rather than a state of ecstatic happiness, this cannot reasonably be characterized as a disaster or a catastrophe. The difference between these two states does not carry great moral weight. By contrast, the difference between sleeping and being tortured *does* carry immense moral weight, and the realization of torture rather than sleep would indeed amount to a catastrophe. Being forced to endure torture rather than dreamless sleep, or an otherwise neutral state, would be a tragedy of a fundamentally different kind than being forced to "endure" a neutral state instead of a state of maximal bliss.

Accepting the qualitative and moral asymmetry presented in this section implies that reducing suffering should always take priority over increasing happiness. Increasing happiness may be fine in itself, yet if it comes at the price of increasing (or not preventing) suffering, it is wrong.

---

68   This is what David Pearce advocates for: the abolitionist project. I say more on this project in chapter 13.
69   *If*, that is, suffering had been abolished for good for sure. We may, of course, assume such a hypothetical in this thought experiment, yet it is worth noting that, in the real world, a deep sigh of relief would never be justified, as there will always be risks, and one can always work to reduce such risks. I say a bit more on this point in section 13.3.
70   Mayerfeld, 1999, p. 118.

1.5 Asymmetries in Knowledge

The final asymmetry between happiness and suffering we shall review in this chapter is an asymmetry at the level of our knowledge. As English essayist Samuel Johnson wrote: "[I]t is, commonly, easier to know what is wrong than what is right; to find what we should avoid, than what we should pursue."[71] In other words, it is easier to identify what is bad and wrong than it is to identify what, if anything, is positively good and right (as opposed to what is *negatively* good and right — i.e. reducing that which is bad and wrong).

This asymmetry is also reflected, for instance, in Aristotle's defense of the goodness of pleasure. For the core premise of Aristotle's argument is not our certainty in the goodness of pleasure, but rather the badness of pain: "[I]t is agreed that pain is bad and to be avoided ..."[72] And he then proceeded to argue that, since pleasure is the opposite of pain, pleasure must be good.[73] (Though to be sure, this argument by no means establishes that the presence of pleasure, as a positive good, is of comparable value to the absence of suffering as a negative good.)[74]

Psychologist Jordan Peterson has expressed a similar asymmetry in knowledge, as he argues that the badness of unnecessary suffering is uniquely indisputable, and, by extension, so is the goodness of preventing it:

---

71 Johnson, 1774.
72 Aristotle, 350 BC, Book 7, chap. 13. This is similar to the argument made by Sam Harris in his book *The Moral Landscape*, which takes a condition he calls "the worst possible misery for everyone" as the starting point. We can agree this scenario is bad, and we should aim, Harris argues, to get as far away from this scenario we can: "I have argued that the value of avoiding the worst possible misery for everyone can be presupposed—and upon this axiom we can build a science of morality ..." Harris, 2010, p. 202. The case for moral realism provided in Hewitt, 2008, chap. 3 also proceeds in a similar way, with the badness of pain as its starting point.
73 Aristotle, 350 BC, Book 7, chap. 13. As Aristotle scholar Dorothea Frede summed up his argument: "[T]he badness of pain is a proof of that pleasure must be good ..." Natali, 2009, p. 185.
74 After all, Aristotle's argument could also be applied to the neutral absence of pain, which is also in a relevant sense the opposite of pain. Yet, as is immediately clear in this case, the fact that these states are in some sense opposites by no means implies it is worth creating neutral states absent of pain (*de novo*) at the price of creating more pain. That would be a *non sequitur*. I say more on this in section 8.5.

> What can I not doubt? The reality of suffering. It brooks no arguments. Nihilists cannot undermine it with skepticism. Totalitarians cannot banish it. Cynics cannot escape from its reality. Suffering is real, and the artful infliction of suffering on another, for its own sake, is wrong. ...
>
> Each human being understands, *a priori*, perhaps not what is good, but certainly what is not. And if there is something that *is not good*, then there is something that *is good*. If the worst sin is the torment of others, merely for the sake of the suffering produced—then the good is whatever is diametrically opposed to that. The good is whatever stops such things from happening.[75]

The list of sources and forms of suffering whose alleviation would clearly be good is indeed long and diverse. Consider, for instance, the suffering endured by humans because of natural disasters, infectious diseases, cancer, poverty, starvation, depression, anxiety, heartache, loss, accidents, chronic pain, periodic pain (e.g. cluster headaches), genetic disorders (e.g. paroxysmal extreme pain disorder), domestic violence, street violence, warfare, slavery, rape, and child abuse.[76] Each entry on this list covers suffering on an unfathomable scale, and yet this list is, of course, still a very far cry from being an exhaustive list of forms and sources of suffering that are obviously worth reducing.[77]

In contrast, it is much less clear which sources or forms of happiness we ought to cultivate, let alone which of them, if any, are as important to cultivate as the prevention of the bad things listed above (the asymmetry presented in the previous section indeed suggests none of them are). An anecdotal case in point is that YouTube videos purported to display "the best of humanity" almost invariably show people preventing

---

75 Peterson, 2018, pp. 197-198.
76 Similar lists are found in Benatar, 2006, pp. 88-92 and Mayerfeld, 1999, p. 107.
77 For instance, it wholly excludes the suffering endured by the vast majority — more than 99.99 percent (Tomasik, 2009d) — of sentient beings on the planet, namely non-human animals, whose cumulative suffering easily dwarfs the cumulative suffering endured by humanity by orders of magnitude on virtually any measure. And this is true even if we only consider the non-human suffering caused by humans alone, which is itself dwarfed by non-human suffering due to natural causes, ibid; Iglesias, 2018.

or ameliorating tragic circumstances rather than promoting some positive good.

As philosopher Bruno Contestabile puts it: "It is easier to find a consensus on the kinds of suffering to be combated than on the kinds of happiness to be promoted."[78] And even in cases where we can identify kinds of happiness that do seem worth actively promoting, such as the prosocial pleasures of altruism[79] and of loving kindness,[80] it is not clear that these are worth promoting for the sake of the happiness itself, as opposed to their beneficial instrumental effects. Yet the forms and sources of suffering we can agree to combat are clearly worth reducing just for the sake of avoiding the suffering itself.

It is worth noting that one can make two rather different and independently plausible cases for an asymmetry in knowledge. First, one can argue that it is easier to identify *the particular sources and forms* of suffering worth preventing than it is to identify the sources and forms of happiness worth promoting.[81] Second, one can argue that there is an asymmetry when it comes to our certainty that suffering, *in general*, is bad and worth preventing versus our certainty that happiness is good and worth promoting (relative to a neutral state).

For example, even if one is not wholly convinced by the qualitative asymmetry argued for in the previous section, it is still *more plausible* that suffering is intrinsically bad and worth preventing than that happiness is intrinsically good and worth creating. Likewise, it is significantly *more plausible* to say that the prevention of suffering carries strictly greater

---

78 Contestabile, 2005. Similarly, it is easier to point to a life clearly not worth living than it is to point to a life clearly worth living. Althaus, 2018 makes a similar point at the level of collective future outcomes: "[C]onsider the number of macroscopically distinct futures whose net value is extremely negative according to at least 99.5% of all humans. It seems plausible that this number is (much) greater than the number of macroscopically distinct futures whose net value is extremely positive according to at least 99.5% of all humans."
79 Dunn et al., 2008; Dunn et al., 2011.
80 Fredrickson et al., 2008.
81 A similar point has been made by scholar of Buddhism Damien Keown: "It is … easier to agree on what is a case of physical suffering than it is to agree on which particular aspect of happiness should be maximised." Keown, 1992, p. 174.

importance than it is to make the inverse claim that the creation of happiness is strictly more important than the prevention of suffering.

These asymmetries in knowledge are reflected in commonly held views. As philosopher R. I. Sikora noted, it is a common intuition that "pain prevention should count more heavily than the promotion of pleasure"[82] — and empirical surveys bear out this claim.[83] By contrast, the intuition that the promotion of pleasure should count more heavily than the prevention of pain is rare.

Beyond that, there is also a strong asymmetry in that very few seem to have seriously questioned the value and moral importance of preventing suffering,[84] while it seems fairly common to doubt the importance of increasing happiness. As psychologist Daniel Kahneman notes:

> [W]hat can confidently be advanced is a reduction of suffering. The question of whether society should intervene so that people will be happier is very controversial, but whether society should strive for people to suffer less — that's widely accepted.[85]

Indeed, many philosophers have rejected that there is value in creating happiness (for the untroubled). These include philosophers such as Epicurus and Arthur Schopenhauer, as well as many Eastern philosophers for whom *moksha*, liberation from suffering, is the highest good. (We shall explore the core view defended by these philosophers in the following chapter.)

This asymmetry in consensus becomes even starker when we consider potential beings. For example, virtually everyone agrees that a life can be so bad that we have strong moral reasons not to create it, yet many doubt whether a life can be so good that we have strong moral reasons to start it. Likewise, a number of philosophers defend the antinatalist view that no

---

82 Sikora, 1976, p. 587.
83 Future of Life Institute, 2017.
84 But didn't Nietzsche doubt the disvalue of suffering? I would not claim that nobody has done so, yet for an argument that Nietzsche's view was distorted by bias, see the quote from Derek Parfit in section 7.3.
85 Mandel, 2018.

life can ever be good enough to be worth starting.[86] Yet no one defends the opposite position — that a life can never be too bad to be worth starting — which is indeed far less plausible (an individual who is tortured for their entire life should count as a trivial example of a life not worth starting).

These asymmetries in knowledge also count as reasons for prioritizing the reduction of suffering. Indeed, each of the asymmetries we have seen arguments for in this chapter lends strong, independent support to the view that the reduction of suffering should be our main priority in practice. In combination, they make a more compelling case still.

---

86 See e.g. Cabrera, 1996; 2019; Benatar, 2006; Akerma, 2010; 2014.

2

Happiness as the Absence of Suffering

What matters about an experience, in terms of its intrinsic value, is that it is free from suffering. By extension, the intrinsic value of happiness lies chiefly in its absence of suffering. In this chapter, I shall review various versions of, and arguments for, this view. The view has been defended by a number of philosophers in the West, including Epicurus and Arthur Schopenhauer, and it is arguably a core tenet of many Eastern traditions, including Buddhism.[1] In recent times, the view has been defended under different names, including "anti-hurt"[2] and "tranquilism",[3] both of which are neatly descriptive.

2.1 Anti-Hurt and Perfectionist Axiology

The term "anti-hurt" was coined by philosopher Dan Geinster, who describes the nature of value in terms of a simple dichotomy: hurt (i.e. suffering) and the absence of hurt. The less hurt there is, the more things are as they should be. As Geinster writes:

---

1   Contestabile, 2010; 2014; Breyer, 2015.
2   Geinster, 2012.
3   Gloor, 2017.

> Only the phenomenon of *hurt* actually *does* hurt, and only its absence can be regarded as '*bliss*' ... hurt simply *should-not-be*, while bliss *should-be* ... the greater the hurt reduced, the greater the bliss.[4]

In other words, all states of happiness have the same intrinsic value as all other states that are absent of suffering — in Geinster's words, these are all equally states that do not bother anyone. Hurt, or suffering, on the other hand, is intrinsically problematic, and what matters in terms of the intrinsic value of experiences, on Geinster's view, is only the degree to which this problematic aspect is absent. With respect to the idea that states of happiness and pleasure are more valuable than other states wholly absent of suffering, Geinster argues that this is an illusion, akin to believing that one can have more than 100 percent of something.[5]

An essentially identical view has been explored by philosopher Bruno Contestabile, albeit under the name "perfectionist axiology"[6] — a name that hints at the inherent perfection (according to this view) of states absent of suffering, including the state of non-existence. (It is worth noting that Socrates seemed to express a similar view in Plato's *Apology*, as he spoke of a state wholly absent of consciousness as being "an unspeakable gain" relative to the life of even the happiest person.)[7]

---

4   Geinster, 2012.
5   Ibid. As we shall see below, Lukas Gloor suggests that this putative illusion may be explained by the fact that pleasure is often the way in which we experience temporary relief from suffering and dissatisfaction, Gloor, 2017. For an outline of the view that many pleasures in fact have subtly negative value, see Knutsson, 2019d.
6   Axiology refers to the study or theory of value.
7   Plato, 399 BC, 40c-e. This sentiment is also found in the Bible, Ecclesiastes 4: "And I declared that the dead, who had already died, are happier than the living, who are still alive. But better than both is he who has not yet been ..." The same view permeates the work of Italian philosopher and poet Giacomo Leopardi. For example, the final verse of his 1829 poem *La quiete dopo la tempesta* ("The Calm After the Storm") reads as follows: "Gracious nature, these / Are the gifts you grant us, / These the favors you lavish / On mortal men and women. For us, / Pleasure means escape from pain. / Sufferings you scatter / With prodigal hand; unhappiness / Needs no prompting; and that / One touch or two of joy / That like a miracle or nine-day marvel / Springs from sorrow / Is our rich reward. Mankind, / Darling of the gods! Happy to find / Some breathing space / Between griefs; and truly blest / If all your ills are cured by death." Leopardi & Grennan, 1997, p. 51.

Contestabile notes that the view has roots in Hinduism, and that it is shared by some forms of Buddhism.⁸ The latter claim is echoed by philosopher and scholar of Buddhism Daniel Breyer, who argues that the cessation of suffering is considered the highest good in the Pali tradition of Buddhism in particular:

> [I]t is not the positive state of nirvāṇa that counts as the ultimate good according to the Pāli Buddhist tradition, but its negative counterpart—the cessation and elimination of suffering. In fact, nirvāṇa of either kind is valuable only because it represents a very specific achievement—the utter eradication of suffering.⁹

And not only is the cessation of suffering the *highest* good according to the Pali tradition, it is also, on Breyer's interpretation, the *only* intrinsic good, implying that "everything else that counts as good is only instrumentally or extrinsically good insofar as it contributes to the cessation of suffering."¹⁰

2.2 Suffering as Tied to Desire

This view of the cessation of suffering as the ultimate good is closely related to the first three of the Four Noble Truths of Buddhism: roughly, that life naturally contains suffering and dissatisfaction (first truth) due to cravings and desires (second truth), and that by ending our cravings and desires, we can eliminate suffering (third truth).¹¹

Epicurus defended a similar view, according to which a state of *ataraxia* (tranquility) — an unperturbed state without mental or bodily pain¹² — is the ultimate good:

---
8   Contestabile, 2014.
9   Breyer, 2015, p. 558. Indeed, the liberation from suffering (*moksha*) is central to most of the well-known Eastern traditions, such as Buddhism, Hinduism, Jainism, and Sikhism.
10 Ibid., p. 542.
11 Contestabile, 2010. (The fourth truth is that the cessation of suffering can be achieved by following the Eightfold Path.) This view of desires bears close resemblance to Christoph Fehige's antifrustrationist position described in section 1.1.
12 Strictly speaking, *ataraxia* refers to a state absent of mental pain and worry, while *aponia* refers to a state absent of physical pain (though one may argue that the former

> A steady view of these matters shows us how to refer all moral choice and aversion to bodily health and imperturbability of mind, these being the twin goals of happy living. It is on this account that we do everything we do — to achieve freedom from pain and freedom from fear. When once we come by this, the tumult in the soul is calmed and the human being does not have to go about looking for something that is lacking or to search for something additional with which to supplement the welfare of soul and body. Accordingly we have need of pleasure only when we feel pain because of the absence of pleasure, but whenever we do not feel pain we no longer stand in need of pleasure.[13]

Epicurus shared the above-mentioned Buddhist view that the best way to attain a tranquil state absent of suffering is to limit one's desires rather than to satisfy (unnecessary) desires.[14] (Philosopher John Stuart Mill is quoted, apocryphally, as saying something similar about his own happiness: "I have learned to seek my happiness by limiting my desires, rather than in attempting to satisfy them.")[15]

A similar view of the relationship between desires and happiness was defended by Arthur Schopenhauer, as he argued that "satisfaction or gratification can never be more than deliverance from a pain, from a want."[16] Hence, according to Schopenhauer, happiness is simply the absence of desire and discomfort:

---

implies the latter, since if one is in a perfectly tranquil and unbothered state of mind, then one is not bothered by physical pain either).
13   Strodach, 1963, p. 182, as quoted in Gloor, 2017. Dan Geinster makes a similar point to the one Epicurus makes here about pleasure, as he writes that we "seek the bliss in happiness and pleasure to dispel the hurt of discontentedness or desire, without which we probably wouldn't bother." Geinster, 2012.
14   Contestabile, 2014.
15   *The Phrenological Journal and Science of Health*, September 1887, p. 170.
16   Schopenhauer, 1819, vol I, p. 319.

> [E]vil is precisely that which is positive, that which makes itself palpable, and good, on the other hand, i.e. all happiness and gratification, is that which is negative, the mere abolition of a desire and extinction of a pain.[17]

Thus, the view that the value of an experience lies in its absence of suffering, and that suffering is tied to desire, is shared by Epicurus, Schopenhauer, and some forms of Buddhism.

A modern proponent of this view is philosopher Lukas Gloor, who follows Epicurus in the name he has given this view: tranquilism. What matters on the tranquilist view "is not to maximize desirable experiences, but to reach a state *absent of desire.*"[18] In other words, tranquilism holds the intrinsic value of an experience to be dependent only on the degree to which a craving for change is present, where states wholly absent of such a craving for change are considered optimal. This gives rise to a value scale of a singular nature:

> Instead of having a scale that goes from negative over neutral to positive, tranquilism's value scale is homogeneous, ranging from optimal states of consciousness to (increasingly more severe degrees of) non-optimal states.[19]

In this way, tranquilism also implies that all states absent of suffering — be they states of euphoric bliss, peaceful contentment, or non-existence — are equally optimal in terms of their intrinsic value. Gloor is careful to point out, however, that he does not intend his tranquilist position to be a standalone theory of value or ethics, since it only says something about the intrinsic value of experiences. It says nothing about other things one may ascribe intrinsic value to, such as virtues or the accomplishment of life goals. Tranquilism is thus readily compatible with other such values.[20]

---

17 And he continued: "Since pleasure and well-being is negative and suffering positive, the happiness of a given life is not to be measured according to the joys and pleasures it contains but according to the absence of the positive element, the absence of suffering." Schopenhauer, 1851, pp. 41-43.
18 Gloor, 2017.
19 Ibid.
20 Ibid.

2.3 Distinguishing Different Anti-Hurt Views

It is worth distinguishing a few different views of the kind explored in this chapter. These views have practically the same implications concerning the nature of value, yet they are not identical. A relevant distinction is that between 1) anti-hurt views that consider suffering inextricably tied to desire, and 2) anti-hurt views that do not. Tranquilism would fall into the first category, as it holds that "a state of consciousness is negative or disvaluable if and only if it contains a craving for change."[21] Yet one can hold an anti-hurt view without agreeing with this particular view of the relationship between suffering and cravings.[22] For example, one can think that there can be suffering without any "craving for change" (e.g. a state of severe depression),[23] or one can think that a craving for change need not imply a negative state.

Another important distinction is that between 1) views that claim that the intrinsic *value* of happiness lies in its absence of suffering, and 2) views that claim that happiness simply *is* the absence of suffering. Views of the former kind make an evaluative claim whereas the latter make an empirical (or definitional) claim: if a conscious mind is absent of suffering, then it is in a happy state.[24]

This empirical claim was defended by Schopenhauer (see the previous section), as well as by Epicurus, who considered it among his sovereign maxims that "[t]he magnitude of pleasure reaches its limit in the removal of all pain."[25] William James also expressed this view:

---

21 Ibid.
22 On my reading, Geinster seems to lean more toward a traditional hedonistic view (or rather an "algonistic" view; *algo* is Greek for pain) than a desire/craving view. See also Knutsson, 2019d.
23 Yet see Gloor, 2017, 4.4 for a discussion of depression in relation to tranquilism.
24 There is, of course, a big difference between *defining* happiness as the absence of suffering (as Dan Geinster, for instance, can be interpreted as doing) and making *the empirical claim* that the state of happiness — the particular feeling we sometimes feel when things go well — merely *is* or *results from* the absence of suffering. Both views say that happiness merely consists in the absence of suffering, yet they define happiness in rather different ways.
25 Laertius, ca. 230, p. 665. Philosopher Thomas Hurka also attributes this view of happiness to Plato, Hurka, 2010, though see the next note for more on Plato's view.

> Happiness, I have lately discovered, is no positive feeling, but a negative condition of freedom from a number of restrictive sensations of which our organism usually seems the seat. When they are wiped out, the clearness and cleanness of the contrast is happiness. This is why anaesthetics make us so happy.[26]

If one holds that the intrinsic value of an experience is determined by where it falls on the continuum of more or less (un)pleasant states, then this view that happiness literally *is* the absence of suffering does indeed imply the evaluative view mentioned above: that the *value* of happiness lies in its absence of suffering. But the converse does not hold true. That is, one may consider happiness to be more than just the absence of suffering — i.e. the presence of something positive — yet still not consider such a positive state to be more valuable than any other state wholly absent of suffering.[27]

Alternatively, one may hold such positive states to be *infinitesimally* more valuable than neutral states, which highlights another relevant distinction, namely that between 1) views that consider all states absent of suffering to be equally optimal, and 2) views that consider the absence of suffering of chief importance while still considering some states of happiness better than others.

Views of the first kind can be visualized with a scale ranging from negative to neutral states, with all states absent of suffering occupying the neutral zero-point (such views may be called pure anti-hurt views). The second view, by contrast, can be visualized with a scale that ranges from negative to positive states, yet where improvements at the negative end

---

26 James, 1901. Voltaire wrote something in the same spirit: "Happiness is only a dream, and pain is real" (see Schopenhauer, 1819, vol II, p. 576). Similarly, Plato argued that it is common for people to experience the mere relief of a negative condition as a positive condition. In the words of Jamie Mayerfeld, Plato accused the average person of mistaking "the recovery of good health as an occasion of great pleasure, when in fact it only signifies a release from the pain of illness." Mayerfeld, 1999, p. 35. Although Plato did, on my reading, argue against James' claim that *all* happiness merely consists in being relieved from pain, he still argued that "the more numerous and violent pleasures which reach the soul through the body are generally of this sort — they are reliefs of pain." Plato, 380 BC, p. 595.

27 Geinster, for example, seems to hold this view with respect to pleasure: "I must concede … that pleasure can be much more *enjoyable* than absolute bliss (zero hurt), … but I suggest that enjoyment has no priority over absolute bliss because one is equally and absolutely *content* with either — contentment being the [operative word] here." Geinster, 2012.

of the scale are always more valuable than improvements at the positive end.[28] We may call this the impure anti-hurt view.

Among philosophers who hold this impure view, both at the level of axiological and moral value,[29] are David Pearce and Clark Wolf.[30] In Wolf's words, "the value of relieving suffering is ... prior to the value of providing additional happiness to the well-off."[31] One may also read G. E. Moore as having endorsed such an asymmetrical view of value in his *Principia Ethica*:

> [T]he consciousness of intense pain ... can be maintained to be a great evil. ... The case of pain thus seems to differ from that of pleasure: for the mere consciousness of pleasure, however intense, does not, *by itself*, appear to be a *great* good, even if it has some slight intrinsic value. In short, pain (if we understand by this expression, the consciousness of pain) appears to be a far worse evil than pleasure is a good.[32]

Although the views distinguished above differ in some important ways, they all agree that there is an asymmetry in the value of reducing suffering versus increasing happiness (relative to a neutral state), where the value of the former is always incomparably greater.

---

28 A way to formalize this view is to represent the value of states of suffering with negative real numbers while representing the value of states of happiness with hyperreal numbers greater than 0, yet smaller than any positive real number. This allows us to assign some states of happiness greater value than others while still keeping this difference smaller than any difference we could make on the negative end of the scale. On the pure anti-hurt view, in contrast, all states of happiness would be assigned exactly the value 0.

29 Philosophers tend to distinguish between 1) evaluative/axiological views that describe things in terms of good and bad, valuable and disvaluable, and 2) normative/moral views that describe things in terms of right and wrong. The anti-hurt views presented above have all been phrased in axiological terms.

30 Pearce, 1995, chap. 2; Wolf, 1997.

31 Wolf, 1997, VIII. Wolf calls his view the "Impure Consequentialist Theory of Obligation" (ICTO). Note that Wolf employs a different definition of suffering than the one we gave in the previous chapter, as he defines it as "things that make life go ill", not as momentary experiential states, Wolf, 1997, III. Yet, as Wolf notes, these two definitions are closely related.

32 Moore, 1903, p. 212. Alternatively, Moore may be read as having a weak negative axiology, *cf.* Knutsson, 2016d.

2.4 Implausible Implications?

To some, the views outlined above may seem counterintuitive, at least at first sight. For instance, one may object that most beings actively seek pleasure and happiness most of the time, often at the seemingly justified cost of increasing their own pain and suffering. Yet one can frame this search for happiness in a way that is consistent with the views explored here, namely by viewing it as an attempt to escape suffering and dissatisfaction.

For example, one may argue that our experience is often tainted by a subtle backdrop of dissatisfaction, which may be hard to notice because we have grown accustomed to it.[33] And because we misinterpret such subtly dissatisfied states as being perfectly neutral, we wrongly believe our attempt to escape dissatisfaction to be a positive pursuit of happiness. In other words, what appears to be a move from a neutral to a positive state is really a matter of going from a state of dissatisfaction, however subtle, to a state relieved from this dissatisfaction.[34]

On this view, when we visit a friend we have desired to see for some time, we do not go from a neutral to a positive state, but instead just remove our craving for their company and the dissatisfaction caused by their absence. The same applies to the pleasure of physical exercise: it relieves us from the bad feelings that come when we fail to exercise. Or even the pleasure of falling in love, which provides refreshing relief from the boredom and desire that otherwise plague us. Here is how Lukas Gloor explains it:

---

33 Gloor & Mannino, 2016, III.
34 Note in this context that mere dissatisfaction and frustrated desires need not imply suffering in the sense of a bad overall experience, yet they can still be worth avoiding and feel strongly in need of relief. For example, the sensation of having to urinate rarely gives rise to an overall bad experience (i.e. suffering as defined here), yet it is still worth being relieved of this sensation. Thus, a more complete encapsulation of the views outlined here would be "happiness as the absence of suffering, discomfort, and dissatisfaction".

Chapter 2

> In the context of everyday life, there are almost always things that ever so slightly bother us. Uncomfortable pressure in the shoes, thirst, hunger, headaches, boredom … When our brain is flooded with pleasure, we temporarily become unaware of all the negative ingredients of our stream of consciousness, and they thus cease to exist. Pleasure is the typical way in which our minds experience temporary freedom from suffering, which may contribute to the view that happiness is the symmetrical counterpart to suffering, and that pleasure, at the expense of all other possible states, is intrinsically important and worth bringing about.[35]

A similar point can be made with respect to the negative states we endure in our pursuits of happiness: they are worthwhile because we would experience even greater dissatisfaction and suffering otherwise. For example, the negative experiences we may endure during physical exercise are likely less bad than the pain and suffering we would experience otherwise due to bad health, chronic back pain, dissatisfying looks, etc. Likewise, the negative experiences most of us may incur in pursuit of a romantic partner, such as fear of rejection, are plausibly less bad than the negative states that would result otherwise, such as loneliness and sexual frustration.

This view of the nature of our strivings finds some support in the psychological literature, as it has been found that "[t]here are many more techniques people use for escaping bad moods than for inducing good ones."[36] And, furthermore, that "people exert disproportionate amounts of energy trying to escape from bad moods …"[37] These findings support the claim that our strivings tend to primarily be aimed toward the avoidance of negative states rather than the attainment of positive ones.

Another objection is that it seems implausible that states of mere contentment have the same value as states of the greatest euphoric bliss. In response to this objection, it should first be noted that not all the views outlined above imply that ecstatic joy has *exactly* the same value as contentment — the impure anti-hurt view, as defended by Pearce and Wolf,

---

35   Gloor, 2017.
36   Baumeister et al., 2001, p. 332.
37   Ibid.

does indeed deem some forms of happiness better than others. The difference in value between such states is just always trumped by any difference found at the level of negative states.

Second, whether it is implausible to claim that "mere" contentment is optimal depends on the eyes that look. For if someone experiences contentment without any negative cravings,[38] and thus does not find their experience insufficient or suboptimal in any way, who are we to say that they are wrong about the value of their state? Indeed, who are we to say that they should want something "better"? The tranquilist view, as well as all other anti-hurt views that measure the value of an experience along a homogeneous scale, would deny that such a "merely" content person is wrong to claim that their state is optimal. Thus, these views are at least in perfect agreement with this person's own perspective, which one may argue is the most relevant perspective to consider in this context. A proponent of tranquilism may argue that this implication appears implausible only from the perspective of someone who is *not* perfectly content — one who desires the existence of euphoric bliss, and who feels bad about its absence.[39]

In a similar vein, one may be tempted to dismiss anti-hurt views on the grounds that they appear to imply that happiness is not really that wonderful, and that the best experience one has ever had was not really that great. Yet it is important to make clear that anti-hurt views imply no such thing. On the contrary, all anti-hurt views imply that experiences of happiness are indeed — together with all other experiential states absent of suffering and dissatisfaction — experiences of the most wonderful kind. The distinctive implication of these views is just that the intrinsic value of happy states is primarily due to their absence of negative features, and hence that the creation of happiness cannot outweigh the creation of suffering.

---

38 The term "negative cravings" avoids the complication that there might be non-problematic cravings.
39 See also Gloor, 2017, 4.3. Gloor's response to this objection is that many peak experiences seem valuable because they "condense" many other things we value, such as achieving goals and gaining deep insights, into a single moment. Thus, we should be careful not to confuse any value we may ascribe to such achievements with the value of the positive experiences that accompany them. As Gloor notes, if the peak experiences in question were merely created in an experience machine, most people would probably feel less sure about the value of such experiences, which suggests that it is not the pleasure *per se* we find (most) valuable in peak experiences, but perhaps rather other goods that they represent (e.g. achievement, self-realization, the fulfillment of deep desires).

2.5 Are Anti-Hurt Views Bleak?

It may seem rather pessimistic to say that, in terms of the intrinsic value of conscious states, the absence of suffering is the greatest aim we can achieve. Yet one can easily turn this sentiment on its head and argue the exact opposite. For example, it is hardly bleak to say that most of the world is in an optimal state, and yet this is precisely the evaluation of the world that follows from anti-hurt views.[40] This stands in stark contrast to views that consider it just as valuable (in principle) to turn neutral states into pleasure as it is to alleviate suffering.[41] According to such views, a neutral state absent of pleasure that could be turned into a state with "10 units" of pleasure is just as bad and problematic as a state of "10 units" of suffering that could be a neutral state, which in turn implies that much more of the world is in a truly problematic state than just those states that contain suffering.[42] Thus, in terms of how much of the world is thought to be in a problematic state, anti-hurt views are indeed among the most positive and optimistic views.

Beyond that, the adoption of anti-hurt views may also have psychological benefits, as it may remove the need to always be seeking something beyond "mere" contentment — a seeking that may, ironically, just keep contentment at bay.[43] This is quite different, again, from views that consider the promotion of happiness just as important as the reduction of suffering, as such views are practically insatiable, both at the personal and the collective level. For example, at the collective level, one can always turn more inanimate matter into happiness.[44] The satiability of anti-hurt views is another weak reason to consider them less bleak than the insatiable alternatives.

---

40 Although the impure anti-hurt view maintains that some states of happiness are better than others, it still does consider states absent of suffering to be optimal in the most relevant sense.
41 Classical utilitarianism, as commonly conceived, would count as such a view.
42 A similar point is made in Anonymous, 2015, 1.4 & 2.2.1. For an attempt to explain why such a view may seem appealing, and why I used to hold it myself, see Vinding, 2018f.
43 *Cf.* the paradox of hedonism and Burkeman, 2012.
44 The same point is made in Wolf, 1997, I: "[T]he positive utilitarian imperative to 'maximize happiness' is insatiable, while the negative utilitarian command to 'minimize misery' is satiable: no matter how much happiness we have, the positive principle tells us that more would always be better."

In any case, whether a view is bleak should not be considered evidence against it. If anything, the fact that we consider a view bleak is a reason to think we are biased against it (due to our tendency toward wishful thinking). Hence, we have good reason to seek to control for any anti-bleakness bias that may distort our evaluations of seemingly bleak views.

And the truth is that many people do find anti-hurt views quite bleak, even as we make clear that such views do not imply that happiness is not wonderful, and even as we point out that anti-hurt views consider most of the world to be perfect. For most of us would probably like to think that there exist experiences that carry truly positive intrinsic value with equal and opposite weight to the intrinsic disvalue of suffering, and which may thus in some sense outweigh suffering.

Yet being motivated to reject anti-hurt views in this way, based on what we would *like* to believe, should only make us that much more keen to give anti-hurt views a fair hearing. Moreover, the fact that Eastern traditions that specialize in paying close attention to the nature of conscious experience have converged on such views — together with other prominent traditions and philosophers, such as Epicurus and Schopenhauer — should give us pause with respect to any inclination we may have to reject anti-hurt views out of hand.

The implications of anti-hurt views are clear: creating more happiness for those who do not suffer is never of greater value than the alleviation and prevention of suffering. Thus, holding an anti-hurt view, or even just accepting that anti-hurt views contain a significant grain of truth, can be another way to arrive at the conclusion that our main priority, in practice, should be to alleviate and prevent suffering.[45]

---

45 Indeed, one can argue that a view of this kind is the underlying explanation behind many of the asymmetries we saw in the previous chapter — why it is important to avoid bringing miserable lives into the world but not to bring about happy ones; why the worst of suffering is much more disvaluable than the best of happiness is valuable (relative to a neutral state); why there is a strong asymmetry in consensus concerning the badness of suffering versus the goodness of happiness; etc.

3

Creating Happiness at the Price of Suffering Is Wrong

"Pleasure is the greatest incentive to evil."

— Attributed to Plato by Plutarch[1]

In this chapter, I shall present various thought experiments and arguments in favor of the view that it is wrong to create happiness at the price of suffering.[2]

3.1 Convergent Arguments

Imagine that we could create great pleasure for a large crowd by torturing a single person — for instance, as part of a sadistic bloodsport, but televised so that billions of people can enjoy watching the torture.[3] If we

---

1   See e.g. Partington, 1838, p. 643.
2   Note that this view follows, for instance, from the moral asymmetry between happiness and suffering defended by Karl Popper, David Pearce, and Clark Wolf. It also follows from other anti-hurt views, provided that one construes them in moral terms. Yet one can accept a version of the view defended in this chapter without subscribing to any of the anti-hurt views described in the previous chapter. For example, one may think that it can be good to increase one's own happiness, for its own sake, at the price of one's own suffering (anti-hurt views would contradict this), yet still maintain that it is wrong to create happiness for some beings at the price of suffering for others.
3   There are various versions of this example. A common one is a case where gladiators

think happiness can always morally outweigh suffering, it follows that we are morally obliged to perform such torture (provided the ensuing pleasure is "sufficiently great"). Yet that seems utterly wrong. A similar example to consider is that of a gang rape: if we think happiness can always outweigh suffering, then such a rape can in principle be justified, provided that the pleasure of the rapists is sufficiently great. This implication, too, is abhorrent.[4]

One may object that these thought experiments bring other issues into play than merely the moral value of happiness versus suffering, which is a fair point. Yet we can, as it were, control for such confounding factors by making the reduction of suffering the purpose of the acts in question. So rather than the torture of a single person being done for the enjoyment of a crowd, it is now done in order to prevent an entire crowd from being tortured in even worse ways; rather than the rape being done for the pleasure of, say, five people, it is done to prevent the suffering of five people who will otherwise be raped (for a longer duration and with even more intense suffering being experienced throughout).[5] While we may still find it unpalatable to permit such preventive actions, it nonetheless seems plausible that torturing a single person in order to prevent the torture of many would be the right thing to do, and that having less rape occur is better than having more. At the very least, it is far more plausible to say that such harmful acts can be justified if they prevent greater suffering than to say that they are justified for the sake of creating pleasure.

Another thought experiment along the same lines is a version of the utility monster described by philosopher Robert Nozick, namely an

---

have to fight for the enjoyment of a full colosseum, which is often raised as a problematic case for classical utilitarianism (see e.g. Scarre, 1996, p. 156).
4   This thought experiment has also been invoked by Richard Ryder, Ryder, 2005; 2009a; 2011, chap. 3.
5   If one objects that it is difficult to construct a case where we have two perfectly analogous scenarios that enable us to only test happiness versus suffering, here is one: imagine we are third-person observers who can determine whether the following scenarios will materialize with the push of a button. We can 1) make A torture/rape B in order to create "even greater" pleasure for C, or 2) make A torture/rape B in order to prevent even more torture/rape for C (assume that C knows nothing about A or B in both cases). The point is that it seems highly plausible to say that only the latter can be permissible, regardless of how much pleasure we may create for C in the first case.

Chapter 3

otherwise well-off creature who attains happiness at the price of imposing suffering on others.[6] If such a creature were to enjoy happiness "much greater" than the suffering we feed it, would it then be right to bring more suffering into the world for the sake of this creature's happiness? In particular, as David Pearce asks, if a sentient being were offered a super-exponential increase in happiness at the price of some other sentient being undergoing a "merely" exponential increase in suffering, would it really be permissible, let alone morally obligatory, to accept the offer?[7]

There are admittedly some complications here, as there are presumably limits to the level of happiness and suffering any single being can experience. Yet we can readily phrase Pearce's question in terms that avoid such complications. For example, if we were offered to bring about a super-exponential increase in the number of extremely happy beings at the price of a "merely" exponential increase in the number of beings who spend their whole lives being tortured, would it then be right to accept the offer? I believe most people would say "no".

Indeed, many, including proponents of anti-hurt views, dispute that the notion of "greater happiness" invoked above is even meaningful. Here is Dan Geinster objecting to it:

> [No] amount of bliss [can] "justify", "outweigh", or "cancel out" any amount of hurt, as when people say that the joys of this world outweigh its sorrows … Indeed, to say that bliss justifies hurt is like saying that the vast emptiness of space somehow outweighs all the suffering on earth, which makes no sense at all.[8]

By contrast, if we imagine the converse scenario[9] in which we have a *dis*utility monster whose suffering increases as more pleasure is experienced by beings who are already well-off, it seems quite plausible to say that the disutility monster, and others, are justified in preventing these well-off

---

6 Nozick, 1974, p. 41.
7 Pearce, 2017, "On Classical Versus Negative Utilitarianism".
8 Geinster, 2012.
9 The converse scenario is relevant to consider to control for variables other than happiness versus suffering that may influence our moral judgments, such as consent (which is what the present section seeks to control for).

beings from having such non-essential, suffering-producing pleasures.[10] In other words, while it does not seem permissible to impose suffering on others (against their will) to create happiness, it does seem justified to prevent beings who are well-off from experiencing pleasure (even against their will) if their pleasure causes suffering.

Indeed, such preventive actions would be in line with an intuitively appealing principle due to Derek Parfit, the "compensation principle", which holds that one person's burdens cannot be compensated by benefits to another person who is already well-off. (Parfit himself wrote that this principle "cannot be denied" and is "clearly true".)[11] The conclusion above can also be considered congruent with the "harm principle" defended by John Stuart Mill in *On Liberty*, which states that "the only purpose for which power can be rightfully exercised over any member of a civilized community, against his will, is to prevent harm to others."[12]

The preceding discussion relates only to tradeoffs between the suffering and happiness of different people, yet one can make similar arguments regarding what we are justified in doing to others for their own sakes. For example, philosopher Seana Shiffrin defends the following moral principle: it is permissible to harm someone in order to prevent greater harm to them, even without their consent, but never permissible to harm someone without their consent to provide them with a pure benefit (i.e. a benefit whose absence causes no harm).[13] In particular, this principle implies that it is wrong to impose suffering on someone (without their consent) in order to provide them with happiness or pleasure.

---

10 There is a close analogy between this case and humanity's exploitation of non-human animals for palate pleasure.
11 Parfit, 1984, p. 337; Wolf, 1997, I. Parfit did make one qualification, however, which is that he thought one person's harm could be outweighed by a benefit for someone this person loves, Parfit, 1984, p. 337.
12 Mill, 1859, p. 8. Indeed, Mill considered it the purpose of his essay to assert this "one very simple principle". To be clear, however, Mill's purpose in defending this principle was primarily to defend personal liberty, not to defend a moral asymmetry between harms and benefits.
13 Shiffrin, 1999. See also Benatar, 2006, pp. 49-54.

3.2 Intra- and Interpersonal Claims

It is important to distinguish between intrapersonal and interpersonal versions of the claim that it is wrong to create happiness at the price of suffering. That is: whether it is wrong to accept such a tradeoff in one's own life versus accepting it for others. For even though some moral views will say it is always wrong to create happiness at the price of suffering, no matter who experiences it,[14] many other views will say it depends crucially on *whose* happiness and suffering we are talking about. For example, some philosophers accept the intrapersonal claim that happiness can outweigh suffering within the same person's life, while they staunchly reject the interpersonal claim that one person's happiness can outweigh *another* person's suffering.[15]

A similar example would be Parfit's compensation principle, which also implies that one person's suffering cannot be compensated by the happiness of another, whereas it says nothing about intrapersonal tradeoffs.[16] Relatedly, Jamie Mayerfeld, who defends a general moral asymmetry between happiness and suffering, argues that we can be significantly *more* confident about this moral asymmetry at the interpersonal level compared to the intrapersonal level.[17] Karl Popper seemed to agree: "[P]ain cannot be outweighed by pleasure, *and especially not one man's pain by another man's pleasure*" (emphasis mine).[18]

The deeper point here is that even if one finds it plausible that happiness can outweigh suffering within one's own life, this need not imply that it is also plausible across different lives. (And this is true even if one holds a reductionist view of personal identity.)[19] Indeed, philosopher P. J. Kelly argues that even classical utilitarianism as defended by Jeremy Bentham, which is usually thought to be among the positions that discriminate the

---

14 Such as the negative utilitarian view defended by David Pearce, Pearce, 1995, chap. 2; 2017, part II.
15 See e.g. Ryder. 2011, chap. 3; Harnad, 2016.
16 Parfit, 1984, p. 337.
17 Mayerfeld, 1999, pp. 131-133, pp. 149-158, p. 176.
18 Popper, 1945, chap. 9, note 2.
19 For although it is tempting to conclude that the distinction between intrapersonal and interpersonal tradeoffs must collapse under reductionist views of personal identity, such views can, in fact, still make some sense of our common-sense notions of personal identity — e.g. as relating to particular streams of consciousness-moments — and thus still allow us to deem certain tradeoffs permissible across one set of consciousness-moments, yet not across others.

least between intra- and interpersonal tradeoffs, would in fact forbid at least some interpersonal tradeoffs between happiness and suffering, such as the torture of some for the purportedly greater happiness of others.[20]

3.3 The Ones Who Walk Away from Omelas

Another case worth considering is the scenario described in Ursula K. Le Guin's 1973 short story *The Ones Who Walk Away from Omelas*. The story describes an almost utopian city, Omelas, in which everyone lives an extraordinarily happy and meaningful life — except for one single child who is locked in a basement room, fated to live a life of squalor:

> The child used to scream for help at night, and cry a good deal, but now it only makes a kind of whining, "eh-haa, eh-haa," and it speaks less and less often. It is so thin there are no calves to its legs; its belly protrudes; it lives on a half-bowl of corn meal and grease a day. It is naked. Its buttocks and thighs are a mass of festered sores, as it sits in its own excrement continually.[21]

The story ends by describing some people in the city who appear to find the situation unacceptable and who choose not to take part in it anymore: the ones who walk away from Omelas.[22]

---

[20] Kelly, 1990, p. 81. Kelly argues that Bentham's conception of justice would forbid such tradeoffs because he sees Bentham as being fundamentally committed to personal liberty and the separateness of persons.
[21] Le Guin, 1973.
[22] The theme of this story is not original to Le Guin. It also appears in Charles Dickens' 1854 novel *Hard Times* (see Wolf, 1997), as well as in Dostoyevsky's *The Brothers Karamazov* (1879, p. 291): "Imagine that you are creating a fabric of human destiny with the object of making men happy in the end, giving them peace and rest at last, but that it was essential and inevitable to torture to death only one tiny creature ... would you consent to be the architect on those conditions?" Similarly, William James asked us to consider "a world in which Messrs. Fourier's and Bellamy's and Morris's Utopias should all be outdone, and millions kept permanently happy on the one simple condition that a certain lost soul on the far-off edge of things should lead a life of lonely torture, ... how hideous a thing would be its enjoyment when deliberately accepted as the fruit of such a bargain?" James, 1891, p. 68.

The question for us to consider here is whether *we* would "walk away from Omelas". Or more to the point: whether we would choose to bring a world like Omelas into existence in the first place.[23] Can the happy and meaningful lives of the other people in Omelas justify the existence of this single, miserable child? Some might say it depends on how many happy people live in Omelas. Yet to many of us, the answer is a clear "no" — the creation of happiness is comparatively frivolous and unnecessary, and it cannot justify the creation of such a victim enduring such suffering.[24]

3.4 What About Small Amounts of Suffering?

Most of the arguments in this chapter seek to establish that it is wrong to impose some considerable amount of suffering on someone — torture, rape, lifelong isolation and squalor — for the sake of creating happiness for others. The plausibility of these claims is roughly proportional to how great the suffering in question is: the more extreme the suffering, the more plausible it is that it cannot be outweighed by happiness. Yet even in the case of the imposition of the mildest of suffering — say, a pinprick that results in a mildly bad overall feeling[25] — for the sake of creating happiness, it is still far from clear, upon closer examination, that this is permissible, much less an ethical obligation.

---

23 In terms of how Omelas compares to our world, it should be noted that our world obviously contains vastly more intense suffering, both in absolute and relative terms. Beyond that, even if we focus only on the beings who are not miserable, there is still a stark contrast to Omelas, since most of the non-miserable beings in our world appear much closer, for the most part, to experiencing states of mediocrity than to enjoying intensely happy and meaningful moments (a similar point is made in Benatar, 2006, pp. 70-80).

24 And even though some people will insist that the child's suffering is a worthy sacrifice, the fact that it only takes a single miserable life to bring the value of a whole paradisiacal city into question for most of us is testimony to the strong asymmetry between the (dis)value of happiness and suffering. By contrast, it would be wholly uninteresting to read a story about a single being who lives a happy and meaningful life at the expense of many beings who must live miserable lives. Such a story would raise no interesting ethical questions whatsoever.

25 And it is indeed important that the pinprick gives rise to an overall bad feeling. Otherwise, it would not involve suffering as I have defined it here, and it may instead merely conjure up associations of an aversive component, which is something else entirely. I say more on this in section 8.9.

Indeed, Arthur Schopenhauer explicitly denied that even mild suffering could ever be compensated by happiness, even intrapersonally:

> *Mille piacer' non vagliono un tormento.* ("A thousand pleasures do not compensate for one pain.")[26]
>
> For that thousands have lived in happiness and joy would never do away with the anguish and death-agony of one individual; and just as little does my present well-being undo my previous sufferings.[27]

Albert Camus seemed to echo this sentiment in his novel *The Plague*: "For who would dare to assert that eternal happiness can compensate for a single moment's human suffering?"[28]

This view appears particularly compelling when we consider what we are allowed to do to others. For would it really be right to impose a small amount of suffering on someone in order to create pleasure for ourselves or others (as Parfit's compensation principle forbids),[29] or even for the very person we impose the suffering on,[30] *provided that* whoever would gain the happiness is doing perfectly fine already? Looking only from the perspective of that moment's suffering itself, the resulting state would indeed be bad. And the question is then what could morally justify such badness, given that the alternative was an entirely trouble-free state. If we maintain that being ethical means to promote happiness *in the place* of suffering, rather than to create happiness *at the price* of suffering, then the answer is "nothing".

---

26 Schopenhauer here quotes Italian renaissance poet Francesco Petrarca, although he alters the poet's original meaning, Mayerfeld, 1999, p. 76.
27 Schopenhauer, 1819, vol II, p. 576. This view of Schopenhauer's is a natural implication of his view that happiness is always negative — the mere absence of desire and pain (see section 2.2).
28 Camus, 1947, p. 224.
29 Parfit, 1984, p. 337; Wolf, 1997. It should be noted that Parfit did believe that some bad lives could be compensated by the good lives of others, Parfit, 2011, vol II, pp. 611-612. Yet he failed to explain how this can be compatible with his ("clearly true") compensation principle.
30 As Shiffrin's ethical principle cited above would forbid, Shiffrin, 1999.

4

The Principle of Sympathy for Intense Suffering[1]

No positive good can outweigh the very worst forms of suffering. This common view lies at the heart of the ethical principle I shall argue for in this chapter. What this principle says, roughly speaking, is that we should prioritize the interests of those who experience the most extreme forms of suffering. In particular, we should prioritize their interest in not experiencing such suffering higher than we should prioritize anything else. I call this the "principle of sympathy for intense suffering".[2]

---

1 This chapter is an expanded version of a chapter with the same title in Vinding, 2018a.
2 I do not claim that this principle is original to me. For example, it bears strong similarity to what Brian Tomasik calls "consent-based negative utilitarianism", Tomasik, 2015a, as well as to the ethical views defended by Ingemar Hedenius (Hedenius, 1964; Knutsson, 2019c), Joseph Mendola (Mendola, 2006), and Jonathan Leighton (Leighton, 2011). An essentially identical view is also explored in Gloor & Mannino, 2016, II. Beyond that, the principle I outline here has strong similarities to Richard Ryder's painism (Ryder, 2005), which says that we should "concern ourselves primarily with the pain of the individual who is the maximum sufferer." Jamie Mayerfeld, too, has expressed a view similar to the one I present in this chapter, Mayerfeld, 1999, p. 148, p. 178. And philosopher Ragnar Ohlsson has defended a duty-based principle along similar lines, Ohlsson, 1979.

4.1 Motivation and Outline

Something that may help motivate us to take this principle seriously is to ask, quite simply, why we would suppose it to be otherwise. Why should we believe that the most extreme forms of suffering can somehow be outweighed or counterbalanced by something else? After all, there seems no reason, *a priori*, to suppose this to be the case.[3] That is, before we look at the particulars, if we consider only what we know about the world at large, we have little reason to assume that the most extreme suffering should be "outweighable". By all appearances, the world was not designed to make the well-being of sentient beings "net positive".[4] Nor does anything we know about the universe at large guarantee that such "net positive" well-being is even a possibility in principle.[5] In short, we have no *a priori* reason to assume a positive story in this regard.

It may be objected that we have no reason to assume a negative story either. And this is true. The point here is just that we should make no strong *a priori* assumptions in either direction.[6] What I shall argue, however, is that when we proceed to look at the relevant particulars — especially the felt experience of extreme suffering — we do indeed, as sympathetic beings, find overwhelming reason to draw a negative conclusion.

A first glance at the particulars may appear to suggest the opposite conclusion. After all, common sense would seem to say that if a conscious subject considers some state of suffering worth experiencing in order to attain some given pleasure, then this pleasure is indeed worth the suffering. And this view may work for most of us most of the time.[7] Yet it runs into

---

3 In what sense do I mean that it could "be the case" that extreme suffering cannot be outweighed? In this chapter, I argue from the position of what well-informed beings would consider acceptable upon reflection. In the next chapter, I shall make an explicitly moral realist case for the view that extreme suffering has superior moral significance relative to everything else.
4 Assuming we can even make sense of such a statement in the first place, *cf.* Knutsson, 2016b.
5 For example, pure anti-hurt views would deny such a possibility.
6 And it is indeed important that we explicitly set the scale equal from the outset, as we may well implicitly make optimistic assumptions otherwise. After all, it is well-documented that humans have a tendency to engage in wishful thinking, Bastardi et al., 2011.
7 Though a proponent of anti-hurt views would, of course, question whether this is a matter of pleasures outweighing some suffering as opposed to a matter of enduring suffering so as to prevent even greater suffering that would have occurred otherwise (see section

serious problems, not just in the interpersonal case,[8] but also in cases where subjects consider their suffering unoutweighable by any amount of pleasure.

For what would the common-sense view say in such a situation? That the suffering indeed cannot be outweighed by any pleasure? That would seem an intuitive suggestion. Yet the problem is that we can also imagine the case of an experience of some pleasure that the subject, in that experience-moment, considers so great that it can outweigh even the worst forms of suffering, which leaves us with mutually incompatible value claims (although one can reasonably doubt the existence of such positive states, whereas, as we shall see below, the existence of correspondingly negative experiences is a certainty).[9] How are we to evaluate these claims?

The common-sense method of evaluation invoked above has clearly broken down at this point, and is entirely silent on the matter. We are forced to appeal to another principle of evaluation. And the principle we should employ is, I maintain, to sympathize with those who are the worst off. Hence the principle of sympathy for intense suffering: we should sympathize with the evaluations of those subjects who experience suffering so intense that they 1) consider it unbearable — i.e. they cannot consent to it even if they try their hardest — and 2) consider it unoutweighable by any positive good, even if only for a brief experience-moment.[10] More precisely, we should minimize the amount of such experience-moments of extreme suffering.[11]

2.4), or to accomplish some life goal one may value independently (recall that anti-hurt views can be compatible with value pluralism, Gloor, 2017).
8   As we saw in the previous chapter, it is not clear that common sense generally allows us to create happiness for some beings at the price of suffering for others (see also section 8.9).
9   And we can have even stronger doubts about whether anyone could ever endorse the positive value claim upon reflection (i.e. not just in that purportedly all-outweighing happy moment, but also afterwards), whereas again, as we shall see shortly, some have indeed endorsed the negative view upon reflection.
10 Both being necessary conditions for deserving such maximum moral priority.
11 Note that, as I defend this principle, it applies both intrapersonally and interpersonally, yet one may also accept it only in the interpersonal case (which is the most morally relevant case at any rate).

4.2 Common-Sense Support

This principle has a lot of support from common sense. For example, imagine two children are offered to ride a roller coaster — one child would find the ride very pleasant, while the other would find it very *un*pleasant. And imagine, furthermore, that the only two options available are that they either both ride or neither of them ride (and if neither of them ride, they are both perfectly fine).[12] Which of these options should we ideally realize?

Common sense would seem to say we should sympathize with and prioritize the child who would find the ride very unpleasant, and hence choose the outcome in which there is no harm and no victim. The mere pleasure of the "ride-positive" child does not justify a violation of the interest of the other child not to suffer a very unpleasant experience.[13] The interest in not enduring such suffering is far more fundamental, and hence has ethical primacy. Indeed, one can argue that there is no genuine interest to have a very pleasant experience if the absence of such an experience is also considered perfectly okay and unproblematic (of course, children in the real world who want roller coaster rides rarely consider it wholly unproblematic if they do not ride).

Arguably, common sense even suggests the same in the case where there are many more children who would find the ride very pleasant, while still only one child who would find it very unpleasant (provided, again, that the children will all be perfectly fine if they do not ride). And yet the suffering in this example, a very unpleasant experience on a roller coaster, can hardly be said to count as extreme, much less an instance of the worst forms of suffering — the forms of suffering that constitute the strongest support for the principle of sympathy for intense suffering. Such intense suffering, even if balanced against the most intense forms of pleasure, only demands even stronger relative priority. However bad we may consider the imposition of a very unpleasant experience for the sake of a very pleasant one, the imposition of extreme suffering for the sake of extreme pleasure must be deemed far worse.

---

12 A similar example is often used by the suffering-focused advocate Inmendham.
13 This is, of course, essentially the same claim we saw a case for in the previous chapter: that creating happiness at the price of suffering is wrong. The principle I defend in this chapter is simply a special case of this claim, namely the special case in which the subject deems the suffering unbearable and irredeemably bad.

4.3 The Horrendous Support

The worst forms of suffering are so terrible that merely thinking about them for a brief moment can leave us in a state of horror for a good while. Thus, we naturally prefer not to contemplate these things. Yet if we are to make sure that we have our priorities right, and that our views about what matters most in this world are as well-considered as possible, then we cannot shy away from the task of contemplating and trying to appreciate the disvalue of these worst of horrors. This is no easy task, and not just because we are reluctant to think about the issue in the first place, but also because it is difficult to gain anything close to a true appreciation of the reality in question. As David Pearce writes:

> It's easy to convince oneself that things can't *really* be that bad, that the horror invoked is being overblown, that what is going on elsewhere in space-time is somehow less real than *this* here-and-now, or that the good in the world somehow offsets the bad. Yet however vividly one thinks one can imagine what agony, torture or suicidal despair must be like, the reality is inconceivably worse. Hazy images of Orwell's 'Room 101' barely hint at what I'm talking about. The force of 'inconceivably' is itself largely inconceivable here.[14]

Many torture victims have echoed this sentiment of inconceivability and inexpressibility. For example, Belgian resistance worker Jean Améry, who was caught and tortured by the Nazis, reported that nothing could have prepared him for the first blow inflicted on him by the Gestapo, as if it revealed a whole new, previously inconceivable dimension of existence:

---

14 Pearce, 1995, 2.7. A personal anecdote of mine in support of Pearce's quote is that, although I write a lot about reducing suffering, I am *always* unpleasantly surprised by how bad it is when I experience even just borderline intense suffering. I then always get the sense that I have no idea what I am talking about when I discuss suffering in my usual happy state, although the words I use in that state are quite accurate: that it is *really* bad. It truly is inconceivable, as we simply cannot simulate that badness in a remotely faithful way when we are feeling good, analogous to the phenomenon of binocular rivalry, where we can only perceive one of two visual images at a time.

> One may have known about torture and death in the cell [before being tortured], without such knowledge having possessed the hue of life ... But with the first blow ... a part of our life ends and it can never again be revived.[15]

A similar report was given by journalist Jacobo Timerman, who was captured and tortured by the Argentine military regime of the late 1970s:

> In the long months of confinement, I often thought of how to transmit the pain that a tortured person undergoes. And always I concluded that it was impossible. It is a pain without points of reference, revelatory symbols, or clues to serve as indicators.[16]

These sobering remarks notwithstanding, we can still gain at least some (admittedly very limited) appreciation of the horror of extreme suffering by considering some real-world examples of it. (What follows are examples of an extremely unpleasant character that may be triggering and traumatizing.)

We can begin to approach such appreciation by considering what it is like to undergo "death by sawing", an execution method used on humans in many parts of the world in the past, and which is still used on non-human animals in some parts of the world today.[17] The victim is tied up and then sawn or chopped in half with a saw or a machete, either transversely or midsagittally — in the latter case, it has both been done from the groin up as well as from the skull down.[18]

---

15 The quote is from Améry's *At the Mind's Limits: Contemplations by a Survivor on Auschwitz*, as quoted in Mayerfeld, 1999, p. 38.
16 The quote is from Timerman's *Prisoner Without a Name, Cell Without a Number*, as quoted in Mayerfeld, 1999, p. 42. Author Barry Hannah expressed a similar sentiment in his novel *Yonder Stands Your Orphan*: "If you are able to explain suffering ... you weren't really there." Hannah, 2001, p. 323.
17 Baker, 2015.
18 See e.g. Busnot, 1714, chap. 8. Beyond such intentionally caused deaths, similar deaths in which the victim is cut or torn apart also happen without human intention, such as due to traffic and industrial accidents, as well as predation. Indeed, such unintentional deaths are far more frequent than intentional ones, and may well be just as intense and protracted in many cases.

Chapter 4

A similarly excruciating way to die is to be tortured to death inside a brazen bull: a hollow metal bull designed to contain a person inside while a fire is burning underneath, which slowly roasts the person inside to death. Many people have been reported to die in this way in ancient times.[19] And many more beings have died, and continue to die, in similar torturous ways, such as by being burned or boiled alive, which happens countless times every day. Indeed, the latter fate — being boiled to death — happens to a million beings each year in the slaughterhouses of the United States alone.[20]

Another horrifying example of torturous suffering is what happened to Kuwaiti Ahmad Qabazard, who, while only a teenager, was captured by Iraqi soldiers and tortured brutally for weeks because of his involvement with the Kuwaiti resistance movement. The soldiers sought to make Ahmad reveal the names of fellow resistance fighters, yet he refused to do so. Finally, Ahmad's parents were told that he would soon be released. They heard a car approaching and went to the door:

> When Ahmad was taken out of the car they saw that his ears, his nose and his genitalia had been cut off. He was coming out of the car with his eyes in his hands. Then the Iraqis shot him, once in the stomach and once in the head, and told his mother to be sure not to move the body for three days.[21]

No less horrible is the tragic fate of the Japanese girl Junko Furuta, who was kidnapped by four teenage boys in 1988, at the age of 16. According to their own trial statements, the boys raped her hundreds of times; inserted

---

19 For instance, the Romans are reported to have killed Christians with the brazen bull, and the bull is also reported to have been used on overthrown tyrants, such as Burdunellus, who was reportedly killed in this way in 497, Collins, 2004, p. 35. Some have, however, disputed whether the brazen bull has been used nearly as frequently as reported, and some even doubt whether it has been used at all. Yet even if it happened to be the case that a brazen bull has never been used (as I dearly hope), the point I am here trying to convey still stands, namely that suffering can be as horrible as we can imagine death inside a brazen bull would be (and indeed far worse, since again, we *cannot* accurately imagine what extreme suffering is like).
20 Dockterman, 2013.
21 Report by Julie Flint, *Observer*, March 3, 1991, as quoted in Glover, 2000, p. 32.

scissors and skewers into her vagina and anus; beat her with golf clubs, bamboo sticks, and iron rods; tied her hands to the ceiling and used her as a punching bag; set fireworks into her anus, vagina, and ear; burned her vagina with cigarettes; tore off her left nipple with pliers; and more. Eventually, she was no longer able to move from the ground, and she repeatedly begged the boys to kill her, which they eventually did, after 44 days, by pouring lighter fluid on her face and body, and setting her on fire.[22]

A much more common example of extreme suffering, indeed something that occurs every second of every day, is being eaten alive — a process that can sometimes last several hours with the victim still fully conscious of being devoured. A harrowing example of such a death that was caught on camera (see the following note) involved a baboon eating and tearing apart the hind legs of a baby gazelle who remained alive and conscious for an unbearably long while.[23] A few minutes of another such protracted death — a baby elephant eaten alive by lions — can be seen via the link in the following note.[24] And a similar death of a man eaten alive by lions can be seen via this note.[25] The man's wife and two children were sitting in a car next to him while it happened, yet they were unable to help him. Knowing this probably only made the man's experience even more horrible, which ties into a point made by Simon Knutsson:

> Sometimes when the badness or moral importance of torture is discussed, it is described in terms of different stimuli that cause tissue damage, such as burning, cutting or stretching. But one should also remember different ways to make someone feel bad, and different kinds of bad feelings, which can be combined to make one's overall experience even more terrible. It is arguably the overall unpleasantness of one's experience that matters most in this context.[26]

---

22 A brief report of the murder can be found in Hawkins, 2013 (unauthenticated source). The official trial documents for the case (in Japanese, yet copyable for machine translation) can be found at: courts.go.jp/app/files/hanrei_jp/261/020261_hanrei.pdf
23 youtube.com/watch?v=PcnH_TOqi3I ["Graphic content warning: Baboon eating gazelle alive"]
24 youtube.com/watch?v=Lc63Rp-UN10 ["Graphic Content Warning: Lions Eat Elephant Alive"]
25 abolitionist.com/reprogramming/maneaters.html
26 Knutsson, 2015b.

Chapter 4

After presenting a real-world example with several layers of extreme cruelty and suffering combined, Knutsson goes on to write:

> Although this example is terrible, one can imagine how it could be worse if more types of violence and bad feelings were added to the mix. To take another example: [Brian] Tomasik often talks about the Brazen bull as a particularly bad form of torture. The victim is locked inside a metal bull, a fire is lit underneath the bull and the victim is roasted to death. It is easy to imagine how this can be made worse. For example, inject the victim with chemicals that amplify pain and block the body's natural pain inhibitors, and put her loved ones in the bull so that when she is being roasted, she also sees her loved ones being roasted. One can imagine further combinations that make it even worse. Talking only of stimuli such as burning almost trivializes how bad experiences can be.[27]

Another example of extreme suffering is what happened to airplane pilot Dax Cowart. In 1973, at the age of 25, Dax went on a trip with his father to visit land that he considered buying. Unfortunately, due to a pipeline leak, the air over the land was filled with propane gas, which is highly flammable when combined with oxygen. As they tried to start their car, the propane ignited, and the two men found themselves in a burning inferno. Dax's father died, and Dax himself had much of his hands, eyes, and ears burned away; two thirds of his skin was severely burned.[28]

The case of Dax has since become quite famous, not only because of the extreme horror he experienced during and after this explosion, but also because of the ethical issues raised by his treatment, which turned out to be about as torturous as the explosion itself. For Dax himself repeatedly said, immediately after the explosion as well as for months later, that he wanted to die more than anything else, and that he did not want to be subjected to any treatment that would keep him alive. Nonetheless, he was forcibly treated for a period of 14 months, during which he tried to end his life several times.

---

27 Ibid.
28 See the following video for a description of the accident by Dax himself: youtube.com/watch?v=M3ZnFJGmoq8 ["Dax's Case"]

After his treatment, Dax managed to recover and live what he considered a happy life — he successfully sued the oil company responsible for the pipeline leak, which left him financially secure; he earned a law degree; got married; and reported to have had "some very, very good experiences" after the accident.[29] Yet even from this position of an accomplished and self-reportedly happy life, he still wished that he had been killed rather than treated. In Dax's own view, no happiness could ever compensate for what he went through.[30]

This kind of evaluation is exactly what the ethical principle advocated here centers on, and what the principle amounts to is essentially a refusal to claim that Dax's evaluation, or any other like it, is wrong. The principle of sympathy for intense suffering maintains that we should not allow the occurrence of such unbearable suffering that the subject finds unoutweighable by any positive good, and hence that the prevention of such suffering should be our highest priority.

And it is indeed worth reflecting on what a rejection of this view would entail. For if one holds that such extreme suffering *can* be outweighed by some positive good, one ought to clarify how. Specifically, according to whom, and measured by what criteria, is such suffering outweighable by positive goods? The most promising option that lies open in this regard, it seems, is to prioritize the assessments of beings who say that their happiness, or other good things about their lives, do outweigh and justify such extreme suffering endured by others.[31] Yet that, I maintain, would be a profoundly unsympathetic choice — not least because it would contradict Parfit's compensation principle: that a benefit for some individuals cannot compensate for harms endured by others, least of all for harms of the most extreme kind.[32]

I shall spare the reader from further examples of extreme suffering here in the text, and instead refer to sources, found in the following note, that contain additional cases that are worth considering to gain an appreciation of the moral significance of extreme suffering.[33] And the crucial question we

---

29 Engel, 1983.
30 Ibid.; Benatar, 2006, p. 63.
31 After all, if such happy beings themselves deny that the good things in their lives can outweigh extreme suffering, it hardly seems plausible for us to say that they do.
32 Parfit, 1984, p. 337; Wolf, 1997.
33 reducing-suffering.org/the-horror-of-suffering/

Chapter 4

must ask ourselves in relation to these examples is whether the creation of happiness or any other purported good could ever justify the creation of, or the failure to prevent, suffering this bad and worse. If not, this implies that our priority should not be to create happiness or other alleged goods, but instead to prevent extreme suffering, regardless of where in time and space it may risk emerging.

4.4 A Clarifying Note

One may object that not all the examples above constitute clear cases in which the suffering subject is unable to consent to their suffering. More generally, one may object that there can exist intense suffering that is not deemed so bad that no positive good could outweigh it, either because the subject is not able to make such an evaluation, or because the subject just chooses not to evaluate it that way. What would the principle of sympathy for intense suffering say about such cases? It would say the following: we should always prioritize reducing the suffering that would be deemed unbearable and unoutweighable (what we may call "unendurable suffering") over suffering that is intense, yet to which the sufferer is able to consent (we may call this "endurable suffering"). And in cases where the sufferers cannot make such evaluations (e.g. non-human animals), we may say that suffering at a level of felt intensity comparable to the suffering deemed unoutweighable and impossible to consent to by subjects who can make such evaluations should also be considered unoutweighable, and its prevention should be prioritized over all less intense forms of suffering.

Yet this is, of course, all rather theoretical. In practice, even when subjects do have the ability to evaluate their experience, we will, as outside observers, usually not be able to know what their evaluation is — for instance, how someone who is burning alive might evaluate their experience. In practice, all we can do is make uncertain assessments of where

---

reducing-suffering.org/on-the-seriousness-of-suffering/
simonknutsson.com/the-seriousness-of-suffering-supplement
youtube.com/watch?v=RyA_eF7W02s ["Preventing Extreme Suffering Has Moral Priority"]

unendurable suffering is likely to occur, and then act to reduce the greatest amount of unendurable suffering in expectation.

4.5 Objections

Among the objections against this view I can think of, the strongest, at least at first sight, is the sentiment: but what about that which is most precious in your life? What about the person who is most dear to you? If anything stands a chance of outweighing the disvalue of extreme suffering, surely this is it. In more specific terms: does it not seem plausible to claim that saving the most precious person in one's life could be worth an instance of the very worst suffering?

Yet one has to be careful about how this question is construed. If what we mean by "saving" is that we save them from extreme suffering, then we are measuring extreme suffering against extreme suffering, and hence we have not pointed to a distinct value entity that might outweigh the disvalue of extreme suffering. Therefore, if we are to point to such a distinct entity, "saving" must here mean something that does not itself involve extreme suffering. And if we wish to claim that there is something wholly different from the reduction of suffering that can be put on the scale, the fate we are saving this person from (at the supposedly worthwhile price of extreme suffering) should preferably involve no suffering at all. So the choice we should consider is rather one between 1) the mixed bargain of an instance of the very worst of suffering, i.e. unendurable suffering, and the continued existence of the most precious person one knows, or 2) the painless discontinuation of the existence of this person, yet without any ensuing suffering for others or oneself.

Now, when phrased in this way, choosing 1) may not sound all that bad to us, especially if we do not know the one who will suffer. Yet this would be cheating — nothing but an appeal to our all too partial moral intuitions. It clearly betrays the principle of impartiality,[34] according to which it should not matter whom the suffering in question is imposed

---

34 Or one could equivalently say that it betrays the virtue of being consistent, as it amounts to treating similar beings differently.

upon; it should be considered equally disvaluable regardless.[35] Thus, if we abide by the principle of impartiality, we may equivalently phrase the choice above as being between 1) the continued existence of the most precious person one knows, yet at the price that this person has to experience a state of unendurable suffering — a state they themself would consider so bad that, according to them, it could never be outweighed by any intrinsic good — or 2) the discontinuation of the existence of this being without any ensuing suffering.

When phrased in this way, it actually seems clearer to me than ever that 2) is the superior choice, and that we should adopt the principle of sympathy for intense suffering. For how could one possibly justify imposing such extreme and, according to the subject, unoutweighable suffering upon the most precious person one knows, suffering that this person would, in that moment, rather die than continue to experience? In this way, for me at least, it is no overstatement to say that this objection against the principle of sympathy for intense suffering, when considered more carefully, actually ends up being one of the strongest arguments in its favor.

Another seemingly compelling objection would be to question whether an arbitrarily long duration of intense, yet, according to the subject, outweighable suffering is really less bad than even just a split second of suffering that is deemed unendurable. Counterintuitively, my response, at least in this theoretical case, would be to bite the bullet and say "yes". After all, if we take the sufferer's own evaluations as the highest arbiter of the disvalue of experiential states, then the unendurable suffering cannot be outweighed by anything, whereas the suffering that is considered outweighable can. Also, it should be noted that this thought experiment likely conflicts with quite a few sensible, real-world intuitions we have. For instance, in the real world, it seems highly likely that a subject who experiences great, but initially not unbearable suffering will eventually find it unbearable, contrary to the hypothetical case we are considering.[36] Beyond that, our intuitions

---

35   I make a more elaborate case for this claim in Vinding, 2017b.
36   This case highlights the importance of not thinking too one-dimensionally about this issue. For example, a constant physical stimulus (say, being burned with a hot object of constant temperature) usually does not translate into a constant experience. For this

may be further confounded by our knowledge that most things in the real world tend to fluctuate in some way, and hence, intuitively, it seems like there is a significant risk that a person who experiences endurable suffering for a long time will also experience some unendurable suffering (again contrary to the actual conditions of the thought experiment).

Partly for these reasons, my response would be rather different in practice. For again, in the real world, we usually cannot determine whether someone is experiencing endurable or unendurable suffering, which means that we have to take uncertainty into account. After all, even if we knew that a subject considered their suffering endurable at one point, this would not imply that they will feel the same at a later time, even if they were exposed to roughly the same aversive stimuli. For in practice we no doubt should expect that significant fluctuations will occur, and that constant aversive stimuli will be felt as worse over time. Indeed, if the suffering caused by such stimuli is intense from the outset, the sufferer will all but surely deem it unbearable eventually.

Thus, in the real world, any large amount of intense suffering is likely to also include unendurable suffering in particular, and therefore, regardless of whether we think some unendurable suffering is worse than any amount of endurable suffering, the only reasonable thing to do in practice is to avoid getting near the abyss altogether.[37]

The principle of sympathy for intense suffering defended here stems neither from depression nor resentment. Rather, as the name implies, it simply stems from a deep sympathy for intense suffering.[38] It stems from a firm

---

reason, it can easily be much worse, in terms of the overall intensity and "consentability" of suffering, to be burned for a long duration with a less scorching object (say, 100 degrees Celsius) than to be burned with a hotter object (say, 200 degrees Celsius) for a short duration, as the experience of unbearableness may only emerge in the former case. This is perfectly consistent with the view I defend, as this view pertains to the overall intensity and "consentability" of experiences, not to external stimuli.

37 I shall say more in response to a similar objection in sections 5.6 and 8.10.
38 Though it is important to note that this sympathy need not stem from compassion (although it may, *cf.* section 6.12). It can also be defended purely with reference to consistency: *I* would want others to sympathize with and prioritize *my* extreme suffering more than anything else, and hence, by consistency, I should do the same with respect to the extreme suffering of others.

choice to side with the evaluations of those who are superlatively worst off. And while it is true that this principle has the implication that it would have been better if the world had never existed, I think the fault here is to be found in the world, not the principle.

Some pockets of the universe are in a state of insufferable darkness. Such suffering is like a black hole that sucks all light out of the world. Or rather, if all the light of the world has any intrinsic value, it pales in comparison to the disvalue of this darkness. Yet, by extension, this also implies that there *is* a form of light whose value *does* compare to this darkness, and that is the kind of light we should aspire to become: the light that brightens and prevents the unendurable darkness of the world.[39]

---

39 I suspect both the content and phrasing of the last couple of sentences are inspired by the following quote I saw written on Facebook by Robert Daoust: "What is at the center of the universe of ethics, I suggest, is not the sun of the good and its play of bad shadows, but the black hole of suffering."

5

A Moral Realist Case for Minimizing Extreme Suffering

> *"Whatever else our ethical commitments and specific constraints are, we can and should certainly all agree that, in principle, the overall amount of conscious suffering in all beings capable of conscious suffering should be minimized."*
>
> — Thomas Metzinger[1]

In this chapter, I shall make a moral realist case for the view that we ought to minimize extreme suffering. In other words, I will argue that we in a sense *truly* and *objectively* ought to reduce extreme suffering as much as we can. This is my honest view, and I shall here seek to clarify why and in what sense I hold it.

The view I present here can be seen as a moral realist version of the principle argued for in the previous chapter, as it defends a version of this principle as a moral truth (in a qualified sense). Yet it is worth being clear that the acceptance of this principle, and of the general claim that we should grant the reduction of suffering special priority, is not predicated on moral realism. That is, one can be a moral anti-realist and still find the arguments I present here plausible and compelling.

---

1 Metzinger, 2003, p. 570. It should be noted that Metzinger is not a moral realist.

5.1 The Map Is Not the Territory

A preliminary remark worth making in this context, if for no other purpose than to reduce the sense of weirdness and skepticism provoked in many people upon encountering a moral realist view, is that the map is not the territory.[2] All theories that purport to say something about the world have limitations. They are expressed in terms of concepts meant to reflect some aspect of the world, and these concepts can at best serve as pointers relative to reality at large, a reality that is in many ways much more complex than concepts can capture. This applies to all theories, and in one sense it is a trivial point. Yet as conceptually-thinking creatures, we can nonetheless easily overlook it. And the point is perhaps especially easy to overlook in the context of moral realist views, probably in large part because such views have traditionally been presented as infallible gospel rather than as fallible and refinable hypotheses.[3] The view I defend here is explicitly the latter: a moral hypothesis that seeks to track reality as accurately as possible with inescapably limited and imprecise concepts. It reflects the view of ethics I have found most compelling so far, and to which I would welcome any qualified criticism and refinement.

5.2 Does Moral Realism Matter?

Another issue worth a brief visit is the relevance of moral realism versus anti-realism. For why bother to argue for a moral realist view if it makes absolutely no difference in practice? My view is that it does make a significant difference. After all, if we do not believe suffering is *truly* bad and morally important, why should we bother to reduce it? Indeed, if we hold a particular ethical view while also believing that ethics is ultimately subjective and arbitrary, what is to prevent us from adopting another ethical view the moment we derive inconvenient and demanding conclusions from our original view? Such a convenient change seems much easier to justify in the absence of moral realism.

---

2   This remark is often attributed to scientist and philosopher Alfred Korzybski.
3   Religions have traditionally done this, of course, yet even in a secular context, it is plausible that we have strong, natural incentives to express our views on values in an overconfident manner for signaling reasons, *cf.* Simler & Hanson, 2018.

More generally, it seems natural to expect that moral realism is better able to motivate moral behavior. And this conjecture finds support in empirical studies. For example, one study in which participants were primed toward either moral realism or anti-realism found that:

> Participants primed with realism were twice as likely to be donors [to charity], compared to control participants and participants primed with antirealism. … [In sum:] priming a belief in moral realism improved moral behavior.[4]

Thus, I think we have reason to believe that moral realism matters.[5] Yet it should be noted that I do not believe in moral realism *because* believing it seems to have good consequences. Rather, it is in a sense the other way around: it is because I think there is such a thing as truly better or worse consequences in the first place that I am a moral realist. The potential motivating force of realist views just gives me additional reason to try to convey my view.

5.3 The Nature of My Argument

My moral realist argument for minimizing extreme suffering rests on two premises. The first premise is that suffering is intrinsically disvaluable and carries normative force. In particular, any subject experiencing a state of extreme suffering will be forced to conclude that this state, by its very nature, is *truly* disvaluable and that it *truly* ought not be.[6] The second premise is that the disvalue and normative force of extreme suffering is qualitatively greater than anything else, and hence the extent to which our actions minimize such suffering is the supremely most important thing

---

4 Young & Durwin, 2013. See also Rai & Holyoak, 2013, which found that merely being exposed to arguments in favor of the view that right and wrong are subjective and culturally contingent appears to "make individuals more likely to engage in immoral behaviors", such as cheating, compared to when they were exposed to the view that morality is objective and universal.
5 For more discussion on the relevance of moral realism, see Hewitt, 2008, chap. 1; Colebrook, 2018, 2.4.
6 Even beings without conceptual capabilities would, I submit, realize this in a preconceptual manner.

about them. In sum: minimizing extreme suffering carries *genuine* and *supreme* normative force.[7]

These premises are difficult to argue for, as opposed to just blankly state. And although I will attempt to justify these statements in the following sections, I think their truth can ultimately only be verified through direct experience. That is, the claims I am making here are really claims about the properties of conscious experience as felt directly, and such claims cannot be definitively confirmed in any other way than through direct conscious experience itself (for instance, one cannot know what the experience of red is like if one has never actually experienced it). This is not to say I cannot present supportive arguments that help render my claims plausible, as I shall, of course, attempt to do below. The point is just that these arguments can never provide anything close to the forcibly compelling justification that direct experience can.[8]

5.4 Suffering Is Inherently Disvaluable

The view that suffering, including extreme suffering in particular,[9] is by its nature disvaluable and something that ought to be reduced has been defended by various thinkers, including many of the philosophers we have visited in previous chapters. For example, as we saw in the first chapter, Karl Popper described suffering as something that "makes a direct moral appeal" for help, and something whose alleviation and prevention carries

---

7   My view thus has strong similarities with the view presented in section 1.4 ("Asymmetries in Quality"), according to which the reduction of suffering is always more important than the creation of happiness. It should be noted, however, that the view I defend in this chapter is not a utilitarian view as such, as it is compatible with pluralist views of value and ethics. To say that extreme suffering carries supreme disvalue and normative force is not to say that nothing else carries any value or normative force whatsoever.

8   A relevant analogy might be the way in which theoretical arguments rendered the existence of the Higgs boson plausible although experiments were still required to definitively confirm it. All I can do here is to present the abstract theoretical arguments for my view.

9   What I write in this section applies to suffering in general as well as to extreme suffering in particular. Only in the next section do I draw a distinction between extreme and non-extreme suffering.

urgency.[10] Consequently, the task of reducing suffering has, in Popper's words, "little to do with 'matters of taste'".[11]

Jamie Mayerfeld holds essentially the same view, as he also maintains that the moral importance of reducing suffering follows directly from its intrinsic nature. In Mayerfeld's words, "suffering cries out for its own abolition".[12] It is, quite simply, "bad and ought not to occur", and hence "everyone must act so as to eliminate suffering".[13] Mayerfeld describes this view as obvious to him, yet he also notes that he cannot supply an argument for it. That suffering is intrinsically bad, and bad in such a way that we ought to reduce it, is for him a rock-bottom observation.

Richard Ryder holds a similar view: "At some point, … justification [for a moral theory] must end. But where? I believe it ends upon the reality of pain."[14] So did utilitarian philosopher Henry Sidgwick, who considered it a fundamental ethical principle that "all pain is to be avoided".[15] And a similar view is found in Eastern philosophy, such as in the writings of 8th-century Buddhist scholar Shantideva: "I should dispel the pain of others, just as I do my own, based on the fact that it is pain."[16]

On my account, this is simply a fact about consciousness: the experience of suffering is inherently bad, and this badness carries normative force — it carries a property of *this ought not occur* that is all too clear, undeniable even, in the moment one experiences it.[17] We do not derive this property.[18] We experience it directly.

---

10   Popper, 1945, chap. 9, note 2; chap. 5, note 6.
11   Ibid., chap. 5, note 6.
12   Mayerfeld, 1999, p. 111.
13   Ibid., p. 111, p. 189.
14   Ryder, 2011, chap. 3. Note that Ryder defines pain "broadly to cover all types of suffering whether cognitive, emotional, or sensory", Ryder, 2009b, p. 402.
15   Sidgwick, 1879, p. 30. Sidgwick here merely spoke of the intrinsic moral disvalue of pain. As a classical utilitarian, he did believe that pain can (in principle) be morally outweighed by happiness.
16   This is from his Bodhicaryavatara, as quoted in Todd, 2012, p. 16.
17   This view is also defended in Pearce, 1995, chap. 2; Hewitt, 2008, chap. 3. However, Hewitt's view differs from mine (and Pearce's) in that she appears to consider happiness and suffering morally symmetric, and fails to address the many arguments against this view.
18   And our inability to derive or explain, as opposed to merely experience, this property is not a deep problem. For just as red can correctly be categorized as a color, even if we cannot specify why exactly, suffering can, I contend, correctly be characterized as

In my view, this is what bridges the "is-ought gap" that is said to prevent us from deriving statements about how the world ought to be from statements about how the world *is*. The statement "suffering is, by its nature, something that ought not occur" is a statement about how the world *is*, and it *does* say something about how the world ought to be. We are only forced to accept a gap between "is" and "ought" if we accept the premise that there are no states of the world — no states of what *is* — that have intrinsically normative properties, a premise I firmly reject.

By analogy, consider mathematical lines and vectors. Saying that "ought" cannot be found anywhere in the realm of what *is* is akin to saying that there are only lines, whereas vectors, things that point in some direction, do not exist. I disagree. When we look closer, we find that vectors — mathematical as well as ethical ones — indeed do exist in a very real sense (though this is not to say they exist in any Platonic sense).[19] The world is richer than our ordinary narrow conceptions suggest.[20]

One may object, however, that the *ought-not-occur* property found in suffering only exists and only carries normative force *for* the person experiencing it, not for others. Yet this objection faces many problems. First, the fact that experiences with this directly felt property of *ought-not-occur* do not exist within our own minds in the present, but only "out there" in the minds of others, in no way implies that this property does not exist "for us" in the most relevant sense. For even if we cannot feel this property directly, the property still exists out there just the same, in the mind-brains of those who do have such experiences. This is a fact about the world as real as any other. And as with all actual facts about the world, it is indeed also a fact "for us", regardless of who we are and whether we manage to connect with it. As David Pearce puts it:

---

something that inherently ought not be, even if we cannot specify why in more exact or reductive terms — its phenomenal nature just renders it self-evident. In my view, to object to this claim and to ask for proof for it is rather like objecting to and asking for proof for the claim that red is a color.

19   See Vinding, 2017b; 2018c for non-Platonic accounts of ethical and mathematical truths respectively.

20   Arguments against the existence of an is-ought gap are also found in Pearce, 1995, chap. 2; Fodor, 2014; 2019.

> [U]nless modern science is hopelessly mistaken, then ... I'm not really special, and neither are you. If agony and despair are bad for me — and they are! — then they are objectively bad for anyone, anywhere. One's own epistemological limitations don't deserve elevation into a metaphysical principle of Nature.[21]

As this quote of Pearce's hints, another reason to reject the notion that the *ought-not-exist* property of others' consciousness is irrelevant "for me" — unlike when it occurs in one's own consciousness — is that it is inconsistent. It amounts to treating the same thing differently, like saying that two plus two equals four for me, yet not for you. In other words, it seems tantamount to granting oneself a special ontological status compared to all other beings.

Another problem with the claim that suffering is only bad and worth avoiding for the person who suffers is that it rests on a deeply suspect view of personal identity.[22] For what, in the end, demarcates one sentient being from another in a sense strong enough to bear such moral relevance? To the best of our understanding, the different states our own mind assumes are distinct physical states distributed over time and space. Yet the same is true of the minds of others. And why should one sliver of such states outside our present consciousness-moment — i.e. the consciousness-moments of what we usually consider our future self — be considered more important than other consciousness-moments that are equally external to our present one? After all, in the present moment, we experience our past and future states of mind just as little as we experience the minds of (those states of the world we usually call) others. To our present mind, our past and future states of mind are also, in a very real sense, "others". Sure, we do in some sense experience them indirectly via memory and expectations. Yet memory and expectations hardly constitute the morally relevant difference we are searching for here, since it is most doubtful that other beings should

---

21 Pearce, 2018. For a more elaborate explanation of Pearce's realist view, see Pearce, 1995, chap. 2.
22 For an elaborate argument for this claim, see Vinding, 2017b. See also Parfit, 1984, chaps. 14-15; Siderits, 2003; Kolak, 2004.

be granted greater intrinsic moral value ("to us") if they shared more of our memories and expectations.

As a specific challenge to the notion that "their suffering only matters to them", consider a case where someone has the two hemispheres of their brain disconnected. Imagine this gives rise to two experiential subjects within a single skull.[23] Should this imply that the left hemisphere suddenly has less reason to prevent suffering for the right hemisphere than before, when they were still connected? This seems implausible. Yet if such a disconnect does not imply less reason for these two disconnected systems to help each other, why should this brain as a whole have less reason to help equally disconnected brains found in other skulls? After all, which particular skull a mind-brain happens to occupy hardly carries great moral relevance either. Specifying the boundaries that are supposed to render "our suffering" more relevant "to us" than the suffering of "others" is tricky. Indeed, I would argue it is impossible.[24]

The truth, I contend, is that there are just different consciousness-moments distributed over space and time, and our notion that some of these are "more us" than others in some deep sense that carries great moral relevance is simply an illusion.[25] Moreover, contrary to what common sense may suggest, the reality is that the only consciousness-moments we can ever act to benefit are consciousness-moments different from our present one. For our actions are never instantaneous. When John at time t_1, or John$_1$, is experiencing extreme suffering and acts on its *ought-not-occur* property, he is really taking action to help John at time t_2, or John$_2$, a closely located yet different state in space and time. And if we concede that such an action to reduce the suffering of another consciousness-moment, John$_2$, carries

---

23 One may dispute whether such a split of consciousness indeed happens in real life when the two hemispheres are disconnected. Yet this is of little relevance here. Such a division of a conscious subject into two does seem possible in principle given a physicalist view, which is all the current thought experiment assumes.

24 Again, a more elaborate case for this claim is found in Vinding, 2017b. See also Siderits, 2003; Kolak, 2004.

25 In practice, however, our common-sense notions of personal identity do indeed have significant relevance in many respects, Vinding, 2017b, "The Field View: Non Sequiturs". See also Korsgaard, 1989; 2009. Korsgaard argues that we cannot make sense of ethics if we think about persons purely in terms of separate consciousness-moments, and that our common-sense notions of personal agency seem necessary for moral deliberation.

normative force for John$_1$ — again, that is the only thing the felt normative force of John$_1$'s suffering could possibly make him act for: to prevent suffering for another consciousness-moment — the task is to explain why reducing the suffering of every other distinct consciousness-moment does not carry the same normative force. I maintain that no satisfying explanation can be given. The difference, we may say, is just that John$_1$ understands the importance of helping John$_{2, 3, 4, …}$ in a much clearer, more direct way than he understands the importance of helping other strings of consciousness-moments. Only an epistemological limitation that hides the true felt reality of the suffering of these other strings makes their suffering seem less important.

So am I saying people are mistaken if they are not motivated to reduce the extreme suffering of others, and, if so, in what sense are they mistaken? I am saying they are mistaken in the same sense that they would be mistaken not to be motivated to prevent themselves, in the usual narrow sense, from experiencing extreme suffering (and I suspect most people would indeed consider the latter a genuine mistake, to put it mildly). Just as we have compelling reason to prevent future suffering for ourselves, closer examination reveals that we have the same good reason to reduce the suffering of others. That is really the essence of the view I am arguing for here.

One may, of course, debate whether "moral realism" is the most appropriate term for this position, yet it seems to me the best fit. On my account, there really is an "ought" inherent to extreme suffering, indeed an "ought" more significant and forceful than anything the word "ought" can ever come close to capturing.

Put another way, one may think of the imperative to reduce extreme suffering as a vindicated hypothetical imperative.[26] For nobody doubts that we can talk meaningfully about hypothetical imperatives: *if* we want to achieve a certain goal, *then* we ought to act in a certain way. That is, once we grant the "if", the "ought" follows. And my point here is simply that the "if" in "if we want to avoid extreme suffering" indeed does obtain, and obtains universally. It *is* truly in our[27] interest to avoid extreme suffering.

---

26 The notion of a hypothetical imperative was first introduced in Kant, 1785, "Second Section".
27 "Our" as in relating to the collective "we" implied by the arguments in Kolak, 2004; Vinding, 2017b.

Or expressed in impersonal terms: wherever they are realized, throughout the universe, states of extreme suffering are intrinsically disvaluable and carry normative force.[28] Consequently, we ought to act so as to minimize them. Or at least, we ought to minimize them if nothing else has similar or greater moral weight, which leads to my second premise.[29]

5.5 Extreme Suffering Has Supreme Normative Force

Of the two premises underlying my argument, this latter one is admittedly the more difficult one to establish.[30] For unlike the first premise defended above, this second premise does not merely say something about suffering *per se*, but says something about extreme suffering relative to all other value entities: extreme suffering has strictly greater normative force than *everything else*. This is a rather extensive claim. So how may we go about defending it?

---

28 I defend this impersonal view at greater length in Vinding, 2017b. William James (James, 1891, II) also phrased ethics in such impersonal terms: "If we must talk impersonally, to be sure we can say that 'the universe' requires, exacts, or makes obligatory such or such an action, whenever it expresses itself through the desires of such or such a creature." See also Sidgwick, 1874, book 3, chap. 13, §3.

29 A similar argument to the one I have made in this section can be found in the canon of Buddhism, where the so-called reductionist view of personal identity I outlined briefly in the text is commonly accepted. In particular, Shantideva wrote: "All sufferings are ownerless because all are devoid of distinction [between 'mine' and 'other']. Because it is suffering, it is to be prevented; how can any limitation be imposed? Why then is suffering to be prevented? Because it is agreed upon without exception by all. Thus if it is to be prevented, then indeed all of it is to be prevented." (As quoted in Siderits, 2003, p. 203.) Another verse in this same passage of Shantideva's emphasizes consistency as a reason to reduce others' suffering, without making any claims about the nature of personal identity: "The suffering of others should be eliminated by me, / Because it is suffering like my own suffering. / I should help others / Because they are sentient beings, as I am a sentient being." (As quoted in The Cowherds, 2015, p. 59.) Such arguments based purely on consistency can be considered of a somewhat broader kind than those based on reductive views of personal identity, since arguments based on consistency do not in general hinge on any particular view of personal identity. For instance, even if one assumes that A and B are different persons in some fundamental sense, one can still reasonably deem it inconsistent for anyone to consider A's suffering more morally significant than B's.

30 Though I believe someone who has actually experienced the very worst states of suffering directly would agree with this premise, *cf.* the report of Dax Cowart, Engel, 1983; Benatar, 2006, p. 63.

A first step may be to argue that all moral value ultimately resides in the realm of consciousness: something can ultimately only have moral value if it affects the experience of a sentient being. On this account, moral value is purely internal to consciousness, like the experience of redness. And although value may *appear* to exist external to consciousness, just like redness may appear to do so, closer examination will always reveal that it is in fact wholly internal to consciousness.[31]

If we grant this step, all we would need to do to justify this second premise is to establish that extreme suffering has superior moral significance relative to all other states within the realm of consciousness. Within this realm, happiness appears the most plausible candidate for a positive good that can morally outweigh extreme suffering. Yet we have seen many arguments against the view that happiness can morally outweigh extreme suffering in previous chapters, including that suffering carries a moral urgency that renders its reduction qualitatively more important than increasing happiness (for those already well-off); that the presence of suffering is bad, or problematic, in a way the absence of happiness is not; that experiences are primarily valuable to the extent they are absent of suffering; that the creation of happiness at the price of suffering is wrong; and that we should sympathize with and prioritize those who experience the worst forms of suffering. Together, I submit, these arguments make a compelling case against the notion that happiness can morally outweigh extreme suffering.[32]

To establish that extreme suffering has supreme moral importance compared to all other states of consciousness, we also need to establish that it has supreme moral significance relative to less severe states of suffering. Yet since there is quite a bit to be said about this issue, I shall postpone this discussion to the following section so as to not derail the more general argument I seek to make here.

---

31 The same view of moral value is defended in Pearce, 1995, chap. 2; Hewitt, 2008, chap. 3. I happen to agree with this view, yet as I point out below in the text, one can reject this view while still maintaining that extreme suffering carries supreme normative force.
32 More supporting arguments are found in the next chapter and in section 8.5, as well as in Mayerfeld, 1996; 1999, chap. 6.

It is important to note that the view that extreme suffering has overriding normative force is by no means predicated on the view that all moral value is found within the realm of consciousness. For instance, one can believe that things such as knowledge, art, and virtues have intrinsic moral value not reducible to their effect on conscious subjects while still believing that the reduction of extreme suffering has supreme importance.

One way to defend this view might be to again consider two different planets. To one planet, we may add all the non-experiential goods we want (assume that this planet is inhabited by conscious beings who can possess these goods), whereas to the other planet, the very worst forms of suffering must be added for some amount of the goods we add to the first planet. If we add nothing to the first planet, no suffering ensues anywhere. The question, then, is whether the addition of non-experiential goods to the first planet can justify increasing the amount of extreme suffering on the other. Even if one places great value on non-experiential goods, it seems highly plausible to say "no". Indeed, one can argue that placing high intrinsic value on a good like virtue should alone lead one to not allow any extreme suffering to be added to the second planet, as allowing such suffering, even for the sake of increasing virtue elsewhere, would not be a virtuous act.[33]

For a similar argument, consider the following thought experiment concerning the importance of increasing knowledge (for its own sake) versus preventing extreme suffering. Before us we have two separate rooms. Inside the first room, the greatest scientists who will ever live are collected with all the tools they need to make progress at the frontier of knowledge, potentially at the verge of making the greatest of discoveries at any time. (Assume that this knowledge will never be instrumentally useful, such as by helping us reduce suffering; it is only the intrinsic value of knowledge we wish to consider.) In the other room, we find a single person who is burning alive indefinitely, or at least as long as we allow the scientists in the first room to keep on researching. Now, how long should we allow these scientists to keep on researching? Even if we value knowledge for its own sake very highly, it seems clear that we should stop the scientists immediately, regardless of how great their rate of knowledge production may be. In other words, it seems

---

33 *Cf.* the view of virtues described in Breyer, 2015, p. 541.

clear that the moral importance of reducing extreme suffering is superior to the importance of increasing knowledge for its own sake.

Such a juxtaposition can be made with respect to any value-bearing entity — whether within the realm of consciousness or outside it — whose moral significance we may wish to pit against the moral significance of extreme suffering. And it seems plausible to say that the prevention of extreme suffering is more important than any other thing we may place in the room next door.[34] Indeed, the view I defend here is that this is not only plausible but *correct*.

In what sense do I maintain it is correct? In the sense that it is a fact about the intrinsic nature of extreme suffering that it carries disvalue and normative force unmatched by anything else.[35] It is not merely a fact about our beliefs about extreme suffering. After all, our higher-order beliefs and preferences can easily fail to ascribe much significance to extreme suffering. And to the extent they do, they are simply wrong: they fail to track the truth of the disvalue intrinsic to extreme suffering. A truth all too evident to those who experience such suffering directly.

One may say that the experience of extreme suffering forces our higher-order beliefs to comply and admit that it has supreme disvalue. The same is not true about extreme happiness, which represents yet another important asymmetry between suffering and happiness: suffering can be too extreme for us to bear, whereas happiness cannot be "too extreme" in a remotely analogous way. In fact, one can experience extreme happiness without being tempted in the least to claim that one's experiential state warrants

---

34 George Orwell expressed a similar intuition in *1984*, part 3, chap. 1: "Never, for any reason on earth, could you wish for an increase of pain."

35 A fact that, I maintain, is verifiable via direct experience, at least in principle, *cf.* the emphasis on the difference between *answers in practice* and *answers in principle* found in Harris, 2010. In this way, my moral realist argument rests on a foundationalist moral epistemology, with direct conscious experience constituting the underlying foundation. Note that the argument we saw in the previous chapter is not predicated on such a moral epistemology, or indeed on any kind of moral realism. The principle of sympathy for intense suffering merely rests on the premise that we should choose to sympathize with, and give prime priority to, the evaluations of those who experience the most extreme suffering. This can be maintained regardless of whether we think the intrinsic nature of extreme suffering is normatively compelling in the strong, realist sense I claim here.

overriding moral priority. By contrast, someone who experiences extreme suffering will *always* find it immensely bad and important.

Indeed, for many of us it is enough to merely witness a case of extreme suffering from the outside to realize that if we do not give foremost priority to the reduction of extreme suffering, we are, in an all too real sense, deeply out of touch with reality.[36]

5.6 Extreme Versus Non-Extreme Suffering

As noted above, the claim that extreme suffering carries greater moral importance than everything else also requires us to establish its superior importance relative to mild suffering. For a simple case for this claim, consider an instance of extreme suffering induced by torture — say, an experience of being roasted in a brazen bull deemed unendurable by the subject — compared to a mild headache that gives rise to a bad overall experience. I claim there is a *lexical* difference between the moral disvalue of these two: a single instance of such extreme suffering is worse and more important to prevent than *arbitrarily many* instances of such mild suffering.[37] If we had two rooms before us, one in which the worst torture conceivable is occurring, and one in which an arbitrarily large number of mild, bearable headaches occur, and if we could stop the suffering in only one of these rooms, we should end the torture.[38]

This claim may not seem all that problematic in itself, but one may wonder whether it forces us to accept an implausible implication, namely that we must specify a particular point at which a slight increase in the

---

36 Such a realization may be provoked by witnessing the extreme suffering found in Tomasik, 2016a, although I must warn that at least one person has been severely traumatized by doing so.

37 Author Jonathan Leighton defends the same view: "One person suffering intensely, such as at the hands of a torturer, is qualitatively different and … incomparably worse than a million people suffering from a mild hangover." Leighton, 2011, p. 85.

38 Note that I do not distinguish between different kinds of extreme suffering in this chapter. This is not because questions concerning different levels of extreme suffering are irrelevant. They just lie beyond the scope of this chapter, which merely seeks to establish that the broader class of states we can categorize as extreme suffering constitutes the primary locus of moral value relative to everything else.

severity of suffering makes this slightly more severe suffering worse than arbitrarily large[39] amounts of slightly less severe suffering.[40] The answer is "no", for various reasons.

First, one can readily formulate views according to which there is no point of discontinuity between sufferings of similar intensity, yet where there nonetheless is a discontinuity between very different intensities of suffering — say, extreme torture and mild headaches.[41] For example, one can maintain that states of suffering sufficiently close to each other in severity cannot be deemed better or worse relative to each other, not just in practice but also in principle.[42] On this view, it is only on a sufficiently coarse-grained scale, at the level of clearly different intensities of suffering, that value lexicality between different states of suffering can obtain.

Second, even if we were to grant that there exists a point of discontinuity at which suffering suddenly becomes lexically worse, this would not require us to be able to say exactly where it lies. For example, one may place a probability distribution between states of mild headache and states of extreme torture and then assign some low yet non-zero probability to each distinct level of severity in between as the place where the hypothetical point of discontinuity lies — say, two percent probability that it lies between -10 and -20 (on some arbitrary suffering severity scale); three percent probability that it lies between -20 and -30; and so on. (A natural

---

39   Naively, one might be tempted to say "infinitely worse", yet 1) this is not a very precise term, as it can be interpreted in various ways, and 2) the most straightforward of these interpretations are not equivalent with the statement made in the text (which concerns arbitrarily large amounts of less severe suffering). For instance, one may take "infinitely worse" to mean that any amount of A is worse than an infinite amount of B. Yet this is a stronger claim than saying that any amount of A is worse than an arbitrarily large amount of B, as "arbitrarily large" merely refers to any finite number (the difference, in formal terms, lies in whether we include the notional infinity point at the "end" of the real line; this difference could be relevant in the context of infinite ethics, cf. Bostrom, 2011b). For more senses in which discontinuities in value between two value entities need not imply that one of these is infinitely better than the other, see Arrhenius & Rabinowicz, 2015, 12.5, 12.8.
40   In the philosophical literature, the argument against lexicality I just alluded to — that we appear forced to accept some breaking point between states that seem similar in some sense — is referred to as the sequence argument, Knutsson, 2016e; 2019b.
41   See Arrhenius & Rabinowicz, 2015, 12.5, 12.7; Knutsson, 2016e, "Thresholds" (and the references found there); 2016g, "The structure of lexicality"; 2019b; Vinding, 2020a.
42   Mayerfeld, 1999, p. 29, pp. 63-65.

point to place it is the point at which the suffering gets so unbearable that it becomes impossible to consent to even if one tries one's hardest.)[43] And when we add up the probabilities in the entire interval, they should sum to a hundred, or whatever our credence in the value lexicality between the two ends of the interval may be.

Another response to this seemingly implausible implication is that it is phrased in a somewhat question-begging manner, as it seems to assume that a discontinuous step in disvalue must be found between two similarly severe forms of suffering. Yet one can reject this assumption, and maintain that a large qualitative jump is found in the severity of suffering itself at some point, and hence in its moral disvalue. Thus, on this view, when suffering gets any more severe at some point, it gets qualitatively more severe, not just "slightly" more severe.[44]

One may say that suffering must, on such a discontinuous view, get qualitatively worse when some particular *physical stimulus* changes just slightly, yet that is very different from claiming that it must get qualitatively worse because of a slight change in the *severity* of suffering.[45] And the former claim about small changes in physical stimulus leading to large differences in consciousness is indeed hardly implausible upon reflection. After all, physics is replete with examples of large qualitative differences resulting from minute changes. For example, a spring will exert a pull with a certain force depending on how far we stretch it, yet at a certain point, if we pull the spring just a tiny bit further, the spring will break and its pull

---

43 *Cf.* the principle argued for in the previous chapter. That the inability to consent seems a natural breaking point is also defended in Tomasik, 2015a, "Consent-based negative utilitarianism?" One reason to think it is a plausible breaking point, even in purely algo-hedonic terms, is that the ability to consent to an experience itself is a strong determinant of its felt quality. One can perhaps think of the ability to consent to an experience of suffering as a net that helps contain its badness. And if such consent cannot be maintained, this may be considered akin to the net breaking, upon which the experience of suffering itself jumps into another dimension of badness. (Note, however, that this breaking point need not be found at a specific intensity of stimulus or level of pain; I say more on this in Vinding, 2020b.)
44 That is, it only gets "slightly more severe" in the sense of being the next step in a notional ordered sequence of increasingly severe states of suffering. Yet to assume that the increase in severity found in each such step must be small is question-begging.
45 Moreover, the claim that such a lexical discontinuity must result from a slight change in stimulus is actually not true, Vinding, 2020b.

will go abruptly to zero.[46] Likewise, consider the discrete energy levels of atoms, where just a tiny difference in how much energy we bombard an atom with can mean a qualitative difference — a literal quantum leap — between two discretely different states with nothing in between.

Indeed, it is a general fact about standing waves of many different kinds that they can assume qualitatively different shapes (with no states in between) as a result of small changes in stimulus, and this is relevant in this context since it has been proposed that different states of consciousness correspond to different kinds of standing waves in the brain.[47] Thus, on this particular theory of how the brain works, it seems quite plausible that a small difference in stimulus intensity may lead to a large, qualitative difference in the severity of suffering. Or phrased in terms of waves: it is plausible that a small change in stimulus could suddenly give rise to a new and qualitatively distinct screaming "overtone" of suffering.

To claim that it is strange that such a screaming overtone should emerge is not much different from saying that it is strange that any disvalue should emerge at all. For example, if suffering has *any* disvalue, one can argue that the emergence of this disvalue faces the same problem: in one state, suffering *almost*, yet still does not quite exist; then we make a tiny physical change, and suddenly it emerges. We have a "strange step", one may claim, where we go from nothing to something. And this step has the same total significance, in that no amount of states similar to the state we had just before the suffering emerged — i.e. neutral states — can be added up to have comparable disvalue to this new (in physical terms) just slightly different state.[48] If we consider this discontinuity wholly unproblematic, it is not clear why we should consider it deeply problematic to have a similar discontinuity between mild and extreme forms of suffering where, I maintain, a similarly unique form of moral disvalue emerges.[49]

---

46 This breaking point is somewhat analogous to the remarks from Jean Améry (quoted in section 4.3) about what happens in the encounter with torturous suffering — "a part of our life ends and it can never again be revived".
47 Atasoy et al., 2017; Johnson, 2018.
48 At least in terms of purely algo-hedonic value.
49 Note, however, that one can reject value lexicality between mild and extreme suffering while still accepting the rest of the argument I have made in this chapter. One would then substitute "extreme suffering" with "suffering" in the second premise of my argument, upon which one gets a moral realist view according to which the reduction of suffering in

The argument I have made in this chapter may, I realize, do little to convince the skeptic. As noted from the outset, words alone can provide only limited support for the premises of my argument. Beyond that, I realize that the view I have laid out here is less than perfectly detailed — I have not, for example, provided a precise definition of extreme suffering (at least nothing more precise than "suffering so unbearable that it becomes impossible to consent to").[50] Yet these shortcomings are not fatal. Indeed, I would argue they are not even shortcomings. For again, the map is not the territory: it is bound to be less than perfectly precise. More generally, the fact that the map is less than perfectly detailed and that arguments alone cannot convince everyone of its validity does not imply that the map is useless or false. I submit the map I have outlined here is both useful and true.[51]

---

general carries supreme moral importance. This latter view is essentially negative utilitarianism as commonly construed, except that it is consistent with the claim that other things besides suffering have moral value as well, albeit lexically inferior moral value. Note also that one may consider my moral realist case for minimizing extreme suffering to be "correct" for all intents and purposes even if one holds such a negative utilitarian view, or indeed even if one holds a classical utilitarian view — provided that the moral disvalue one assigns to extreme suffering is so great that, given the prevalence of extreme suffering, other things will not have greater importance in practice, even if they could in principle. I know of at least one classical utilitarian who holds roughly this view (and such a view also finds some support in the empirical data presented in Emilsson, 2019).

50 It is not clear to me how one could provide a significantly more precise definition of extreme suffering, in phenomenological terms, than this.

51 Once again, it is important to note that one can accept the core claim I defend in this first part of the book — that we should grant the reduction of suffering special priority in practice — without accepting the stronger, more specific views I have defended in this chapter and the previous one.

6

Other Arguments for Focusing on Suffering

The arguments we have seen in previous chapters are by no means an exhaustive catalog of arguments in favor of prioritizing the reduction of suffering. The purpose of this chapter is to present some of the many other arguments that have been made in favor of the same conclusion. These arguments demonstrate how a focus on reducing suffering can be supported by a diverse range of views and intuitions.

6.1 Egalitarianism and Prioritarianism

Egalitarianism is a moral view characterized by the claim that we should reduce inequality and give special priority to the interests of those who are worse off.[1] This view has become increasingly popular among moral and political philosophers in recent decades.[2] And from this view, a strong focus on reducing suffering follows quite naturally. That is, egalitarianism holds we should prioritize those who are worse off in the most morally relevant sense, and since those who suffer the most are clearly among those who

---

1   Horta, 2016, p. 111.
2   Ibid.

are worse off in the most relevant sense, it follows that egalitarians should give special priority to reducing the suffering of the greatest sufferers.[3]

Note how this egalitarian case for prioritizing suffering is quite distinct from the arguments we have seen in previous chapters, as it says rather little about suffering from the outset. The starting point for egalitarianism is only that we should reduce inequality by helping those who are worse off, and the priority it grants to the reduction of suffering is then derived from this principle. It is a derivative priority that only becomes apparent when we examine the specific ways in which some individuals are worse off than others.

A similar yet distinct moral stance is prioritarianism, which shares with egalitarianism the view that we should prioritize the interests of those who are worse off. However, unlike egalitarianism, prioritarianism is phrased in absolute rather than relative terms. That is, egalitarianism holds that we should give priority to those who are worst off out of all individuals while prioritarianism holds that benefiting beings matters more the worse off these beings are, period (regardless of how badly off others may be).[4]

Prioritarianism thus provides a similar case for prioritizing suffering to the one egalitarianism provides. The fundamental intuition that animates it says nothing about suffering *per se*, but pertains instead to particular beings and how well or badly off these are in a more general sense — and the worse these particular beings are doing, the more important it is to help them.[5]

(Note that egalitarianism and prioritarianism further imply that we should generally give priority to non-human animals, as they tend to be worse off than humans.)[6]

---

[3] I have here phrased egalitarianism in moral rather than axiological terms, yet one may also phrase it in axiological terms. The same applies to my remarks below on prioritarianism.
[4] Derek Parfit discussed this prioritarian view, what he called the "Priority View", and its relation to egalitarianism in Parfit, 1995.
[5] A discussion of the difference between grounding concern for suffering in the intrinsic badness of suffering versus grounding it in this prioritarian view can be found in Mayerfeld, 1999, pp. 149-152. As Mayerfeld notes: "The difference is that whereas the intrinsic property view emphasizes the intrinsic awfulness of suffering, the priority view emphasizes the harm that suffering does to persons." Ibid., p. 150. Yet although these ways of grounding concern for suffering are distinct, there is no conflict between them. Indeed, they are perfectly complementary.
[6] Faria, 2014; Horta, 2016.

6.2 Other Values More Plausibly Have Diminishing Returns

Various philosophers have argued that many of the positive goods we value have diminishing returns as we add more of them. For example, philosopher Thomas Hurka argues that adding additional well-off people makes an outcome better when the population is small, yet with this value diminishing as the population level increases.[7] Similar arguments have been made with respect to increasing happiness, both within a single life as well as in all beings in total: as more happiness is added, the additional value it adds — to a life or to the world as a whole — decreases.[8]

The same plausibly applies to various accomplishments, to the extent one values these. The hundredth sub-ten-second hundred meter run was not as great an addition to the canon of human achievements as the first one, the twentieth painting of Mona Lisa indistinguishable from Da Vinci's is not as valuable as the original, the tenth proof of an important mathematical theorem is not as significant as the first, etc.[9]

The point here is that such diminishing returns seem much less plausible, indeed repugnant, when it comes to the value of reducing suffering. As Lukas Gloor and Adriano Mannino note:

---

[7] Hurka, 1983.

[8] The views defended by Hurka in ibid. imply diminishing returns in value not just as population levels rise, but also as total happiness increases. See also Rabinowicz, 2003; Knutsson, 2016e, "Thresholds". Mayerfeld defends a similar view with respect to the (dis)value and moral weight of happiness and suffering in general: "[S]uffering possesses greater moral weight than happiness, and ... as suffering increases in intensity its moral weight increases at a faster rate than its intensity." Mayerfeld, 1999, p. 135. This view is also discussed in Hurka, 2010, and at the level of what is valuable for individuals, it is defended in Mathison, 2018, chap. 2.

[9] These examples all pertain to accomplishments achieved by a population of individuals, yet the point can also be made with respect to accomplishments and experiences within a single life: one's hundredth kiss is usually not as valuable as the first (with the same person), one's hundredth derivation of a given theorem does not carry the same personal significance as the first one, etc.

> By contrast [to people's beliefs about the importance of increasing happiness and happy populations], people are much less likely to place diminishing returns on reducing suffering — at least insofar as the disvalue of extreme suffering, or the suffering in lives that on the whole do not seem worth living, is concerned. Most people would say that no matter the size of a (finite) population of suffering beings, adding more suffering beings would always remain equally bad.[10]

Derek Parfit, too, explicitly endorsed this sentiment:

> When we consider the badness of suffering, we should claim that this badness has no upper limit. It is always bad if an extra person has to endure extreme agony. And this is always just as bad, however many others have similar lives. The badness of extra suffering never declines.[11]

Yet Parfit did consider it plausible, or at least significantly more plausible, that the addition of happiness to the world only adds diminishing value to it.[12]

This asymmetry in (the plausibility of) diminishing returns is thus another reason to grant particular priority to the reduction of suffering. And this is especially true in a world where there is a risk that suffering may become far more prevalent in the future.[13] For if increasing positive goods has diminishing returns while the prevention of suffering does not, it follows that the latter becomes far more important in the limit, if we increase both the total amount of positive goods and suffering, as humanity may well do in the future. Thus, on this view, it can be far more important to avoid creating a large civilization full of suffering than to create a large utopia full of positive goods, even if one assumes these things have equal value in small amounts. The larger we expect our future to be, the more this view supports a focus on reducing suffering.

---

10 Gloor & Mannino, 2016.
11 Parfit, 1984, p. 406.
12 Ibid., chap. 17.
13 Tomasik, 2011; Althaus & Gloor, 2016. I say more on this in chapter 14.

6.3 Impartiality

Philosophers often distinguish between agent-relative and agent-neutral values — things that are good for a person alone versus things that are good from an impartial perspective. And it has been argued that suffering is among the strongest candidates for something that is disvaluable from an impartial perspective: something that has agent-neutral as opposed to mere agent-relative disvalue.[14] Thomas Nagel defended this view in his book *The View From Nowhere*:

> [P]ain can be detached in thought from the fact that it is mine without losing any of its dreadfulness. It has, so to speak, a life of its own. That is why it is natural to ascribe to it a value of its own.[15]

Jamie Mayerfeld, too, defends this view: "Suffering is bad ... not only for the individual whom it afflicts, but bad from an impersonal point of view. Its occurrence makes the world that much worse."[16]

This is then another way in which one can defend a moral asymmetry between suffering and happiness: by arguing that suffering carries significant moral disvalue from an impartial perspective, whereas pleasure and happiness carry value only in an agent-relative sense. David Benatar seems to hold such a view, in that he argues that "happiness is [only] valuable because it is good for people—because it makes people's lives go better",[17] while he maintains that the absence of pain and suffering is good even if there is no one who enjoys it.[18]

---

14   See Nagel, 1986, pp. 159-162. Nagel mentions both pleasure and pain as (dis)valuable from an impartial perspective, yet his discussion centers mostly on pain and suffering.
15   Ibid., p. 160.
16   Mayerfeld, 1999, p. 111. See also ibid., pp. 84-89. Indeed, Mayerfeld argues that "attention to suffering makes it hard to preserve skepticism about impersonal values." Ibid., p. 87.
17   Benatar, 2006, p. 37.
18   Ibid., p. 30. See also Jules, 2019.

6.4 Deontic Asymmetry

A similar way to defend a moral asymmetry between happiness and suffering is to say that, regardless of the axiological value we may ascribe to happiness and suffering, we still generally have a greater *duty* to prevent suffering than to create a "corresponding" amount of happiness. In other words, even if we believed that happiness and suffering were equally valuable in one sense, we may still maintain that the *moral importance*[19] of reducing suffering is greater than the moral importance of producing ("equal") happiness. Such a "deontic asymmetry" between happiness and suffering has been defended by philosopher W. D. Ross, among others.[20]

Asymmetries of this kind may be defended at the level of the intrinsic moral importance of happiness versus suffering, yet they can also be defended in a prioritarian way, as is in fact quite common.[21] For example, even if one thinks that a move from a neutral state to a very happy state in some sense carries comparable value to a move from a very miserable state to a neutral state, one may still think that our moral duties pertain primarily to moves of the latter kind, because they help beings who are worse off.

Regardless of how plausible we consider such a decoupling of value and moral duties to be, it seems significantly more plausible to think that such a decoupling should favor a duty to prevent suffering over a duty to create happiness than *vice versa*.

---

19 As mentioned in an earlier note, philosophers tend to distinguish between 1) that which is valuable (axiology), and 2) that which we have moral obligations to bring about or do (ethics), and one need not assume that the former implies or is coterminous with the latter.
20 Mathison, 2018, 2.5. While the thinkers we visited in section 1.4, such as Karl Popper and David Pearce, as well as Clark Wolf (introduced in section 2.3), all endorse a moral asymmetry of this kind, these thinkers also, on my reading, maintain that there is a strong asymmetry at the level of the intrinsic (dis)value of happiness and suffering. Indeed, Pearce and Wolf both seem to consider the moral asymmetry they endorse wholly derivative from an asymmetry in (dis)value. Thus, unlike the view of W. D. Ross, the views of these thinkers do not appear to entail a strong decoupling between the intrinsic (dis)value of suffering and happiness and the moral duties pertaining to these respective states.
21 Mathison, 2018, 2.5.1.

6.5 The Golden Rule

Another way to support a special concern for suffering is by appealing to the Golden Rule: "Do unto others as you would have them do unto you."[22] For while the Golden Rule surely pertains to more than just suffering, a strong case can be made that it implies especially strong obligations when it comes to relieving others' suffering.[23] If *we* were in a state of extreme suffering, we would sorely want others to prioritize the relief of our torment higher than anything else. Hence, if we are to adhere to the Golden Rule, we should give especially high priority to the alleviation of the extreme suffering of others.

6.6 The Categorical Imperative

The categorical imperative of Immanuel Kant holds that we should act only according to maxims that we can will to be a universal law.[24] Kant considered this precept the bedrock of morality, and argued that it implies a duty to help those in distress.[25] A prosperous person who does not help someone in distress would not be acting in accordance with the categorical imperative because "it is impossible to will that such a principle should have the universal validity of a law of nature."[26] For if an unhelpful person were suffering and in need of help, they could not wish others to be similarly unhelpful, and hence, according to Kant, such a person's will contradicts itself.[27]

---

22 According to philosopher Simon Blackburn, this rule is "found in some form in almost every ethical tradition", Blackburn, 2001, p. 101.
23 Mayerfeld, 1999, p. 114.
24 Kant famously stated his categorical imperative in two different ways that he considered "essentially identical": 1) "Act only on that maxim whereby thou canst at the same time will that it should become a universal law", and 2) "act in regard to every rational being (thyself and others), [in such a way] that he may always have place in thy maxim as an end in himself", Kant, 1785, "Second Section". And some philosophers have argued that the second formulation of the imperative supports an antinatalist position. Bringing a being into the world, they argue, cannot be done for that being's own sake, and hence to bring beings into the world is to treat them as means to an end rather than as ends in themselves, Benatar, 2006, pp. 128-131; Akerma, 2010.
25 Kant's original formulation of the categorical imperative only pertained to rational moral agents, yet one can expand it so that it relates to all sentient beings, Korsgaard, 2018.
26 Kant, 1785, "Second Section".
27 Ibid.

Chapter 6

There are clear similarities between the Golden Rule and the categorical imperative, both in terms of their content in general as well as the way in which they support a special concern for suffering in particular. As Mayerfeld notes: "Arguments from the Golden Rule and the categorical imperative both claim, more or less, that the relief of suffering is willed by us if we look at matters in a certain way."[28]

Nonetheless, the two precepts *are* distinct and should not be conflated. Indeed, Kant himself argued that the Golden Rule could be misapplied because it was insufficiently universal.[29] Whereas the Golden Rule merely asks us to do unto others as we would have them do unto us, the categorical imperative asks us to do unto everyone as we would have everyone do unto everyone.

6.7 Contractualism

In the context of moral philosophy, contractualism refers to a class of moral theories that hold that the legitimacy of moral rules must be grounded in respect for the will of each person to whom they pertain. On this view, the ultimate test of the validity of a moral principle is whether each person would be able to sign on to it.[30]

One of the philosophers most strongly associated with contractualism is T. M. Scanlon.[31] In his book *What We Owe to Each Other*, Scanlon argues that the only moral principles we should accept are those that "no one could reasonably reject as a basis for informed, unforced, general

---

28 Mayerfeld, 1999, p. 115.
29 Simon Blackburn gives the following examples of problematic (purported) implications of the Golden Rule that the categorical imperative might avoid: "A criminal can throw [the Golden Rule] at a judge, asking him how he would like it if he were being sentenced — yet the sentence may be just, for all that. A person in good circumstances may gladly agree that others should not benefit him, if he could be excused from benefiting them. He apparently abides by the Golden Rule. So something with more structure is needed." Blackburn, 2001, p. 101.
30 Hence Kant's view of morality is usually considered a contractualist one.
31 Indeed, contractualism is commonly used in two senses: a broad sense, which refers to contractualist theories in general, and a narrow sense, which refers to Scanlon's contractualist theory in particular.

agreement."[32] This, Scanlon argues, naturally directs our attention to "those who would do worst" under the rules we may propose, as they will have the strongest complaints against it.[33] And since those who suffer the most must be considered among those who do worst in general, Scanlon's contractualism is yet another view that can ground particular importance to the reduction of suffering, especially of those who suffer the most.[34]

Another prominent contractualist theorist whose views have similar implications is John Rawls, who argued that we would choose the best general principles for a society if we were ignorant about which particular individual we ourselves would be in that society.[35] And from this position, he argued, we would prioritize the interests of those who are worst off.[36] Rawls' argument focuses primarily on principles of justice in particular, yet it can readily be extended to moral principles in general. That is, we can consider what we would do if we had to determine the moral principles guiding all moral agents in the world, but without knowing which particular being we ourselves will be born as.[37] When considering that we could be born as one of the beings who experiences the very worst forms of suffering, it seems plausible that we would follow Rawls and give special priority to those who are worst off, and thus endorse "reduce extreme suffering" as a sovereign moral principle.[38]

---

32 Scanlon, 1998, p. 153.
33 Scanlon, 1982, p. 123. Scanlon himself wrote that he hereby endorses "something like" a prioritarian view, Scanlon, 1998, p. 396.
34 Mayerfeld, 1999, p. 115.
35 In Rawls' now famous terminology, we should imagine ourselves in an "original position" where we are placed behind a "veil of ignorance", Rawls, 1971, chap. III.
36 In particular, in the context of distributive justice, Rawls defended the "Difference Principle" (a form of maximin principle), according to which we should allow inequality only to the extent it benefits those who are worst off (provided certain fundamental conditions of liberty and equality of opportunity are met), Rawls, 2001, part II. Contractualist philosopher Ronald Dworkin defended similar views to Rawls, with similar implications in terms of favoring the worst off, Dworkin, 1981; Mayerfeld, 1999, p. 115.
37 The circumstance presented here is also different from the original position presented by Rawls in that he excluded all sentient beings except humans, Rawls, 2001, part III. For an exploration of the original position that does not exclude non-human beings, see VanDeVeer, 1979.
38 Mayerfeld makes a similar point: "People who could not predict the extent of their vulnerability to suffering in real life might seek protection from the worst eventuality by agreeing on a strong requirement to relieve suffering." Mayerfeld, 1999, p. 115.

Chapter 6

Indeed, the intersection of consent and suffering is a highly relevant one, not least when it comes to states of suffering so extreme that the subject is unable to consent to them. Such states would seem especially relevant from a contractualist perspective, and yet they appear to have received little attention.[39] This is a terrible omission since a strong case can be made that reducing such states should be our highest priority on a contractualist view. For example, say we assume a reductionist view of personal identity[40] and consider the evaluations made by the different consciousness-moments distributed in space and time. It seems that all the consciousness-moments that experience extreme, "unconsentable" suffering should plausibly have a superior claim against any moral principle that allows this suffering to exist. Such experience-moments can, in the words of Scanlon, "reasonably reject"[41] any such moral principle — with supreme force. Hence, one may argue, the moral principles a contractualist should accept are exactly those that minimize the number of these unendurable states of suffering, or at any rate principles that consider the prevention of such states a unique priority.

For a supporting argument in favor of this view, consider the following thought experiment. Imagine if all the consciousness-moments distributed across the world were collected into a single, continuous string of experiences, with all the worst (or least "consentable") states found at the beginning of this string, and the best ones at the end of it. And imagine, furthermore, that we had to determine the moral rules that apply to the world by witnessing, from the outside, the string of experiences that would be produced by these rules: a continuous succession of all the worst states of suffering unfolding until they eventually reach the increasingly less bad states. When we consider the issue in this way — a way that, importantly, does not allow us to ignore the reality of the very worst of states — it seems quite plausible to say that we should choose the set of moral principles that minimize the worst, least "consentable" experience-moments. And

---

39   Brian Tomasik's consent-based negative utilitarianism (Tomasik, 2015a) is an example of a view that does center on such "unconsentable" suffering, yet this view is not explicitly contractualist.
40   As defended in Siderits, 2003; Kolak, 2004; Vinding, 2017b.
41   Scanlon, 1998, p. 153.

that is just looking from the outside; the case would be even stronger if we were forced to go through this string of experiences from the inside.[42]

The Golden Rule, the categorical imperative, and the contractualist views explored above all ask us to consider ethics from an impartial perspective, and they all plausibly imply that we should make the reduction of suffering a foremost moral priority. More than that, they identify our own will, as moral agents, as the source from which this moral priority derives, which, it has been suggested, could help make us more motivated to act on it in practice.[43]

6.8 Rights-Based Ethics

Ethical views that center on rights represent yet another way in which the reduction of suffering can be defended as a unique moral priority.[44] For instance, one may defend Seana Shiffrin's moral principle against non-consensual harm as a proper moral right.[45] That is, one may argue that individuals should have a right not to be harmed without their consent, unless the harm is done to prevent a greater harm. (Such a right would have significant implications.)[46] Similarly, one may also defend a version of Parfit's compensation principle in terms of rights: individuals should have a right not to be harmed for the sake of providing others with a

---

42   Note that the contractualist case outlined here for minimizing extreme suffering is distinct from the moral realist case I made in the previous chapter, as the contractualist case rests primarily on the consent of the sufferers, not the intrinsic badness of extreme suffering. The case made here is thus more akin to the case I made for the principle of sympathy for intense suffering, although it is important to note that the latter is not predicated on contractualism.
43   Mayerfeld, 1999, p. 116; Scanlon, 1982.
44   Rights-based moral views are often derived from contractualist views, yet one need not be a contractualist to embrace a rights-based ethic.
45   Shiffrin, 1999.
46   For example, it has been argued that a moral right of this kind would disallow all procreation, Benatar, 2006, p. 53. And the same argument could be made even if this moral right pertained only to extremely severe harms, since procreation indeed entails a considerable risk of such harms, Singh, 2012; Benatar & Wasserman, 2015, "The Risk of Serious Harm". Note, however, that consequentialists aiming to reduce suffering should probably not push for human antinatalism, Vinding, forthcoming.

benefit. (Such a right, too, would have significant implications in practice; for example, our exploiting and killing non-human animals for the sake of human palate pleasure is clearly at odds with the view that all sentient individuals possess this right.)

A right not to be harmed without one's consent is an example of a so-called negative right — a right to be free from something. Yet one can also defend a corresponding positive right (i.e. a right to be helped), namely a right to have one's suffering alleviated. Indeed, among positive rights, there is arguably no right more plausible and important than the right to receive help and relief when one is in a state of extreme suffering. The same point can be made about rights and extreme suffering in general, whether we speak of positive or negative rights: to the extent we embrace a framework of moral rights, there is no right more important than the right to be free from extreme suffering. As human rights theorists Roberto Andorno and Cristiana Baffone argue, our entire institution of human rights can be seen as an attempt to guard individuals against the worst forms of suffering:

> [H]uman rights norms are primarily focused on preventing the worst forms of human suffering, even if they only concern a small portion of the population. This task has moral priority over the promotion of the maximum well-being of the majority of people. ... the entire human rights enterprise can be regarded as a social response to suffering ...[47]

6.9 Tradeoff-Forbidding Deontology

Deontology, or duty ethics, is the view that certain moral rules are universally valid and should always be obeyed.[48] Kant's categorical imperative is a prototypical example of a deontological principle. Yet there are other

---

[47] Andorno & Baffone, 2014, abstract. See also the approach to human rights defended in William Felice's *Taking Suffering Seriously: The Importance of Collective Human Rights*, Felice, 1996.
[48] Deontology is related to rights-based ethics in that rights are often, though by no means always, conceived of in deontological terms. Conversely, one can be a deontologist without endorsing rights-based ethical views.

philosophers than Kant who have defended deontological principles that imply a special duty to help those in distress. For example, philosopher Ragnar Ohlsson has defended what he calls the "Principle of Unacceptable Tradeoffs", which says the following:

> [T]he wrongness of killing another human being or causing him unbearable suffering or degradation cannot be outweighed by positive consequences befalling persons whose lives would be acceptable at all events. Neither can the wrongness of not saving another human being from death or unbearable suffering or degradation be outweighed by positive consequences befalling persons whose lives would be acceptable at all events.[49]

Ohlsson proposes that some version of this principle should be considered the foremost categorical rule of ethics, while also stressing that the principle "is compatible with a wide range of possible ethical principles and systems".[50]

Animal rights theorist Gary Francione defends a similar, yet more general deontological view, as he holds that it is always wrong to impose death or suffering on *any* sentient being for reasons such as pleasure or convenience, and that it is "absolutely wrong to engage in … exploitation of the vulnerable".[51]

---

49 Ohlsson, 1979, abstract. As in the case of Kant's categorical imperative, this principle can also be extended to non-human beings. Notice how Ohlsson's principle not only implies a duty to avoid causing suffering by commission, but also a duty to actively prevent it.
50 Ibid., p. 96, pp. 115-116. A similar tradeoff-forbidding view often defended by deontologists is the view that torture is always wrong (though one need not be a deontologist to defend this view at a practical level, Mayerfeld, 2008).
51 Francione, 2013, I; 2019. See also Francione, 2000; 2008.

6.10 Universal Kinship

Notions of universal kinship and solidarity are another basis on which a strong concern for suffering can be grounded. Philosopher J. Howard Moore argued for such notions in his books *The Universal Kinship* and *The New Ethics*, based on the naturalistic understanding that all sentient beings share the same origin.[52] In Moore's own words:

> The inhabitants of the earth are bound to each other by the ties and obligations of a common kinship. Man is simply *one* of a *series* of sentients, differing in degree, but not in kind, from the beings below, above, and around him.[53]

Moore held that this implies what he called the "Great Law": act toward others as you would act toward a part of your own self.[54] And this law, he was careful to make clear, should apply not only to humans, but to all beings, including "birds, fishes, and insects".[55] Beyond that, Moore held that our universal kinship requires us to give strong moral weight to suffering in particular, which he considered vastly preponderant in the world.[56]

Similar sentiments of solidarity and concern for suffering are found in the views of Nobel Peace laureate Albert Schweitzer, who held that all sentient beings are part of a shared "community of suffering", and that our membership of this community implies that the heart of ethics lies

---

52 Moore, 1906; 1907. I am grateful to L. Reeves for bringing Moore's work to my attention.
53 Moore, 1907, p. 15. Moore wrote that the doctrine of universal kinship is "as old almost as human philosophy", and argued that figures such as Buddha, Pythagoras, and Plutarch all taught and practiced it, Moore, 1906, p. 322. Philosopher Henry S. Salt defended similar views in *The Creed of Kinship*, Salt, 1935.
54 Moore, 1907, p. 15. This view bears close similarities to the grounding of moral concern for suffering in a reductionist view of personal identity I pursued in the previous chapter, as well as in Vinding, 2017b (and one may indeed read Moore as an open individualist). Yet it is worth noting that concern for suffering based on notions of universal kinship and solidarity need not be predicated on moral realism or a reductionist view of personal identity.
55 Moore, 1907, p. 15.
56 Moore, 1906, pp. 327-328.

in a caring response to the suffering of our fellow beings.[57] As he wrote in his autobiography:

> I cannot help but feel the suffering all around me, not only of humanity but of the whole of creation. I have never tried to withdraw myself from this community of suffering. It seemed to me a matter of course that we should all take our share of the burden of pain which lies upon the world.[58]

6.11 "Do No Harm"

Another widely shared moral principle that can support a focus on reducing suffering is the principle of non-maleficence: do no harm. The principle *primum non nocere* — "first, do no harm" — is emphasized in many cultures in general, as well as in modern medical ethics in particular, where its origins can be traced back to the Hippocratic school of ancient Greece.[59]

Principles of non-maleficence are uniquely prominent in Eastern traditions such as Hinduism, Buddhism, and especially Jainism. These traditions all consider Ahimsa, often translated as "do no harm", to be an important tenet and virtue. The strong emphasis placed on Ahimsa within Jainism derives in large part from the teachings of Mahavira (born around the sixth century BCE), whom Gandhi considered "the greatest

---

57 Martin, 2007, chap. 6. Such a sentiment of solidarity was also expressed by Schopenhauer in his essay "On the Suffering of the World", in which he argued for seeing and sympathizing with other humans as "fellow sufferers", which Schopenhauer argued "reminds us of that which is after all the most necessary thing in life — the tolerance, patience, regard, and love of neighbor, of which everyone stands in need, and which, therefore, every man owes to his fellow." Schopenhauer, 1851, p. 50. Philosopher Edward Payson Evans likewise described and defended "a common bond of brotherhood and benevolent sympathy, which is now slowly expanding so as to comprise ... every sensitive embodiment of organic life." Evans, 1898, p. 4. Similarly, Peter Wessel Zapffe wrote of "the brotherhood of suffering between everything alive" in Zapffe, 1933.
58 Schweitzer, 1933, p. 242. Schweitzer and Moore also both emphasized compassion as a core value, which is a view we shall explore below.
59 The Hippocratic Oath includes a promise of abstaining from doing harm, yet, contrary to common belief, it does not in fact include the precise statement "first, do no harm". Apropos medical ethics, the view that the relief of suffering should be a foremost aim of medical practice has been defended in Cassel, 1991.

authority" on Ahimsa.[60] Mahavira taught that "[a]ll breathing, existing, living, sentient creatures should not be slain, nor treated with violence, nor abused, nor tormented, nor driven away."[61] Indeed, Jains are famous for also extending Ahimsa to insects, and to avoid walking on grass so as to not crush them.[62]

In recent history, an ethic of "do no harm" and non-violence was developed and endorsed by Leo Tolstoy, most elaborately in his book *The Kingdom of God Is Within You*.[63] Tolstoy was inspired by Christianity, which he saw as "fundamentally a creed of Non-violence based on Jesus' Sermon on the Mount".[64] Together with Jain teachings on Ahimsa, Tolstoy's views were an important influence on Gandhi's view of non-violence, which in turn influenced Martin Luther King Jr.[65]

If we generalize the principle "do no harm" to the suffering that our civilization may cause future generations, it follows that we should actively work to reduce such future suffering.

6.12 Compassion as a Core Value

The final motivation for prioritizing the reduction of suffering we shall visit in this chapter is compassion: sympathetic consciousness for the suffering of others accompanied by a wish to alleviate it. Compassion is considered an important virtue in most major religions[66] as well as in many secular traditions. For example, in the tradition of virtue ethics, philosopher Martha Nussbaum has defended compassion as a virtue, and has argued that Aristotle defended it too.[67] Similarly, philosopher Roger Crisp

---

60   Pandey, 1998, p. 50.
61   Acharanga Sutra, Book 1, lecture 4, lesson 1, as quoted in Fox, 1996, p. 262.
62   A modern introduction to Ahimsa is found in Altman, 1988.
63   Tolstoy, 1894.
64   Tahir, 2012, abstract.
65   Ibid., p. 349.
66   Though especially in Jainism and Buddhism. Indeed, the above-mentioned concept of Ahimsa is also often translated as compassion (although "karuna" is the more common word for compassion in both Sanskrit and Pali). For an elaborate survey of the role of compassion in major world traditions, see Lampert, 2005.
67   Nussbaum, 2001, Part II. Compassion has also been defended as a virtue at the level

endorses a compassion-based "sufficiency principle" according to which we should give absolute priority to those who fall below a certain threshold of well-being.[68] And Arthur Schopenhauer even identified compassion as the sole basis of morality.[69]

A moral concern for suffering based on compassion is compatible with — but not identical to — the other motivations we have seen above. For example, one may, contrary to many of the arguments outlined in previous chapters, maintain that happiness and suffering have similar moral (in)significance from an impersonal perspective, yet still hold suffering to be more significant *from the vantage point of compassion* (as that is arguably what compassion itself says). And if one then identifies this vantage point, this particular moral sentiment, as one's core virtue or value, a focus on reducing suffering follows.[70]

Grounding a moral concern for suffering in sentiments of compassion is, it should be noted, quite compatible with a systematic and rigorous approach to ethics in practice, as evidenced by the systematic approaches of many of those who ground their morality in this way.[71] Indeed, in his book *Consequences of Compassion*, scholar of Buddhism Charles Goodman argues that various Buddhist philosophers motivated by compassion have endorsed consequentialist (which is to say systematic and optimizing) moral views, and that the determination to act like a perfect consequentialist who helps all sentient beings is "the heart of Mahayana Buddhism".[72]

---

of political philosophy, such as by proponents of "compassionate conservatism".
68 Crisp, 2003.
69 Schopenhauer, 1840. See also Wolf, 2015; Shapshay, 2019. Schopenhauer's view of the basis of morality bears significant similarities to that of David Hume (Hume, 1751), who has also been interpreted as defending compassion as a core virtue, Swanton, 2000; 2015. Philosopher Tadeusz Kotarbiński likewise defended an "ethics of pity" aimed at the alleviation of suffering, Rabinowicz, 2000. Bertrand Russell can also be interpreted as resting his ethics on compassion, at least in his later years, as he held that ethics must be based on sentiments, and wrote that "what the world needs is Christian love, or compassion" (Russell, 1954, p. ix), and that "every individual in the world who is suffering represents a failure of human wisdom and of common humanity" (ibid. p. 227).
70 For a case for a moral realist view resting on compassion, see Marshall, 2018.
71 A modern such systematic approach to ethics based on compassion can be found in Jonathan Leighton's *The Battle for Compassion*, Leighton, 2011. I believe Brian Tomasik, too, grounds his moral view in roughly this way, and his approach to ethics at the practical level is among the most systematic and calculating approaches I know of.
72 Goodman, 2009, pp. 5-7.

Chapter 6

As is clear from the above, a strong concern for suffering can be supported by many diverse arguments (and the list of arguments outlined here is, of course, still far from exhaustive). The convergence of so many different and independently plausible arguments gives us strong reason to accept that the reduction of suffering should be a foremost moral priority.[73]

---

73   For an extensive list of publications that argue in favor of suffering-focused views, see Center on Long-Term Risk, 2016. Another way one can defend suffering-focused views is to ground them in concern for the dignity of individuals, Pullman, 2002; Mayerfeld, 2008. Unlike suffering, a neutral absence of happiness does not threaten the dignity of individuals. Additionally, one can support suffering-focused views with aesthetic sentiments, such as "small is beautiful" (Tomasik, 2015a), or the sentiment that suffering is revolting in a way the absence of happiness is not. An argument that supports a suffering-focused view based on aesthetic considerations is also found in the appendix in Benatar, 2015.

7

Biases Against Focusing on Suffering

"When we forget pain, or underestimate it, or talk about people 'getting used to it', we are really so far losing sight of what the universe, which we wish to conceive adequately, really is."

— Edmund Gurney[1]

In this chapter, I shall present various biases against giving suffering its due moral weight and consideration. These biases are worth keeping in mind as we form our appraisal of suffering-focused views. Otherwise, we risk rejecting these views for reasons we would not ourselves endorse upon reflection.

7.1 Can We Be Biased Against Values?

It may be objected that it is unclear how one can be biased against a set of values, as opposed to a set of facts. My first response to this sentiment is to note that, on the moral realist view I myself defend, there is ultimately no dichotomy between facts and values. Yet beyond that, there are in fact

---

1   As quoted in Epperson, 1997, p. 140.

many ways in which one can be biased against values.[2] For example, if we refuse to give fair hearing to a moral position because it is shunned by our local culture, and if we would in fact accept this moral view upon deeper reflection, then our dismissal of this view can fairly be said to be biased. That is, relative to our own well-reflected judgment, strong cultural resistance against a given moral position can indeed be a biasing factor, and a rather strong one at that.[3]

Beyond such cultural biases, another source of bias is simply ignorance of the facts. For example, the question of what it is like to experience states of extreme suffering, including how horrible we ourselves would consider them from the inside, is a factual matter, and something we can be very wrong about. If we are wrong about what it is like to experience intense suffering, we risk being wrong about its moral importance.

7.2 Contemplating Extreme Suffering Is Painful

One reason we should expect to be biased against giving suffering its due moral weight is that suffering can be horrifying to behold and think about.[4] In other words, we have a strong personal incentive to avoid exposure to extreme suffering, and this incentive may prevent us from arriving at a well-reflected assessment of its moral importance — i.e. the well-reflected judgment we ourselves would form if only we exposed ourselves to that which we currently hide from our gaze.[5]

---

2 For an elaborate case against the legitimacy of the fact/value-dichotomy, see Putnam, 2002.
3 For a similar, more concrete example, consider political bias, which we can readily talk about in meaningful ways without assuming deep truths about right and wrong. For example, say we accept the premise that the most important thing in politics is that we promote the best policies no matter who endorses them (most people would probably agree with this premise upon reflection). *If* we accept this premise, then tribally-driven tendencies to deviate from this fundamental value — e.g. any tendency to favor a policy when it is proposed by one's own political party while rejecting it when proposed by the opposition — can accurately be called a bias.
4 In particular, empathizing deeply with the suffering of another can be very painful, and this painfulness of empathy may motivate us to look away and disengage. This is one reason for us to primarily cultivate compassion over empathy, Bloom, 2016.
5 Studies have found that direct confrontations with suffering, such as when we observe

Somewhat paradoxically, the horror of extreme suffering can keep us from appreciating the true scope of this horror. Indeed, we commonly turn our heads away from extreme suffering while simultaneously denying, often with confidence, that it carries supreme disvalue. Yet how can we make such a claim about extreme suffering if we do not dare to truly behold it?

It is not only at an individual level that we shun and neglect suffering but also at a societal level, as sociologist Stanley Cohen argued in his book *States of Denial: Knowing About Atrocities and Suffering*.[6] Cohen explores the psychology of denial in the context of suffering — our tendency to suppress it with self-deception and rationalizations because it is too disturbing — and demonstrates how this results in denials of the reality and scope of suffering at an individual, social, and political level.[7] He argues that denial is the norm while awareness of the everyday horrors of reality is a rare aberration.[8]

---

others in pain or experience pain ourselves, generally lead to more sympathetic moral judgments, Xiao et al., 2015. This suggests that hiding suffering from our gaze leads us to have less concern for it.

6   The extent to which the suffering that surrounds us is hidden from our gaze is also described in Alexander, 2015. Alexander describes how we cannot comprehend just how bad things are even in communities that appear relatively well off from the outside. His essay does not even describe the poorest people in the world; nor does it say anything about non-human animals, who suffer in far greater numbers and whose suffering is hidden far more effectively still.

7   A collective neglect of suffering at a social and institutional level, particularly within academia, is also described in Siu, 1988. See also Kleinman et al., 1997; Daoust, 2012.

8   Cohen, 2001. A similar argument is made in Zapffe, 1933, III. Our preference for shoving suffering under the carpet also shines through in much of the philosophical terminology. For example, philosophers usually use the term "well-being" to cover both positive and negative states of "well-being", and rarely use the term "ill-being" (though see Kagan, 2014; Mathison, 2018). And views that consider well-being to be comprised wholly by suffering and pleasure are called "hedonist" views (from the Greek word "hedone" for pleasure), in effect omitting any mention of suffering (inspired by Robert Daoust, I prefer to use the more balanced term "algo-hedonic"). Likewise, views holding that well-being (positive and negative) is all that matters are called "welfarist".

7.3 Cognitive Biases Conspiring

Modern psychology has documented a long list of cognitive biases to which the human mind is prone. And many of these biases plausibly conspire to produce a strong bias against appreciating the true horror of suffering. For one, there is wishful thinking: our tendency to believe as true what we wish were true.[9] In the context of appraising the significance of extreme suffering, this bias likely pulls us toward the belief that extreme suffering can't be *that* bad, that it must be outweighed and compensated for somehow, and that there has to be some grander quest more worth pursuing than to reduce suffering.[10]

Next, there is confirmation bias: our propensity to search for and favor information that confirms our pre-existing views.[11] If we already look away from extreme suffering, and entertain wishful beliefs about it, confirmation bias will serve to maintain this status quo — to keep us shying away from arguments and other sources of evidence that might count against our view. And this status quo can then be further consolidated by our conformity bias, our tendency to conform to our peers. For although most people do agree on reflection that the reduction of suffering is important, relatively few seem to believe it should be a foremost priority in *their* lives, much less act on this belief.[12]

These last two biases can, of course, also work in the other direction. That is, if one already believes that the reduction of suffering should be our foremost priority, and if one's closest peers share this view, then confirmation bias and conformity bias can make us biased against opposing views. Yet we should expect a bias in this opposite direction to be far less common, again since comparatively few people currently consider the

---

9   Bastardi et al., 2011. See also Kunda, 1990.
10 Note that our bias toward wishful thinking is related to, yet still distinct from, the bias of looking away and ignoring described in the previous section. For while the bias described in the previous section primarily keeps us from witnessing and thinking about the true nature of suffering in the first place, wishful thinking (also) leads us to entertain wishful beliefs about suffering even when we do think about it.
11 Plous, 1993, p. 233.
12 This discrepancy explains how reducing suffering can both be highly popular and unpopular at the same time: it is popular at the level of our reflective values (*cf.* Future of Life Institute, 2017), yet unpopular at the level of what we do in practice (e.g. most people spend their resources selfishly and eat beings whom they know have suffered).

endeavor of reducing suffering an overriding priority in their lives, and even fewer are surrounded by people who share this view.

Beyond that, there is also an asymmetry in that wishful thinking, unlike confirmation bias and conformity bias, cannot readily cut both ways. For to say that extreme suffering carries supreme disvalue, and that we should make the reduction of suffering our foremost priority, is hardly a wishful or feel-good proposition for anyone.[13] It is not a view we would want to be true, and hence we should expect our minds to be resistant toward accepting it, even if we would in fact accept it upon reflection.

There is an irony here. We are tempted to dismiss and downplay the disvalue and moral importance of (intensely) bad feelings because acknowledging it might result in (mildly) bad feelings for ourselves. Yet I suspect this ironic dynamic is not uncommon. Indeed, as Parfit noted, it is easy to see how it can be in our self-interest to downplay the badness of suffering in this way:

> When Nietzsche tried to believe that suffering is good, so that his own suffering would be easier to bear, Nietzsche's judgment was distorted by self-interest. But when we believe that suffering is bad, our judgment is not distorted in this way.[14]

Our condition can be made much easier to bear if we believe that extreme suffering is not *that* bad, or that it can readily be outweighed by other things. We should be careful not to let this incentive cloud our judgment.

Another thing to be wary of, in relation to wishful thinking, is the common human tendency of assuming that there must be some great thing that will eventually come about and make all the bad things worthwhile, whether it is some kind of heaven in a life after death, some state of spiritual bliss, or some future utopia we hope might eventually emerge. The independent convergence toward beliefs of this kind across many different cultures suggests that the human mind has a natural proclivity for such

---

13 However, even if this is not a feel-good account of value and ethics, accepting a view of this kind is nonetheless compatible with living a fulfilling life. Indeed, integrating suffering-focused ethics with a healthy personal attitude and lifestyle is paramount if we are to be effective in our efforts to alleviate suffering (more on this in chapter 17).
14 Parfit, 2011, chap. 126.

beliefs, and that we should maintain some skepticism toward expectations that conform to this pattern.[15]

7.4 We Underestimate the Badness of Suffering

"[A]s a rule we find pleasure much less pleasurable, pain much more painful than we expected."
— Arthur Schopenhauer[16]

There are many reasons why we underestimate the badness of suffering.[17] One of them we have already mentioned in a previous chapter: the badness of extreme suffering is simply incomprehensible from the outside when we ourselves are experiencing a relatively pleasant state. Our understanding of conscious states is inherently state-dependent, and consequently a large gap exists between the understanding of extreme suffering we can attain in any bearable state of consciousness versus the understanding that would be revealed to us directly in an actual state of extreme suffering. This so-called "empathy gap" between us and those who suffer intensely means that we can only understand suffering indirectly, through vague hints and symbols, when we are not suffering ourselves.[18]

---

15   I am not suggesting we should be skeptical of the notion that life can get a lot better. Yet this should not be confused with the question of whether any better state we can reasonably expect to bring about — such as a much happier state — can ever morally outweigh all the suffering its creation would entail, including the (risk of) extreme suffering. I say more on this in section 8.6.
16   Schopenhauer, 1851, p. 42.
17   Jamie Mayerfeld provides an elaborate account of some of the ways in which we underestimate suffering in Mayerfeld, 1999, pp. 101-107, pp. 189-193. This section owes a considerable debt to Mayerfeld's account.
18   The term "empathy gap" refers to our inability to understand emotional states very different from our own in general, not just our inability to understand suffering (when we ourselves are okay). Yet pain and suffering have been a prominent focus for studies on the empathy gap. For example, one study of bullying found that people who were not themselves socially excluded consistently underestimated the social pain of those who were, Nordgren et al., 2011. Similarly, research suggests that physicians routinely underestimate the pain of their patients, Marino & Marino, 2014.

Another significant reason we underestimate suffering is that we confuse it with something far milder that masquerades as the real thing. In the words of Jamie Mayerfeld:

> There is a whole subclass of rather common emotions that falsely parade as suffering to win increased attention for themselves. I am speaking not only of anger, but also resentment, spite, and bitterness. It is important to recognize that these emotions often include no suffering at all, although the people experiencing them may wish to describe them that way.[19]

As mentioned earlier, we all too readily confuse an aversive subcomponent of experience for suffering. For example, it is possible to cry intensely and feel a sense of sadness without having a bad overall feeling. And if we mistake an experience like this for suffering, let alone compare it to extreme suffering, we are making a grave mistake indeed. Mayerfeld continues:

> Real cases of suffering, meanwhile, tend to go unheard. This is not only because people who are genuinely suffering typically lack the resources with which to publicize their condition, but also because ... many forms of suffering deprive people of the very ability to express, sometimes even think, the fact that they are suffering.[20]

Being unable to express one's suffering is also the case for the vast majority of sentient beings on the planet: non-human animals. The most numerous of them, such as fish and invertebrates, cannot even scream. We do not even need to cover our ears to ignore their suffering.

---

19 Mayerfeld, 1999, p. 53. A similar quote from Mayerfeld: "It is of the highest importance to be able to distinguish genuine suffering from the pale but deceptive imitation of it. It is of the highest importance to realize that what so often passes for 'suffering,' for want of a richer vocabulary or clearer powers of discernment, in the experience of people who enjoy a firm material and psychological foundation in their lives, is not genuine suffering and can only be called so by the most distant and strained analogy." Ibid., p. 46.
20 Ibid., p. 53.

Chapter 7

Yet, as Mayerfeld hints, the same is true of many humans, since extreme suffering can severely compromise our ability to express ourselves — a phenomenon that has been explored by Gordon and Susan Marino in their essay "Paying Homage to the Silence of Suffering". They argue that "intense and prolonged agony breaks down our linguistic and cognitive capacities",[21] and hence our assessments of pain and suffering are often biased by the resulting "silence of pain".[22]

Most of us indeed have very little sense of proportion when it comes to suffering, which is not surprising given that the mere act of contemplating the many possible levels of suffering can itself be painful. Yet such painfulness notwithstanding, let us try to briefly survey just a few of these levels to get but a vague sense of the possible depths of suffering.

For example, we can start by imagining a person, Jane, who is anxious about an upcoming exam. The anxiety is intense and all-consuming in a way that renders it impossible for her to find any relaxation or sleep. "What could be worse than this?", she is tempted to think. Yet the next day, Jane is informed that her parents have been killed. She now truly suffers. Her sadness hits a level she had no idea existed — as though the word "sadness" has a deeper meaning that she had hitherto known nothing about. She now realizes how blessed her situation had been before, as her current state feels far worse and immeasurably more hopeless. This could hardly be worse. And yet it could.

For next, Jane is kidnapped by a gang of sadistic psychopaths who take her to a torture chamber to impose horrendous torment upon her. Physical and psychological pain at a level that breaks almost everything in Jane, including her ability to think a structured thought and to express, even to herself, what is happening. Jane's world is suffering. She feels she *is* suffering, albeit this suffering has almost no commonality to any suffering she had experienced before. This has to be the peak of badness. But it is not.

For nothing means more to Jane than her two brothers and two sisters whom the evil torturers have now also found and captured. Peak badness suddenly gets stretched radically further, as the torturers begin employing

---

21 Marino & Marino, 2014, abstract.
22 Ibid. A similar case is made in Scarry, 1985.

even worse torture methods on Jane as well as on her brothers and sisters. Nothing can be said. Words have no meaning. "Why?" seems apt yet is misplaced, and inexpressible anyway. Nothing can be worse. Yet, of course, in reality, it can. Indeed, what happens in reality, in every moment of every day, *is* far worse, and certainly far worse than anything this story comes close to conveying.[23]

This is a terrible story to sit and make up, but it does serve to illustrate an important point: when we think suffering can barely get worse, it usually can, and by a lot. We may be experiencing a state of minus nine and think we have reached the absolute bottom, until we experience a state of minus ten and see how wrong we were. Then we experience a state of minus a hundred, which makes us realize how wrong — and relatively blessed — we were in a state of "just" minus ten.[24] And then we experience a state of minus a thousand, and so on. Our conception of suffering would have to be stretched and broken many times for it to conform even remotely to the true extent that the horror of suffering can assume.[25]

Sadly, however, this point remains difficult to convey. Our sense of what it is like to be in the last stage of the ladder of horror described above probably does not come close to capturing the actual horror one would

---

23   Not least due to the enormous number of beings who endure extreme suffering. Yet even if we insist on comparing the suffering of a single individual with the suffering of Jane, it is sadly quite probable that the one being who is doing the very worst on Earth at any given moment suffers significantly more than Jane. Or put more precisely: that the string of the worst consciousness-moments on Earth at any given moment is worse than Jane's.

24   As a case in point, a friend told me that his personal experience with heartbreak made him significantly more sympathetic to suffering-focused ethics. And while such experiences indeed can lend strong support to suffering-focused views, it is worth noting that the experience of heartbreak will still tend to only lie at a very early step in the ladder of horror. The fact that an experience of heartbreak can lead to a significant increase in the concern we give suffering provides a strong indication of how little thought we give to, and how far detached we in fact are from, the reality of the very worst states of suffering.

25   That the intensity of suffering is felt as falling along a logarithmic scale finds support in Emilsson, 2019. How does such a scale fit with the lexicality between different intensities of suffering I defended in the fifth chapter? The claim I sought to defend in the fifth chapter was merely the general claim that intense suffering should take priority over mild forms of suffering. This is compatible with the more specific claim that some forms of extreme suffering are worse, and deserve more priority, than others.

experience even in the mid-stages of this ladder — say, after being informed that one's parents have been killed, or in the earliest stages of progressively worse torture. Again, words and imagination can only take us so far. Yet they can at least help us realize the relative insignificance of most of our daily worries, and thus help sharpen our priorities.

For instance, many of us can probably admit to having felt frustrated by a small stain on a shirt to such an extent that it took up a substantial fraction of our mental energy. And yet the scale of a problem of this kind does not even compare to the first step on the ladder of suffering described in the story of Jane. To be consumed by problems this trivial, as many of us often are, is to be out of touch with reality in a very real sense. It is to be out of touch with the badness of the worst states of suffering. And not only that, it is also to be disconnected from the reality of what we in fact could be doing with our time and resources to alleviate such suffering, which leads us to the next point.

7.5 We Underestimate Our Ability to Reduce Suffering

For beyond underestimating the badness of suffering, we also generally underestimate our ability to prevent it. After all, preventing just a comparatively small duration of extreme suffering each year (say, minutes of it) would surely be worth making a great effort to accomplish, and yet we tend not to realize that we in all likelihood readily could reduce this much suffering — and probably far more[26] — if only we tried. It is as though the extent of our ability to reduce suffering barely interests us, which alone indicates just how much we underestimate it.[27]

Thus, we underestimate both the badness of suffering as well as our ability to reduce it, which in turn leads us to greatly underestimate what Mayerfeld calls our duty to relieve suffering:

---

26 See section 15.2.
27 Mayerfeld writes more about our tendency to underestimate and forget our ability to reduce suffering in Mayerfeld, 1999, pp. 191-193.

[B]y distorting the meaning of suffering and denying its existence, and by overlooking our capacity to prevent it, we interpose a series of screens that permit no more than a faint image of the duty to relieve suffering to come before us.[28]

And this faint image is likely made even fainter by our omission bias. For even if we did have a clear sense of our ability to relieve suffering, most of us would probably still be much more motivated to prevent suffering resulting from our own acts of commission (i.e. suffering caused directly by us) than to prevent an equal, or even much greater amount of suffering due to acts of omission (i.e. suffering that we did not cause directly, yet which we could have prevented).[29] Our natural moral intuitions, which most of the time seem more concerned about not being blamed for behaving badly than about reducing suffering, have a hard time seeing even a remote equivalence between these two kinds of failure to prevent suffering. Indeed, we tend to consider acts of commission far worse, even though we arguably bring about far more suffering by omission in today's world: by not actively working to reduce suffering.[30] These omission-tolerant intuitions thus count as an additional biasing factor preventing us from acting according to our duty to relieve suffering.[31]

---

28 Ibid., p. 213.
29 Again, for elaborate arguments against a strong moral distinction between inflicting harm and failing to prevent harm, see Kagan, 1989, chaps. 3-4; Bennett, 1995. For psychological studies on "omission bias", see Ritov & Baron, 1990; Spranca et al., 1991.
30 Mayerfeld makes a similar point: "Note that the duty to relieve suffering comes in two parts: a prohibition against inflicting suffering, and a requirement to prevent it. What we tend to underestimate is less the former than the latter." Mayerfeld, 1999, p. 189.
31 Again, such a duty, or goal, need not be predicated on moral realism. Nor does this point about omission bias depend on our accepting any particularly demanding moral principle. For instance, merely holding the modest moral premise that we ought to reduce suffering when we can do so at a minimal cost to ourselves would imply that our omission-tolerant intuitions constitute a biasing factor (relative to the practical implications of this premise).

7.6 Novelty Bias and Numbness to the Scope of Suffering

Another biasing factor is that we fail to appreciate the scale at which suffering is always occurring, not to mention the scale at which it risks occurring in the future. There are various reasons for this. First, we appear to have a novelty bias of sorts: when we see a disaster in the news, such as a school shooting or an earthquake, we tend to feel a strong sense of horror and urgency over what has happened — something unusual that demands serious attention. Yet the truth is that the disasters reported in the news, including large ones such as 9/11 or the 2004 tsunami in Indonesia, represent no more than a drop in the ocean of suffering experienced on Earth at any moment.

For example, we rarely hear about the fact that 5.4 million children under the age of five die each year, often in excruciatingly painful ways, and that more than half of these deaths "are due to conditions that could be prevented or treated with access to simple, affordable interventions."[32] And yet human suffering constitutes only a tiny minority of all suffering on the planet. More than 150 million land-living non-human beings experience the horror of being forced into a slaughterhouse and killed for human consumption, and more than three billion aquatic beings are killed in the most agonizing ways for the same purpose — *every single day*.[33]

Disaster on an unfathomable scale is always taking place on Earth. Countless instances of extreme suffering are occurring in this moment — *right now*. Yet because this suffering is so normal and ordinary, simply occurring every day, distributed rather evenly over time and space, it seems less evocative and urgent than the more unusual, more localized disasters, such as school shootings and earthquakes. Almost all the suffering that occurs on Earth can be considered baseline horror, which allows us to ignore it.[34] We simply do not *feel* the ever-present emergency that surrounds us. As George Bernard Shaw observed in relation to the horrors routinely inflicted upon non-human animals: "Custom will reconcile people to any atrocity …"[35]

---

32 World Health Organization, 2019.
33 Mood & Brooke, 2010.
34 A similar point is made in Davidow, 2013.
35 Salt, 1915, preface.

Yet the lack of novelty is not the only thing that keeps our moral intuitions from grasping the scope of the disaster in which we find ourselves. For even when we are presented with a novel atrocity, we still fail to appreciate its horror in a way that is remotely proportional to its scope, a phenomenon known as "scope neglect". And the greater the scope, the greater our failure. Indeed, work by psychologist Paul Slovic suggests that we not only fail to care in proportion to the number of victims involved in an atrocity, but we even seem to care *less* the more victims there are.[36]

A million deaths really is just a statistic at the level of our moral cognition.[37] This dumbfounding-by-numbers blindspot of our minds is one we must make arduous efforts to control for if we are to have an accurate sense of the scope and moral importance of the suffering of the world.

Yet not only do we seem to care less about a group of beings the bigger the group is, we also seem to care less about helping the *same* number of beings affected by a tragedy when the total number of beings affected by the tragedy is higher. That is, we feel more compelled to help ten people out of twenty than we do to help ten out of a hundred, although the absolute impact would be the same in both cases — a "proportion bias", if you will.[38] This constitutes an additional bias to control for, especially given the magnitude of the ever-present baseline horror that exists as a backdrop to any endeavor we may pursue to reduce suffering.

Given this failure to appreciate the scope and urgency of ongoing suffering, we should hardly expect our appreciation of risks of astronomical future suffering to be any better.[39] In fact, we should expect these risks to be even more readily ignored than the ongoing baseline horror, in part due to 1) their far-away and unfamiliar nature; 2) their lack of novelty — we can always work to reduce such risks, and hence it can be difficult to summon moral motivation to do such work now rather than later; and 3) the scope of such risks is orders of magnitude greater than the sum of disasters currently taking place on Earth, implying that our scope neglect

---

36 Slovic, 2007; Cameron & Payne, 2011.
37 The quote "The death of one man is a tragedy, the death of millions is a statistic" is often attributed to Stalin, yet he appears never to have said it.
38 Fetherstonhaugh et al., 1997.
39 See chapter 14, as well as Tomasik, 2011; Althaus & Gloor, 2016; Baumann, 2017e.

may leave us even more dumbfounded by these risks of astronomical future suffering and the ongoing maximal moral urgency of reducing them. This would appear consistent with the low amount of attention we currently devote to analyzing and addressing these risks.

7.7 Perpetrator Bias

Our tendency to overlook the baseline horror always occurring in the world is probably also in part explainable by a "perpetrator bias" of sorts. That is, we seem to care more about suffering when it is caused by a moral agent who has brought it about by intentional action compared to when it is not.[40] Given that we evolved in a social world, it makes sense that our moral sentiments are especially attuned to the transgressions of other moral agents. However, with respect to the goal of effectively reducing suffering for sentient beings, this tendency likely constitutes a significant bias, as the vast majority of suffering in the world is not caused by the intentional actions of moral agents.[41] Indeed, even the term Paul Slovic gave to our tendency to neglect the suffering and death of the masses — "genocide neglect" — itself displays this bias: our "perpetratorless-suffering neglect".[42]

---

40 Tomasik, 2013i.
41 Davidow, 2013. This bias probably clouds our thinking about suffering in the long-term future as well, even as most suffering then may well be caused by moral agents. For most future suffering will probably have systemic causes, and our perpetrator-biased minds generally seem far more active with respect to the actions of a small group of individuals compared to larger, systemic sources of suffering. Take, for instance, the example of factory farming in today's world: our moral sentiments do tend to get exercised about the single farm worker who throws piglets into a concrete floor, yet less so about the institution of factory farming as a whole, although the latter causes far more suffering.
42 The name Slovic used is not so strange given that he chose genocide as the particular case for his study of our tendency to "become numbly indifferent to the plight of individuals who are 'one of many'", Slovic, 2007. Yet the choice of genocide as the point of departure for exploring this phenomenon is itself a case of choosing a relatively small and evocative subset of sources of suffering compared to others that are much bigger and far less evocative, such as the suffering of non-human animals in nature (Tomasik, 2013i; Davidow, 2013), or the many forms of human misery not caused by agents who harm others intentionally (e.g. the human suffering caused by aging and mental illness).

7.8 The Just World Fallacy

A related bias is the "Just World Fallacy", a cognitive bias that leads us to assume that whatever happens in the world must be morally fair, balanced in proportion to what everyone deserves. If something bad happens to someone, they must have done something to deserve it. (Which, again, makes some sense to assume for a brain adapted to a social world, as social agents do indeed tend to punish those who violate norms.)

Belief in a just world can make us cynical and cold toward suffering. For example, in one study where subjects were made to observe an actor apparently receive painful electrical shocks, the subjects would devalue and reject the (perceived) victim when they were unable to intervene, in part, the authors suggest, because of the observers' need to maintain a belief in a just world.[43] As a more recent review of our tendency to believe in a just world put it:

> When [people] cannot help innocent victims and remedy injustice or when help is too costly they tend to downgrade the victims and/or blame them for self-infliction and hence increase victim suffering.[44]

One may, of course, dispute whether the need to maintain a belief in a just world is the main explanation of this observed pattern of downgrading. But whatever its source, our tendency to make such knee-jerk rejections and devaluations of victims and their suffering clearly constitutes an additional bias to control for in our attempts to gain a proper sense of the importance of reducing suffering, especially when the endeavor to reduce suffering appears costly and difficult.

---

43 Lerner & Simmons, 1966, p. 209.
44 Furnham, 2003, 2.4.

7.9 An Optimistic Psychology Built by Evolution

In light of our evolutionary history, we should not be surprised to discover that we have psychological mechanisms that bias us against realizing the badness and scope of suffering. After all, appreciating the badness of others' suffering and prioritizing its reduction was hardly an optimal strategy for gene propagation in our ancestral environment. As Aldous Huxley wrote in his novel *Crome Yellow*:

> [I]f one had an imagination vivid enough and a sympathy sufficiently sensitive really to comprehend and to feel the sufferings of other people, one would never have a moment's peace of mind.[45]

Yet it is not only the suffering of others that we may tend to underestimate and ignore. It has also been argued that our assessments are strongly biased even when it comes to the suffering that has occurred, and will occur, in our own lives. For example, David Benatar argues that many of our cognitive biases conspire to make us greatly overestimate the quality of our own lives, and to downplay the suffering they contain.[46]

Philosopher Thomas Metzinger has proposed a similar picture in his essay "Suffering". Metzinger reports the results from a pilot study he conducted in which students were asked at random times, via their cell phones, whether they would be willing to relive the experience they had the moment before their phone vibrated. On average, the students reported their experience not worth reliving 72 percent of the time.[47] Metzinger

---

45 Huxley, 1921, p. 132.
46 Benatar, 2006, pp. 64-65. Benatar further argues that self-assessments of one's quality of life "are a better indicator of the *comparative* rather than *actual* quality of one's life. One effect of this is that those negative features of life that are shared by everybody are inert in people's judgements about their own well-being. Since these features are very relevant, overlooking them leads to unreliable judgements." Benatar, 2006, p. 68. As a case in point, consider how we would feel about having to defecate if only few people ever did it, as though it were a rare disorder. It seems likely that we would consider this condition a most regrettable one for those who have it, especially considering that it occasionally involves serious pain and complications (e.g. stomach pain, indigestion, diarrhea). Yet since everyone shares this condition, we tend not to see it in this way.
47 Metzinger, 2016, p. 240. David Hume may be said to have reported a similar finding: "Ask yourself, ask any of your acquaintance, whether they would live over again the last ten or twenty years of their life. No! but the next twenty, they say, will be better …"

uses this result (which he himself admits "cannot count as significant") as a starting point for a discussion about how our large-scale narrative about the quality of our lives might be severely out of touch with the reality of our actual felt, moment-to-moment experience:

> If the human organism would not repeat most individual conscious moments if it had any choice, then the logic of psychological evolution mandates concealment of the fact from the self-modelling system caught on the hedonic treadmill. ... a strategy of flexible, dynamic self-representation across a hierarchy of timescales could have a causal effect in continuously remotivating the self-conscious organism, systematically distracting it from the potential insight that the life of an anti-entropic system is one big uphill battle, a strenuous affair with minimal prospect of enduring success. Let us call this speculative hypothesis "narrative self-deception".[48]

In the terminology of Daniel Kahneman, Metzinger's proposal amounts to the claim that our experiencing self (our moment-to-moment experience) is much less happy than our remembering self (our evaluations of past experiences based on memory). And Kahneman's own research in fact strongly supports the claim that our remembering self does not reliably track our moment-to-moment experience, and that it often fails to appreciate the amount of pain the experiencing self has experienced — even to such an extent that, when forced to choose between two different painful experiences endured in the past, the remembering self can easily be manipulated to prefer significantly *more* pain rather than less.[49]

Recent research on the evaluations of the remembering self and the experiencing self also confirms that the former is much more optimistic

---

Hume, 1779, part 10, Demea speaking.
48 Metzinger, 2016, pp. 241-242. Schopenhauer made a similar claim in *The World as Will and Representation*: "If ... we were to bring to the sight of everyone the terrible sufferings and afflictions to which his life is constantly exposed, he would be seized with horror." Schopenhauer, 1819, vol I, p. 325.
49 Kahneman et al., 1993; Kahneman & Riis, 2005; Kahneman, 2011, part 5.

than the latter. As one study reported: "Across all measures, global reports [of well-being] were significantly higher than aggregated daily states."[50]

That our minds are skillfully hiding the actual amount of suffering we experience, as proposed by Metzinger, is in line with the finding that the human mind has a strong proclivity for self-deception and suppression in general.[51] And the view is also well-supported by studies of our perception of the good and bad things in our lives in particular. For example, in their book *The Pollyanna Principle*, psychologists Margaret Matlin and David Stang argue that people tend to report encountering positive stimuli significantly more often than they in fact do, and that we generally remember pleasant experiences more accurately than unpleasant experiences.[52] In Matlin's words: "As our memory for an event fades, the positive components of that event seem *slightly less* positive, whereas the negative components seem *much less* negative."[53]

The tendency of our memories of negative emotions to fade more over time than our memories of positive emotions is known as the "fading affect bias".[54] Research on this bias has also shown that our memories *associated with* negative emotions, such as memories of negative events themselves, also tend to fade more readily than memories associated with positive emotions.[55]

Closely related is the cognitive bias known as "rosy retrospection" — our tendency to rate events more favorably some time after they have occurred than we do while experiencing them.[56] And a similar phenomenon occurs as people age and make backward evaluations of their own lives, which is known as the "age-related positivity effect": "Relative to their

---

50 Newman et al., 2020, abstract.
51 For an accessible review of such self-deception and selective suppression in the human mind, see Simler & Hanson, 2018, part I.
52 Matlin & Stang, 1978.
53 Matlin, 2017, p. 320.
54 Walker & Skowronski, 2009.
55 Skowronski et al., 2014. However, it seems that people with major depressive disorder are an exception to this pattern, as they remember negative stimuli better than positive stimuli, Kaletsch et al., 2014.
56 Mitchell et al., 1997.

younger counterparts, older people attend to and remember more positive than negative information [about their lives as a whole]."[57]

Baumeister et al. summed up the research on optimistic memories in the following way, which lends support to Metzinger's thesis:

> Although both good and bad feelings may fade with time, the bad ones are actively suppressed; whereas the good memories may be cultivated and sustained (e.g., through reminiscence). By the same token, people may treat bad experiences as isolated events while integrating good ones into an ongoing general perception of goodness. In this way, individuals may sustain a broadly favorable view of their lives.[58]

So while our tendency to misremember past suffering can in part be explained by our inability to understand states very dissimilar from our present one (i.e. the empathy gap), it likely also involves a significant amount of active suppression.[59]

Beyond our tendencies to misremember and understate past sufferings and bad events (sometimes collectively referred to as the "positivity bias"),[60] we also have a tendency to form overoptimistic expectations about the future, known as the "optimism bias". That is, we underestimate how likely we are to suffer misfortune and overestimate our likelihood of attaining success. As cognitive neuroscientist Tali Sharot writes:

---

57 Reed & Carstensen, 2012, abstract.
58 Baumeister et al., 2001, p. 361.
59 A first-person account of how this psychology of suppressing and forgetting suffering may occur is found in Mayerfeld, 1999, p. 34. Mayerfeld's account, particularly his claim that we underestimate past suffering more the further in the past it occurred, finds support in Matlin, 2017.
60 See e.g. Sutton, 2009, p. 536.

> [W]e underrate our chances of getting divorced, being in a car accident, or suffering from cancer. We also expect to live longer than objective measures would warrant, overestimate our success in the job market, and believe that our children will be especially talented. This phenomenon is known as the optimism bias, and it is one of the most consistent, prevalent, and robust biases documented in psychology and behavioral economics.[61]

Such biased beliefs may well have been adaptive for the task of propagating genes in the past,[62] yet they probably serve as an impediment for getting a clear picture of the risks of future suffering that face us.

7.10 The Pleasure-Desire Bias

Another reason we may be biased against prioritizing the reduction of suffering is that evolution has built us to crave various sources of pleasure — sex, food, admiration, etc. We are, in a sense, built to be addicts to these sources of pleasure. And this craving, it has been argued, could bias our evaluations of the importance of attaining and increasing pleasure (at least of these kinds) versus avoiding and reducing suffering, since the avoidance of suffering is not something we crave and desire in this same, quasi-addicted way.[63]

This argument ties into the important distinction drawn in neuroscience between "wanting" and "liking" in our reward system. For as neuroscientists Kent Berridge and Terry Robinson note:

---

61 Sharot, 2011, abstract. Optimistic biases of this kind have also been observed in non-human animals, ibid.
62 Ibid. The tendency for overly optimistic beliefs to lead to a greater chance of success (in certain endeavors) is known as the "Pygmalion effect".
63 A version of this argument has often been made by suffering-focused advocate Inmendham. For example, he writes the following on his website donotgod.com: "[T]he only true positive is elimination/prevention of a true negative. [T]he perception of all other positive worth is an illusion of desire which perverts evaluation of the worth of lesser states of discomfort." See also Tomasik, 2016c.

> [T]he brain circuitry that mediates the psychological process of "wanting" a particular reward is dissociable from circuitry that mediates the degree to which it is "liked." Incentive salience or "wanting," a form of motivation, is generated by large and robust neural systems that include mesolimbic dopamine. By comparison, "liking," or *the actual pleasurable impact* [emphasis mine] of reward consumption, is mediated by smaller and fragile neural systems, and is not dependent on dopamine. The incentive-sensitization theory posits the essence of drug addiction to be excessive amplification specifically of psychological "wanting," especially triggered by cues, without necessarily an amplification of "liking."[64]

Thus, there is an important distinction between being pleased by something and wanting something. Indeed, as Berridge and Robinson hint, there can be intense wanting with virtually no accompanying liking. And what the argument outlined above says is that, first, we should be careful not to confuse this pure wanting component of our motivation system for "an actual pleasurable impact". More than that, we should be careful not to be overwhelmed by the strong motivating power of this wanting system, and to not follow its recommendations uncritically — this motivating power being the force that often overrules our willpower and better judgment, and leads us to pursue crude desires (smoking, cheating, bingeing) over our deeper values and ideals. This is not the system we would want as the highest arbiter of our most important decisions.

7.11 Existence Bias

Another reason to expect the human mind to be strongly motivated to reject suffering-focused moral views is that we have a powerful drive — quite distinct from our drive for pleasure — to maintain and extend our existence almost no matter the costs. As Thomas Metzinger describes it:

---

64 Berridge & Robinson, 2016.

Chapter 7

> I claim that our deepest cognitive bias is "existence bias", which means that we will simply do almost anything to prolong our own existence. For us, sustaining one's existence is the default goal in almost every case of uncertainty, even if it may violate rationality constraints, simply because it is a biological imperative that has been burned into our nervous systems over millennia.[65]

Indeed, *if* it happens to be the case that there are strongly life-unfriendly truths about the value of our condition, then any ability to readily acknowledge such truths would likely have faced strong selection pressure, and thus mostly been weeded out of the population. Which is to say that, *if* such truths exist, we should expect to have a very hard time acknowledging them. More than that, we should expect to have an existence bias of the kind Metzinger describes.

The widespread taboo against euthanasia, even in the most hopeless cases, may be considered an expression of such a bias, which highlights the importance of questioning our instinctive inclination to favor existence at any price.[66] From an ethical perspective, we cannot simply assume that existence is worth a lot of suffering, or even that existence is in itself intrinsically good. Indeed, philosopher Philippa Foot argued that "merely being alive, even without suffering, is not a good."[67]

The putative existence bias described by Metzinger could have astronomical implications. For not only should we expect this existence bias

---

[65] Metzinger, 2017. Such an existence bias is also implied by Schopenhauer's concept of the "will to live", which he saw as an underlying psychological force motivating all living beings (Schopenhauer, 1819), and it is also related to the concept of *bhava-tanha* (craving for existence) within Buddhism. Beyond that, there is evidence in the psychological literature for an existence bias of a more general kind. For example, one study, titled "The existence bias", demonstrated that "people treat the mere existence of something as evidence of its goodness." Eidelman et al., 2009.

[66] Indeed, it is highly relevant to control for existence bias on virtually any moral view. For example, if one is a classical utilitarian (i.e. if one thinks happiness can outweigh suffering, and that we should maximize the sum of happiness minus suffering), it seems that one should take great care to make sure that one is not biased by an existence bias to deem a condition net positive when it is in fact net negative. In the worst case, such a mistake could cause a moral disaster on an astronomical scale, also by classical utilitarian standards.

[67] Foot, 2002, p. 42. Philosopher Jonathan Glover has defended the same view, Glover, 1977, pp. 39-59.

to recommend us to incur virtually any cost for the sake of our own continued existence — as well as to vastly overestimate the badness of non-existence[68] — but we should also expect it to endorse the same thing with respect to the continuation and expansion of our notional tribe and species, and possibly even to strongly favor the expansion of sentient life beyond our planet.[69] In light of this possibility, it is paramount that we make sure our thinking about such prospects is guided by reason rather than by crude biological drives.

7.12 Social Signaling: Show Your Best, Hide Your Worst

Much of what we humans do is done to signal things to others about ourselves. In particular, for evolutionary reasons, we like to exhibit positive things about ourselves — crudely speaking, that we are capable and happy winners in life — and to hide the negatives, such as our shortcomings and our unhappiness.[70] And this constitutes yet another reason to expect us to be biased in our thinking about suffering, in various ways.

First, our general tendency to signal positive things about ourselves probably gives us a skewed sense of how much other people suffer. For while we may realize that we ourselves tend to suffer significantly, at least in periods, a casual glance at the lives of other people will reveal a different picture, as people publicly show much less failure and misery (those being bad signals from a biological perspective) and far more success and happiness (good signals) than what they actually experience. Consider social media as an example: we mostly present our best rather than our worst moments to the world. Here is how Schopenhauer described this general phenomenon:

---

68 One may argue there is nothing bad about the non-existence of sentience, in contrast to our feelings about it, *cf.* Knutsson, 2016a; Vinding, 2018f. In Geinster's words: "the only thing that's horrible (hurtful) about [non-existence] is the very *existence* of one contemplating not to exist." Geinster, 2012.
69 *Cf.* Tomasik, 2014e; Dello-Iacovo, 2016.
70 A case for this general claim can be found in Simler & Hanson, 2018.

> [H]uman life ... is covered on the outside with a false glitter; what suffers always conceals itself. On the other hand, everyone parades whatever pomp and splendour he can obtain by effort ...[71]

And when we do share our failures and misery publicly, it is usually the failures and misery of the past, which we can now report from a relatively blessed vantage point that is spared from accurate memories of the suffering we once experienced, and from which we can weave our past misery into a story of eventual success and accomplishment — a story that reflects positively on us. By contrast, the misery that does not lead to great success seems much less willingly reported, and is at any rate far less interesting to hear about.

Second, it is not only our own lives we prefer to present and reinforce a positive narrative about, but also the world at large, which can in turn create an echo chamber of positivity. For example, studies have found that Twitter users have a preference for sharing positive rather than negative information, and that they are more emotionally affected by positive information.[72] This preference and emotional disposition toward favoring positive information is another biasing factor potentially preventing us from giving a fair hearing to views that give primary importance to the reduction of suffering.

Indeed, by telling a positive story about the world at large, one also signals positive things about oneself — that one has a positive mindset, for instance, and that one is not a downer. By contrast, publicly endorsing a view of the world that is all about suffering and the overwhelming importance of its reduction does not signal a positive or happy story about us. This is an additional way in which our preference for signaling positive things about ourselves likely biases us against holding a suffering-focused view, let alone expressing such a view.[73]

---

71 Schopenhauer, 1819, vol I, p. 325.
72 Ferrara & Yang, 2015a; 2015b. A similar finding is reported in Taylor & Brown, 1988: "[B]oth the social world and cognitive-processing mechanisms impose filters on incoming information that distort it in a positive direction; negative information may be isolated and represented in as unthreatening a manner as possible." This is related to the general thesis of suffering suppression defended in Cohen, 2001.
73 A third reason to expect us to be biased against suffering-focused views in relation to social signaling is that we care a lot about recognition and admiration from others. And if we assume that we at some primitive level want to maximize such admiration, yet that we do

7.13 Suffering Is Abstract

Another reason we focus less on suffering than deeper reflection might recommend, and why we fail to reduce it as effectively as we could, is its abstract nature.[74] People often do work to address forms of suffering they have been touched by personally — for instance, one might have seen a close family member suffer and die terribly from a specific disease and then choose to dedicate one's life toward the alleviation of this ailment. Yet it is rare for people to work to reduce suffering *in general*. This is also true of most people who choose to work on reducing forms of suffering that have not touched them personally: they still tend to work on addressing specific forms of suffering (e.g. hunger, domestic violence, child abuse), as these tend to have communities, academic literatures, and sociological momenta supporting them and drawing people to them. By contrast, there is very little academic literature and sociological momentum about the reduction of suffering *in general*.[75]

From a normative perspective, this makes little sense, and is indeed yet another expression of bias. For whether we ourselves happen to have encountered a given form of suffering, or whether society currently focuses on particular forms of suffering over others, should not be what determines our priorities.[76] That would be an expression of an epistemic limitation

---

not think this aim is important on reflection, it follows that we could have a bias to prioritize working toward the creation of a large and happy future population — in a public way, so this large population could admire us for having brought it about — rather than to work toward a future with the least amount of suffering. The latter would probably be a future with fewer sentient beings, and hence with less admiration for us. This argument may seem farfetched, yet note that it mostly rests on the premise that we might at some level be motivated to maximize our own admiration over all time, and this premise is hardly that far fetched.

74 A similar point is made in Mayerfeld, 1999, p. 107.

75 My point is not that we, as a society, focus too much on any of the specific sources of suffering just mentioned. My point is rather that our efforts to reduce suffering tend to be much too narrow and confined, whereby we risk missing more effective ways in which we could reduce suffering in general. For instance, it is conceivable that there are actions that would increase the amount of resources devoted to the reduction of virtually all forms and sources of suffering (a Pareto improvement for a wide range of endeavors to alleviate suffering, if you will), such as by increasing society's concern for suffering in general.

76 To be sure, the priority society gives to the alleviation of a given form of suffering does give *some* indication of its severity, but this indication is, unfortunately, quite weak in the bigger picture, especially relative to the goal of reducing suffering for *all* sentient beings.

and status quo bias respectively, which most of us can agree should not be the animating forces behind our decisions. If by working on alleviating some particular evil, A, we will relieve more intense suffering for a greater number of beings than by addressing another evil, B, then, other things being equal, reason would dictate that we work on addressing A rather than B. Indeed, the choice of addressing A over B might be the most consequential choice we could ever make. And yet, as a society, we spend very little effort trying to get choices of this most consequential sort right.[77]

The abstractness bias reviewed here is probably especially strong in relation to risks of astronomical future suffering, since such suffering is more abstract and general than even all currently ongoing suffering. We do not know what forms such future suffering might take — it could exist in as yet unknown forms and contexts — and this lack of concreteness may well make it even more difficult for us to take these risks seriously compared to ongoing, well-known forms of suffering.

7.14 A Brief Introspective Experiment

To get a clearer sense of how our reasoning might be biased, it may also be worth taking a step back to observe our own mind and the nature of its motivations more directly. The following introspective experiment might help shed some light on the matter: if you observe your mind carefully, and try to internally raise the moral conjecture that extreme suffering carries supreme disvalue and warrants our highest moral priority, what attitude emerges in your mind? Is it an attitude similar to that of a dispassionate, impartial scientist who wants to identify the most plausible theory in light of all evidence, whatever that theory may turn out to be? Or is it more akin to the attitude of, say, a politically motivated partisan who dislikes and seeks to discredit a bothersome proposal that does not fit with the party line? (I can personally testify that my mind was strongly partisan against this moral conjecture in the past, and that it in many ways still is.)

---

77 From a descriptive perspective, however, our priorities make perfect sense. The human mind is not built to reason abstractly from well-reflected first principles, at least not as a first resort.

I believe this exercise is worth doing in relation to any moral view we might ponder, as we can agree on reflection that we should aspire toward the dispassionate attitude of the scientist rather than the motivated reasoning of the partisan. Nonetheless, by (human) nature, we tend to be more like the partisan than the scientist.

7.15 Counterbiases?

Finally, for this exploration of biases to be fair and complete, we should also search for biases that might lead us to overestimate the moral importance of suffering. This is, however, a more difficult task. An obvious candidate, at least judging by its name and common interpretation, would be the "negativity bias". Yet contrary to what its name and popular image might suggest, this so-called bias is not really a counterweight to the positivity bias reviewed above. In fact, it is quite the opposite. For the term "negativity bias" refers to the well-documented tendency reviewed in the study "Bad Is Stronger Than Good" by Baumeister et al., namely: our tendency to *actually feel* the bad more powerfully than the good — that "bad is stronger than good, as a general principle across a broad range of psychological phenomena [including emotions]."[78]

In other words, what this "bias" refers to is the tendency of our actual experiences of bad things to diverge from some idealized symmetry between good and bad.[79] And hence, if anything, the so-called negativity "bias" would seem to count as a reason *in favor* rather than against focusing on the alleviation of suffering in practice. This is not what we were searching for.[80]

---

78 Baumeister et al., 2001, abstract. Another paper described negativity bias as "[t]he principle ... that in most situations, negative events are more salient, potent, dominant in combinations, and generally efficacious than positive events." Rozin & Royzman, 2001, p. 297.

79 This is a rather unusual way to define a bias, since a bias is usually defined in terms of how our expectations fail to track empirical reality, not the other way around. If we adopt this more common definition of what constitutes a bias, it is indeed our *a priori* expectation of symmetry that is biased, i.e. distorted relative to empirical reality.

80 There may seem to be a contradiction between the positivity bias and the negativity "bias", yet the tension is only apparent. Negativity "bias" implies that we tend to experi-

We already noted above how, if one currently grants supreme priority to the reduction of suffering, and if one's peers do the same, confirmation bias and conformity bias could count as biases in favor of suffering-focused views. This seems a legitimate source of bias worth being aware of and controlling for.[81] Yet, as also noted above, biases of this kind will probably tend to be significantly weaker and more rare compared to the confirmation and conformity biases working in the opposite direction (given how little most people in fact prioritize reducing suffering at the level of their behavior).

Another relevant bias is "pessimism bias", which is the opposite of optimism bias — a tendency to overestimate the probability of misfortune and underestimate the probability of success. Again, however, optimism bias is generally much stronger and more prevalent than pessimism bias. Studies indicate that people are generally optimistic, with depressed people being the exception who display a pessimism bias.[82] This suggests that most people should be more concerned about controlling for optimism bias than pessimism bias.[83]

One may dispute whether this is true, as most people do appear to make overly pessimistic assessments about how others are doing in some respects, such as whether the fraction of people living in absolute poverty has declined in recent decades (it has).[84] Yet people also seem to have grotesquely optimistic beliefs that concern much larger numbers of beings. For instance, 58 percent of adults in the United States think that

---

ence negative emotions more powerfully, and become affected more by negative events, whereas the positivity bias implies that our *memories* of negative emotions and negative events are significantly more positive than they in fact were when we experienced them, and indeed that we are more likely to forget negative events altogether (Skowronski et al., 2014), even as such events have a more powerful effect on our mood at the time and after, Baumeister et al., 2001; Rozin & Royzman, 2001.

81   Relative, again, to the ideal of independent reflection.
82   Sharot et al., 2007.
83   Related to this, it has been hypothesized that some degree of depression makes us more realistic (depressive realism), Alloy & Abramson, 1988. Beyond that, it should be noted that the pessimism bias, like the optimism bias, only pertains to the estimation of the *probabilities* of future events, not the badness of those events in themselves, and hence the pessimism bias has little relevance for our attempts to evaluate the intrinsic moral significance of suffering, as opposed to our assessments of its future prevalence. In other words, even if one has a strong pessimism bias, one may still underestimate the moral importance of suffering.
84   See e.g. Rosling et al., 2018.

"most farmed animals are treated well", despite the fact that 99 percent of "farmed" animals in the United States live on factory farms.[85] And people probably have even more unjustifiably optimistic views about the condition of non-human animals in nature, who constitute the vast majority of sentient beings on Earth.[86]

An additional finding that may be relevant is that people with major depressive disorder (MDD) display a "negative perception bias" relative to other people, in that they perceive and rate other people's emotions more negatively than most people rate others' emotions, and rate "interactions with negative emotionality as being more intense" than do people without MDD.[87] Thus, if one has MDD, this might count as a bias to control for in one's appraisal of the prevalence of negative emotions in others. However, one may also argue that most people rate others' emotions too optimistically, and that depressives generally have a more accurate perception of the emotions of others.[88] Indeed, on my reading, the study cited above is equally consistent with this latter interpretation.[89]

Two other tendencies of the human mind that might seem worth reviewing here are "loss aversion" — our tendency to value losses more than (in some sense) equivalent gains — and "risk aversion", our tendency to prefer a safe option over a risky one even when the risky one yields a higher expected value. It seems natural to suspect that these aversions could count as biases in favor of a suffering-focused view. Yet upon closer examination, it is not clear why they should. For loss aversion and risk aversion say rather little about suffering in particular. They are about losses-versus-gains and risks in general, and they are usually studied in the context of monetary

---

85 Sentience Institute, 2017. For some insight into the actual and indisputably horrendous conditions on factory farms, see mercyforanimals.org/investigations.
86 Pinker, 2002, p. 163; Tomasik, 2009b; 2009d; Horta, 2010a; Davidow, 2013; Iglesias, 2018.
87 Kaletsch et al., 2014.
88 Again, some argue that people with depression generally make more accurate assessments, Alloy & Abramson, 1988.
89 The study in question being Kaletsch et al., 2014. "Equally consistent" because people with MDD rate the expression of positive feelings just as positively as other people do, yet they rate the expression of negative feelings (i.e. body movements by actors that portray negative emotions) more negatively, and it is not clear why one of these two groups should be considered more correct in its assessments than the other.

losses and risks, which have little to do with suffering as such.[90] One may, of course, suggest that we prefer to avoid losses and risks because they lead to negative emotions, yet, following the remarks on the negativity "bias" above, such a preference to avoid negative states arguably speaks to their felt disvalue rather than a bias.[91]

All in all, while there are some biases that plausibly do push us toward focusing on the reduction of suffering, these seem comparatively few and weak when compared to the biases that pull us away from such a focus. At any rate, the biases reviewed in this chapter should give us serious pause with respect to any inclination we may have to dismiss the moral weight of suffering and the importance of prioritizing its reduction.

---

90   Indeed, a risk-averse classical utilitarian may (irrationally) make a choice that leads to more rather than less suffering in expectation. Imagine, for instance, a choice between 1) a bet with 95 percent probability of creating 500 "utilons" (a unit of happiness), and 5 percent probability of creating 10 utilons, or 2) creating 1,000,000 utilons and 999,525 "disutilons" (a unit of suffering). These options have an expected value of 475.5 and 475 utilons respectively on the classical utilitarian framework. Yet the risk of an outcome with only 10 utilons keeps the risk-averse classical utilitarian from making the choice with the highest expected value, and which entails no suffering. Thus, risk aversion need not favor less suffering; it can readily favor more of it.

91   That we feel strong negative emotions about risks and losses (compared to foregone gains) is probably in large part explained by the diminishing marginal value of resources. For example, for an individual, being in possession of $100,000 is not ten times as good as having $10,000, and hence getting $10,000 for sure is indeed better (for the sake of our survival) than a 1/10 bet of getting $100,000, although an idealized risk-neutral agent would consider them equivalent. Likewise, in the case of loss aversion, if one has $10,000, then losing this would be much more significant than a gain of another $10,000.

8

Objections Against Focusing on Suffering

Various objections can be leveled against the arguments I have presented in previous chapters. The aim of this chapter is to raise and respond to some of the most common of these objections.

8.1 *The views defended here are absurd because they imply we should seek to end all sentient life.*

First of all, the general claim that we should give special importance to the reduction of suffering in practice does not imply that we should end all sentient life, even if we could do so painlessly (more on this below).

Second, on the more specific views I have defended — the principle of sympathy for intense suffering and my moral realist view — it would indeed, *in theory, in some hypothetical scenario*, be morally right to push a button that ends sentient life if the alternative is to let it keep existing with the extreme suffering it entails. (Though notice that it could be better still, on these views, to push a button that allows sentient life to keep existing without extreme suffering.)[1]

---

1   Whether this would be better depends on what one considers valuable beyond the reduction of extreme suffering. That is, beyond the claim that extreme suffering carries supreme moral disvalue, my moral realist position and the principle of sympathy for intense suffering are both silent on what has moral value, and hence both views are com-

However, it is not obvious that this *theoretical* claim about *hypothetical* scenarios is absurd. Before claiming it is absurd, we should keep in mind the concrete reality of what extreme suffering is in fact like (not to mention the many biases reviewed in the previous chapter, especially Metzinger's existence bias). We should remember that some beings are experiencing suffering so horrible that they consider the end of it more important than anything else. Can we really state with confidence that this assessment of theirs is absurd, or that it is absurd to sympathize and agree with their judgment?[2]

Indeed, if we were forced to directly observe the being suffering the most on the planet right now, a helpless victim in a state beyond excruciating torment, would we still be able to confidently maintain that it is absurd to say that we should push the button? (Not to mention if we had to directly observe *all* the beings who experience extreme suffering on the planet right now, as well as all the future suffering that pushing the button would prevent.)

A related question we should ask ourselves is whether we would push a button to *create* a world that contains such suffering. If not, or if we would have serious hesitations about doing it, we should also be hesitant to consider it absurd to claim that the painless cessation of sentient life would be better than the continued existence of the extreme suffering it entails.[3]

All of this is, of course, wholly theoretical — pertaining to hypotheticals quite detached from the reality of our condition. It is another issue altogether what is optimal to do *in practice* according to these views, when we do factor in the realities of our condition. And here we find many strong reasons to *not* try to end sentient life on Earth, including human civilization in particular.[4]

---

patible with views according to which it would be morally important to sustain life (in the absence of extreme suffering).
2 *Cf.* Knutsson, 2016a.
3 I am not hereby claiming that not creating the world is morally equivalent to ending it. What I do claim is that if abstaining from creating the world with all the suffering it entails is not obviously morally absurd, then we should at least also hesitate to call the pushing of this hypothetical button morally absurd.
4 We should, of course, assign *some* probability to the claim that seeking to end all sentient life is the best we can do given these views, as there is bound to be some uncertainty about what is optimal. Yet it is important to note that this applies to all consequentialist views. That is, on any plausible consequentialist view, there is some probability that the future will be so bad, and our options for preventing bad outcomes so limited, that it would be best if we tried to end all sentient life. Thus, with respect to the question of

One important reason is that it is conceivable that future scenarios in which human civilization persists will generally contain less extreme suffering than future scenarios in which it does not, and there is indeed considerable uncertainty about this.[5] For example, it is conceivable that human civilization may give rise to less extreme suffering than some other civilization — whether that civilization originates from other planets[6] or from other lifeforms on Earth[7] — which might colonize our local region of the cosmos in our stead in case human extinction occurs. If human civilization reduces extreme suffering in expectation, then this constitutes a reason to work to preserve human civilization. And the fact that there is considerable uncertainty about the matter constitutes a strong reason against trying to end human civilization.

Beyond that, even if one believes that the persistence of human civilization is more likely to increase extreme suffering, there are still overwhelming reasons to *not* seek to end human civilization, and to strongly discourage any such attempts. One reason is that any attempt to end all Earth-originating sentient life is likely to backfire, and thus to increase extreme suffering in expectation, in part by decreasing stability and cooperation in the future, and by decreasing compassionate values and concern for suffering.[8] A more elaborate explanation of this point is found in the "Negative Utilitarianism FAQ":

---

whether one should seek to end all sentient life in practice, the only difference between the suffering-minimizing views I have defended and other consequentialist views is the particular credence they assign to an affirmative answer to this question. And what I am arguing here is that these credences would plausibly not differ much: it is highly unlikely that we should seek to destroy the world on any suffering-minimizing view, for reasons I shall now explore in the text. See also Knutsson, 2019a.

5   For some considerations relevant to this question, see Pearce, 1995, chap. 4, 32; Tomasik, 2011, "What if human colonization is more humane than ET colonization?"; 2013a, "Might humans be replaced by other species?"; Vinding, 2015b; Knutsson, 2019a, "Is Killing Everyone More Likely to Become Optimal from a Negative or from a Traditional Utilitarian Perspective?"

6   Tomasik, 2011, "What if human colonization is more humane than ET colonization?"

7   Tomasik, 2013a, "Might humans be replaced by other species?"

8   Tomasik, 2011, "Why we should remain cooperative".

> [Increasing extinction risk would be] very bad even by NU [negative utilitarian] standards. There are important and dominant reasons against doing this. ... The difference between "no future" (i.e. no Earth-originating intelligence expanding into space) and a decent future, where concern for suffering and thwarted preferences plays some role (even though it would likely not be the only value) is much smaller than the difference between a decent future and one that goes awfully wrong. NUs will benefit more by cooperating and compromising with other value systems in trying to make the future safer in regard to (agreed-upon) worst-case scenarios, rather than by trying to prevent space colonization from happening at all. It would be a tragedy if altruistically-concerned people split up into opposing factions due to them having different definitions of "doing what is good", while greed and bad incentives lead the non-altruistically-inclined people in the world [to] win the race. Instead, those who share *at least some significant concern* for the reduction of suffering should join together.[9]

In relation to this point, it appears especially relevant to keep our proportion bias in mind: our tendency to be more eager to help ten out of twenty individuals than to help ten out of a hundred.[10] This bias likely leads us to overestimate the value of ending *all* extreme suffering in a (hypothetical) future that would otherwise contain comparatively little suffering, relative to the value of preventing even a substantial fraction of extreme suffering in a (hypothetical) future scenario with astronomical amounts of extreme suffering. The absolute amount of suffering prevented in the latter case may be far greater, even as the suffering reduced in proportional terms may be modest, and hence unappealing to our biased intuitions.

We should be careful to control for this. If we are trying to minimize extreme suffering in expectation, we should seek to minimize expected suffering in absolute rather than proportional terms, which in turn implies that we should be careful not to overlook risks of future scenarios that

---

9 Anonymous, 2015, 3.2. More elaboration is found in this same piece, as well as in Tomasik, 2011, "Why we should remain cooperative"; 2013a; 2013g; 2014a; Gloor, 2018.
10 Fetherstonhaugh et al., 1997.

contain astronomical amounts of suffering.[11] Also because virtually everyone can get behind efforts to avoid very bad outcomes, which highlights the importance of cooperating with others who are willing to support such efforts, and not least the importance of avoiding uncooperative actions that turn others away and thus hamper these most important efforts to avoid very bad outcomes.

In sum, on any view according to which we should minimize suffering, there are overriding reasons not to seek to end sentient life, including human civilization in particular. Instead, we should seek to engage with others in kind and cooperative ways so as to increase future concern for suffering, and in particular, we should work to reduce the risk of worst-case outcomes that contain astronomical amounts of suffering. How we can best do this is the subject we shall explore in the second part of this book.

Also worth pointing out in response to the objection above is that, as Simon Knutsson has argued, it seems about as likely that strict suffering-minimizing views endorse "destroying the world" as it does that, for example, classical utilitarianism endorses that we should kill people in order to replace them with happier beings.[12] Both are theoretical implications that most people would probably find unpalatable at first sight, and both are courses of action we almost surely should not pursue in practice according to these respective views. Yet if we do not think this latter theoretical implication constitutes a strong reason to dismiss classical utilitarianism,

---

11   That is, when thinking about future priorities, we should be careful not to consider the worst-case scenario something like "suffering will be bound to Earth and things will go on as usual", but instead something like "astronomical suffering at a scale and intensity orders of magnitude greater than anything seen on Earth", and we should realize that incautious pursuits to prevent scenarios of the former kind likely significantly worsen scenarios of the latter kind in expectation.

12   Knutsson, 2019a. Similarly, one can argue that classical utilitarianism has an even less plausible button-pushing implication than do suffering-minimizing views. For if we could push a button that destroyed our world in an armageddon of suffering, by causing the worst torture possible for years for all beings in this world, and if this button in turn created a new world with a "sufficient amount" of pleasure, then classical utilitarianism would oblige us to push this button of torment to create such pleasure (a similar point is made in ibid.). See also David Pearce's discussion of what he calls a "utilitronium shockwave", a shockwave of matter and energy optimized for bliss, the creation of which would, in theory, be a moral obligation according to classical utilitarianism, Pearce, 2017, "On Classical Versus Negative Utilitarianism".

it is not clear why the corresponding theoretical implication of strictly suffering-minimizing views should count as devastating for those views.[13]

One response to these objections is to reject both views, or at least to reject them in their pure form, and instead adopt additional elements in one's moral theory, such as a prohibition against killing innocent beings. Having such a multiplicity of elements in one's moral theory — what is called a pluralist moral theory — is common in modern philosophy, including among defenders of suffering-focused moral views in particular. This relates back to my earlier remark that suffering-focused views do not generally imply that we should end all sentient life even if we could do so painlessly. Indeed, many suffering-focused views entail a maximal prohibition against it. For example, Jamie Mayerfeld defends a strong *prima facie* duty to reduce suffering, and argues that no amount of bliss can justify allowing the lifelong torture of one being.[14] Nonetheless, he still maintains that he is "sure that it is wrong to seek the destruction of sentient life, even if it could be done painlessly."[15] He goes on to note that:

> [T]here may be a crucial difference between thinking that it would have been better if the world had never come into existence, and thinking that we may take it upon ourselves to destroy the life that already exists.[16]

Mayerfeld thus defends an explicitly pluralist account of ethics, according to which we should respect individual autonomy and the intrinsic value of persons, and which holds that it is wrong to seek the destruction of sentient life.[17]

Another prominent defender of suffering-focused ethics with a similar view is Clark Wolf, who defends a pluralist view according to which our prime obligation as far as welfare is concerned is to reduce suffering, while he also notes that he is "convinced that welfarist considerations are not

---

13   Knutsson, 2019a.
14   Mayerfeld, 1999, p. 178.
15   Ibid., p. 159.
16   Ibid., pp. 159-160. David Benatar makes a similar point in MOWE, 2018, around 68 minutes in.
17   Mayerfeld, 1999, pp. 159-160.

the only morally relevant considerations."[18] In particular, with respect to death and the world destruction argument, Wolf writes that:

> [W]e might have a contravening *prima facie* obligation not to kill other people. Such an obligation might then defeat the *prima facie* obligation to alleviate suffering and would provide the basis for a plausible argument against the annihilation of our world.[19]

A similar view seems endorsed within the tradition of Buddhist ethics, as scholar of Buddhism Daniel Breyer explains with the following analogy:

> An oncologist strives to eliminate cancer in her patients, but she does not succeed when they die. Likewise, the Buddhist strives to eliminate suffering, but does not succeed by destroying the world because she can no more cure the world of suffering by annihilating it than the oncologist can cure cancer by killing her patient.[20]

This Buddhist view and the views of Mayerfeld and Wolf are all strongly suffering-focused views that do not permit the destruction of the world.[21] And given that attempts to destroy the world seem so bad in expectation, it is probably optimal to adopt a side-constraint that prohibits such attempts even on purely suffering-minimizing views.[22]

---

18   Wolf, 1997, VIII.
19   Ibid. Wolf has also argued against the world destruction argument with an appeal to rights: "[P]olicy makers simply have no right to make decisions about whether the lives of others are worth living, or whether they should live or die. Since it is clear that policy makers have no right to kill off the miserable and destitute, this response gains support from our moral intuitions." Wolf, 1996, p. 278.
20   Breyer, 2015, p. 555.
21   In a similar vein, author Jonathan Leighton has defended a pragmatic view he calls "negative utilitarianism plus", according to which we should do our best to reduce preventable suffering, yet where we can still "categorically refuse to intentionally destroy the planet and eliminate ourselves and everything we care about in the process …" Leighton, 2011, p. 96. See also Leighton, 2019.
22   Again, the same point can be made about classical utilitarianism and similar moral views: the future could be negative in expectation, and hence destroying the world *could* be optimal given these views, yet it is probably still best to adopt a side-constraint that forbids it. There is not a fundamental difference between classical and negative utilitarianism in this regard, Knutsson, 2019a.

All in all, it is not the case that the views defended here imply that we should seek to destroy the world, whether we speak of the broader moral claim that we should give special importance to the reduction of suffering, or the stronger, more specific moral view that the minimization of extreme suffering carries overriding moral importance. On the contrary: these views strongly imply that we should *not* do this.

8.2 *Giving so much weight to suffering seems to imply that death would be a good thing, and that death is something we should want to occur sooner rather than later. Yet most people do not want to die.*

The short reply to this objection is that none of the views defended here imply that death is generally a good thing. Again, to say that the reduction of suffering should be a foremost priority is not to say that other things do not have value as well. As noted above, one can agree with this general claim while being a pluralist who ascribes intrinsic value to a wide variety of things, including living a moral life and achieving one's life goals, both of which would imply that death is indeed bad.

Furthermore, the view that the reduction of suffering deserves special priority is also compatible with classical utilitarianism, especially if one accepts Adam Smith's point that the potential depths of suffering are far deeper than the heights of happiness, and if one accepts the existence of a significant asymmetry in the ease of realizing states of happiness versus states of suffering, as defended in the first chapter.[23] And classical utilitarianism does not generally consider death good either (even though it does in some cases, and probably quite often relative to what influential Christian views and views animated by existence bias find acceptable).[24]

---

23 As Mayerfeld notes: "[M]ost utilitarians agree we accomplish more by trying to prevent suffering than by trying to increase happiness ..." Mayerfeld, 1999, p. 149. The same view is expressed in Ord, 2013 and Singer, 2018, about 9 minutes in.

24 It is worth noting, however, that classical utilitarianism also has some counterintuitive implications with respect to death. For example, if a person who lives in complete isolation experiences significantly more suffering than happiness (also by their own admission), then, even if this person expresses a strong wish to live on, classical utilitarianism holds that, other things being equal, it would be morally right to end the life of this person (though to be clear, classical utilitarianism would not say we should kill such a person in

Yet even from the perspective of views that consider the minimization of suffering the overriding or only value, it is not the case that death, much less early death, is generally good. For one, early deaths are usually seen as more tragic and plausibly cause more suffering to the bereaved than do later deaths.[25] More significantly, however, a reduced lifespan will also reduce one's potential to reduce extreme suffering, which renders the early death of any moral agent a potentially very bad thing.[26]

Beyond that, early death may give rise to more suffering for other beings, such as wild animals, who may emerge in greater numbers in the dead individual's stead, and whose lives may contain significantly more suffering than would the continued life of the individual who died early.[27] These considerations suggest that early death is also generally a very bad thing even from a pure suffering-minimizing perspective.[28]

---

practice, as other things are *not* equal). This is probably an unacceptable implication for many, even in theory, in which case one might find it necessary to include other things in one's moral theory than just purely welfarist elements, such as respect for consent and a prohibition against killing.

25 One study of "bereaved parents of deceased children (infancy to age 34)" found that "[a]n average of 18.05 years following the death, when parents were age 53, bereaved parents reported more depressive symptoms, poorer well-being, and more health problems and were more likely to have experienced a depressive episode and marital disruption than were comparison parents." Rogers et al., 2008. This plausibly also applies to other species where parents have a small number of children in whom they invest a lot of resources, *cf.* Vinding, 2018e.

26 Vinding, 2015c.

27 Tomasik, 2016b; Vinding, forthcoming. This consideration applies not only to the early death of humans but to all sentient beings, Tomasik, 2017a.

28 It must be conceded, though, that from one's own personal perspective in isolation, views that assign overriding disvalue to extreme suffering do indeed imply that one's continued existence is bad due to the risk of extreme suffering it entails. Yet this theoretical implication is again 1) not a view with great practical relevance, since one can generally expect to reduce much more suffering by staying alive, and 2) hardly that absurd if we really think about what is at stake.

8.3 *The views defended here do not seem to respect personal autonomy and liberty.*

Again, my core claim that suffering deserves special priority in practice is consistent with pluralist views of value, including views according to which liberty and personal autonomy have intrinsic moral value. The same is true of the more specific suffering-minimizing views I have defended, as these views merely hold that the reduction of extreme suffering is what matters *most* — not that it is the *only* thing that matters — and hence these views are also perfectly consistent with the claim that individual liberty and autonomy matter intrinsically.[29]

Beyond that, even if we do not consider liberty and autonomy intrinsically valuable, we should still, on any view that considers the reduction of suffering a priority, value liberty and autonomy for instrumental reasons, since doing so generally has good consequences. On an individual level, respecting the liberty and autonomy of others will generally be a much more effective way for us to engage with the world, as it enables trust and collaboration. Similarly, on a collective and institutional level, we should all want to enforce respect for individual liberty, as it serves as a precondition for open-ended human conversation and peaceful coexistence, which both seem necessary for any successful endeavor to reduce suffering effectively.

---

29 For an argument for the claim that the reduction of extreme suffering should rank higher than respect for individual liberty, consider again two planets, one to which we can add greater levels of individual liberty (for people who do not suffer in the absence of liberty) and one to which we can add extreme suffering. The question is then whether it would be right to increase individual liberty on the one planet (assuming, still, that it does not reduce suffering) while adding some amount of extreme suffering to the other. I maintain it would not. Reducing extreme suffering takes precedence over increasing individual liberty when these are in conflict. A confounding factor, of course, is that these aims are generally not in conflict, as I argue below in the text.

8.4 Reducing suffering only seems overridingly important to us while we experience it. When we do not suffer, other things seem equally or more important. Why should suffering be granted a special status? For example, many people will also, in the moment of eating potato chips, downplay or disregard the importance of other things, such as their health, their figure, the bad feelings that may ensue, etc. Yet we do not consider this a good reason to deem potato-chip eating especially important. Likewise, we should not consider the reduction of suffering overridingly important just because we experience it as such in the moment.[30]

First, it is worth reiterating that the core claim that suffering deserves special importance in practice does not imply that other goals, such as those we tend to pursue when we do not suffer intensely, are not also intrinsically worth pursuing.

Second, even as the problem of suffering is vastly neglected, many people actually do consider the reduction and prevention of suffering uniquely important even when they do not suffer themselves. As a case in point, a survey conducted by the Future of Life Institute, in which more than 14,000 people responded, found that the goal people favored most as the ideal aim of a future civilization was "minimizing suffering".[31] This was the most popular aim by a large margin, ahead of "maximizing positive experiences", and most of the people who favored this goal were probably not suffering while they responded to the survey.

Third, the biases reviewed in the previous chapter may distort our judgment. For example, the empathy gap that makes us unable to really understand the nature and importance of suffering when we are not experiencing it, and the positivity bias that makes our memories of negative states mild compared to our memories of positive states, even though the negative states actually tend to be more dominant.[32] Beyond that, there is the pleasure-desire bias: the potential for our mechanism of pure wanting, as opposed to the actually pleasant sensation of liking, to bias our

---
30 This objection is a paraphrased version of the objection found in Grace, 2012.
31 Future of Life Institute, 2017.
32 See section 7.9; Baumeister et al., 2001.

assessments. And this seems especially relevant with respect to the potato-chip example, since potato-chip eating plausibly tends to be motivated significantly more by wanting than by liking. In other words, it may stem more from *anticipation* of a reward than from an actual sensation of pleasure (not too unlike the actions of an addict, although on a smaller scale).[33] In contrast, when we experience suffering, we are directly experiencing a bad state, and our drive to get away from it is not based on frivolous self-indulgence or "empty" wanting.

When we consider suffering unimportant because we do not ourselves experience it, we do so, I submit, because of an epistemic limitation. The same cannot be said, or at least not to remotely the same extent, about the wanting-driven behavior of eating potato chips. Indeed, potato-chip eating can often be deemed barely enjoyable and without real value even from the inside while one indulges in it (such as if one has already eaten a full bag), whereas intense suffering will *always* be experienced as intensely bad, and its avoidance will *always* be found undeniably important in the moment. This is a big difference.

More generally, we have many crude drives for primeval indulgences that we can easily be caught up in and obsess about, yet most of us can agree that these tend not to stand up to reflective scrutiny, nor warrant a high-minded defense (if anything, these drives usually require the opposite from our cerebral faculties: restraint). The reduction of suffering, on the other hand, does indeed deserve our most sincere endorsement and defense. Most of us can agree, on reflection, that these goals are not on the same footing.

---

33   Pablo Stafforini made a similar point in the comments on Grace, 2012.

8.5 It seems strange to deny a symmetry between happiness and suffering. Why should happiness of a given intensity not be considered as morally good as suffering of the same intensity should be considered morally bad?

Intuitions certainly differ on whether it is more strange to deny or affirm a moral symmetry between happiness and suffering.[34] Recall that R. I. Sikora called it a common intuition that "pain prevention should count more heavily than the promotion of pleasure",[35] while philosopher Gustaf Arrhenius calls it an "important intuition" that it is "more important to relieve suffering than to increase (already happy people's) happiness."[36] And the survey finding that minimizing suffering appears the most favored ideal goal among people also suggests that asymmetrical intuitions are widely shared.[37]

In the interpersonal case especially (which is the most morally relevant one by far), I believe most people would find any supposed moral symmetry between happiness and suffering deeply suspect. For instance, if Bob could gain a maximal level of happiness for an hour at the price of Alice having to experience suffering for an hour at an intensity just below the "corresponding" intensity of suffering, is it really plausible to say that we are morally required to bring about this state of affairs (if the alternative is that Alice and Bob are both in an untroubled, neutral state)?[38] I think most people would deny this, and it is by no means clear why they should not.

---

34 At any rate, one should be careful with appeals to strangeness. For the fact that a proposition seems strange does not imply that the alternatives will seem less strange. Indeed, there is no logical reason why our intuitions should not deem every conceivable position on a given issue strange. So even if it in some sense seems strange to reject a moral symmetry between happiness and suffering, it may well be much stranger still to *accept* such a moral symmetry, especially when we consider its implications.
35 Sikora, 1976, p. 587. James Griffin also wrote that Karl Popper "has answered for the majority" in rejecting a moral symmetry between happiness and suffering, Griffin, 1979, p. 47.
36 Arrhenius, 2000, p. 138.
37 Future of Life Institute, 2017. There may, of course, be other things explaining these responses than just a moral asymmetry between equally intense happiness and suffering, such as asymmetries in potential intensities (see section 1.2) as well as asymmetries in ease of realization (see section 1.3), yet it still seems likely that (implicit) acceptance of such a moral asymmetry is at least part of the explanation.
38 The meaning of the term "corresponding intensity" in this context is itself problematic, as it is not clear how to measure intensities of happiness and suffering in a commensu-

After all, as G. E. Moore wrote in *Principia Ethica*:

> We have no title whatever to assume that the truth on any subject-matter will display such symmetry as we desire to see ... The study of Ethics would, no doubt, be far more simple, and its results far more 'systematic,' if, for instance, pain were an evil of exactly the same magnitude as pleasure is a good; but we have no reason whatever to assume that the Universe is such that ethical truths must display this kind of symmetry ...[39]

Clark Wolf makes a similar point in relation to the assumption that pleasure can outweigh pain:

> [I]t is far from obvious that pains and pleasures are commensurable in this way, and there is good reason to doubt that the twin utilitarian aims [of maximizing happiness and minimizing suffering] are even compatible — at least not without further explanation.[40]

One observation that may seem to favor a moral or evaluative symmetry between happiness and suffering is that we can sometimes have bad and good feelings simultaneously, and it can seem like the good can sometimes overpower or outweigh the bad. If so, why should we not deem them symmetric?

One must be careful here, however. For happiness and suffering as defined here — an overall good feeling and an overall bad feeling respectively — indeed cannot coexist at the same time; only aversive and pleasant components can. And pleasant components can surely dominate aversive components, in effect producing an overall pleasant feeling. This is a clear

---

rable way, let alone in a manner that has interpersonal validity, Knutsson, 2016b. Yet let us assume for the sake of argument that Bob and Alice use the same intensity scale. Note also that the "corresponding level" of suffering need not be close to maximal, *cf.* the asymmetry in potential states defended in section 1.2 and Mathison, 2018, chap. 2.

[39] Moore, 1903, p. 222. Indeed, as quoted earlier, Moore wrote that "pleasure, however intense, does not, *by itself,* appear to be a *great* good, even if it has some slight intrinsic value", whereas "pain ... appears to be a far worse evil than pleasure is a good." Ibid., p. 212.

[40] Wolf, 1997, I.

and well-defined sense in which pleasant components can prevail over aversive components.

Yet to draw implications about suffering from this is, once again, to overlook the monumental gap between a mere aversive component and suffering proper, the former being a merely local experiential property that may well be wholly agreeable, whereas the latter is, by definition, a globally disagreeable state of consciousness. In other words, these are two fundamentally different phenomena (although the former may lead to the latter). And unlike the case of pleasant components dominating aversive components, there is no straightforward sense in which the happiness of many can outweigh the extreme suffering of a single individual, although we may be tempted to (mis)extrapolate like this from the case of aversive components, their vast dissimilarity from suffering notwithstanding.[41]

Pleasure may well be able to *prevent* suffering, such as by keeping suffering at bay in the mind that it occupies, yet that still does not suggest that whatever intrinsic value pleasure might have is comparable to the intrinsic disvalue of suffering, much less that it is justifiable to create pleasure at the price of suffering.

Indeed, the notion that happiness and suffering are morally symmetric deserves our most meticulous scrutiny. It may, of course, seem intuitive to assume that some kind of symmetry must obtain, and to superimpose a certain interval of the real numbers onto the range of happiness and suffering we can experience — from minus ten to plus ten, say. Yet we have to be extremely cautious about such naively intuitive moves of conceptualization. This holds true of efforts to devise theoretical models in general, but it is especially true when our ethical priorities hinge on these conceptual models; when they can determine, for instance, whether we find it acceptable to allow astronomical amounts of suffering to occur in order to create "even greater" amounts of happiness.

First of all, it is worth examining why it can seem intuitive to consider suffering and happiness morally symmetric. One reason may be the terms we usually use to describe these states. As Simon Knutsson notes in a defense of the view that suffering does not have a truly positive counterpart:

---

[41] A similar point is made in Anonymous, 2015, 2.2.5

> [T]he phrases 'negative well-being' and 'negative experiences' are unfortunate because if something is negative, it sounds as if there is a positive counterpart. Better names may be 'problematic moments in life' and 'problematic experiences,' because unproblematic, which seems to be the opposite of problematic, does not imply positive.[42]

Another reason we may consider happiness and suffering opposites is that they, as hinted by Knutsson, *are* opposites in a very real sense: a problematic feeling is indeed the exact opposite of an unproblematic feeling. Yet the fact that two states are each others' opposites in this sense does not imply they are symmetric in the sense of being able to morally outweigh each other or meaningfully cancel each other out. Consider, by analogy, the states of being below and above water respectively. One can certainly say that being below water is the opposite of being above water. In particular, one can say that, in one sense, being 50 meters below water is the opposite of being 50 meters above water. But this does not mean, quite obviously, that a symmetry exists between these respective states in terms of their value and moral significance. Indeed, there is a sense in which it matters much more to have one's head just above the water surface than it does to get it higher up still.

In general, it is simply fallacious to assume that every element in existence necessarily has an inverse element that can meaningfully undo or outweigh it. As Guillaume Chauvat puts it:

> Many symmetric utilitarians assume that things must be symmetric by default; that the existence of negative value almost mathematically implies the existence of positive value. This seems misguided: very often, optimization problems consist in minimizing an error that ideally would be zero, but which in practice has a strictly positive lower bound. I wonder if common intuitions would be different if things were phrased more as an optimization problem?[43]

---

42 Knutsson, 2019a, "How objectionable are the purported implications?"
43 Personal communication.

The view that happiness and suffering are not opposites in the sense of being symmetric counterparts also finds support from psychology and neuroscience. As Baumeister et al. note:

> The distinction between good and bad (pleasant and unpleasant) emotions is well established in psychology and familiar to nearly everyone. Although laypersons typically regard these as opposites, there is some evidence that the two are somewhat independent ...[44]

Philosopher of psychology and neuroscience Adam Shriver sums up the research in the following way:

> Recent results from the neurosciences demonstrate that pleasure and pain are not two symmetrical poles of a single scale of experience but in fact two different types of experiences altogether, with dramatically different contributions to well-being.[45]

And as Shriver notes, it is worth paying close attention to these findings in our ethical theorizing:

> Given the large body of evidence suggesting an asymmetry [between happiness and suffering at the level of the brain], ethicists cannot simply assume that what is said about pleasure has similar implications for pain, and vice versa.[46]

Thus, also when we take into account what we know about happiness and suffering in psychological and neuroscientific terms, we find reasons to doubt that (to use Popper's phrase) we can treat degrees of pain as "negative

---

44 Baumeister et al., 2001, p. 331. See also Diener & Emmons, 1984.
45 Shriver, 2014, abstract. This is not, however, to say that there are not significant overlaps between the circuits that mediate pain and pleasure. For example, as Mike Johnson points out, damage to the ventral pallidum seems able to change reactions toward otherwise pleasurable things into active disliking, and "certain painkillers such as acetaminophen blunt both pain and pleasure ..." Johnson, 2016, pp. 5-6.
46 Shriver, 2014, p. 13 (draft version). The same point is made in Bain & Brady, 2014, 4.3: "We must not ... assume that whatever is said about unpleasantness should simply be inverted and said about pleasantness ..."

degrees of pleasure", and to doubt that pleasure can ethically "cancel out" pain — any more than putting people far above a water surface can cancel out or outweigh the bad of putting people far below it.

Yet far stronger still, I maintain, are the more direct reasons not to accept a moral symmetry between "equally intense" states of happiness and suffering that we have reviewed in previous chapters, such as the fact that there is an urgency to reducing suffering, inherent to the experience itself, while there is no corresponding urgency to increase happiness for those who do not suffer.[47]

This is a real, qualitative difference between the experiential properties of happiness and suffering, and it implies, I submit, that helping someone go from zero to ten on a notional happiness scale (where zero is an entirely unproblematic, neutral state) does not have remotely the same moral importance, if any at all, as helping someone go from minus ten to zero on a "corresponding" suffering scale.

Such a moral asymmetry also finds support in the related fact that the wrongness and problematic nature of suffering is manifest from the inside, inherent to the experience of suffering itself rather than superimposed, whereas the notion that there is something (similarly) wrong and problematic about states absent of suffering must be imposed from the outside. Suffering and happiness are qualitatively different in these regards, whether intense or not.[48]

---

[47] See section 1.4. Again, for concreteness, we can imagine that we have a bunch of pills that we can use to raise happiness to maximally intense levels for a group of otherwise entirely untroubled people for a full day, *or* we can use them to reduce "correspondingly intense" suffering for an equally large group of people, and bring them to an untroubled, neutral state (for the same duration). It seems highly plausible to say that we should use these pills for the latter rather than the former, which is to say that it seems highly plausible to reject the moral symmetry between happiness and suffering supposed by the objection above.

[48] Beyond that, one can argue that, even if happiness and suffering were morally symmetric up to a certain point, this would not imply that suffering of an intensity beyond this point can be morally outweighed by any amount of happiness. Additional arguments in favor of a moral asymmetry between happiness and suffering are found in Mayerfeld, 1996; 1999, chap. 6; Mathison, 2018, chap. 2.

For these reasons, it is far more plausible to add up happiness and suffering separately than to add them up in a single measure, especially from a moral perspective. Cognitive scientist Stevan Harnad defends the same view:

> [Pain and pleasure are] incommensurable ... it makes no sense to add and subtract across both half lines to integrate "net" welfare over both these qualities. ...
>
> It follows that if welfare comparisons or integrations are to be applied across multiple individuals, it can only be done separately for pain and separately for pleasure.[49]

On this view, the only thing that can count as "negative suffering" is the reduction of suffering itself, not the increase of something else. And while there are no doubt also considerable problems with regard to measuring and adding up suffering and happiness separately,[50] such separate measurements are still much less problematic, as they only entail measuring and adding up things of the same fundamental kind — not two qualitatively different things.[51]

---

49 Harnad, 2016, pp. 1-2.
50 Knutsson, 2016b.
51 It is also bound to be less problematic since summing happiness and suffering together into one measure indeed requires that we can add up happiness and suffering respectively, *and* that we can add them up together. The mere fact that this is an additional assumption we have to accept renders such a single sum of happiness and suffering strictly less plausible than the claim that we can add them up separately. See also Anonymous, 2015, 2.2.13.

8.6 The strong focus on suffering argued for here is missing something important: the world is getting better.[52] We have seen poverty decline rapidly over the last few decades, and humanity's understanding and wealth are increasing at a near-exponential pace. In particular, the science and engineering of happiness has only just begun, and it may well be that these endeavors will eventually enable us to create forms of happiness far greater than anything any currently living sentient mind is able to experience. Such states of happiness could have greater moral weight than even the most extreme forms of suffering that biological evolution has created, and our civilization could some day bring about astronomical numbers of beings experiencing such happiness. It would be a myopic shame if we allowed the comparative bleakness of today's world to prevent us from working toward the creation of such a truly awesome future.

First, the fact that the world is getting better in some respects does not imply that things will continue to get better in all morally relevant respects in the future; and any expectation we may have that things will continue to get better should be met with skepticism, especially in light of our tendency to entertain wishful thinking and overoptimistic expectations.[53] Second, the world is in fact not getting better in *all* respects. For example, the number of individuals subjected to the extreme horrors of factory farming — which is about twenty times the number of existing humans, *per year*[54] — is increasing at a roughly exponential rate.[55] So overall, for the sentient beings within humanity's "care", the world is in fact becoming worse every year, with a roughly exponential increase in human-caused suffering.[56]

---

52   Ridley, 2010; Pinker, 2011; 2018; Rosling et al., 2018. Note that none of the arguments I have presented concerning the moral importance of suffering are in tension with the descriptive accounts of human progress in these books. A criticism I would level at these descriptive accounts, however, is that none of them come remotely close to conveying the situation of the vast majority of sentient beings on the planet, which renders these accounts incomplete at best.
53   Bastardi et al., 2011; Sharot, 2011.
54   Mood & Brooke, 2012.
55   Bollard, 2018.
56   This is not to say that this trend could not also be reversed — hopefully it will be — yet it does serve to question the optimistic narrative expressed in this objection, which does not

And even if the world were improving at an exponential pace in every regard, this would not imply that our condition is on the whole "net positive" — such that, say, it is worth spreading to outer space — or that it is on its way to becoming "net positive". The fact that we have reduced some bad things significantly, such as poverty and child mortality, does not imply that we have thereby produced a positive good, much less a positive good that can outweigh extreme suffering. By analogy, imagine a torture chamber in which a thousand people are perpetually subjected to the most horrific torture. If it happened that the number of people tortured in the torture room was brought down to "just" a hundred in a decade, this would surely be amazing progress, at least in some sense. Yet it would not imply that the torture room would now be worth expanding to outer space, or that it ever could be. And our planet undoubtedly contains far more extreme suffering than a torture room that ceaselessly tortures a thousand individuals for a lifetime.

As for the notion that we might be able to create happiness "much greater" than even the most extreme suffering currently possible, it should be noted that we might also create forms of *suffering* even more extreme than what has hitherto been possible, such as in future interrogations powered by technological breakthroughs.[57] In the worst case, we might create such suffering on an astronomical scale.[58]

A more fundamental point, however, is that the possibility that happiness might become much more intense has little relevance to most of the arguments advanced here. As noted in response to the previous objection, no matter how intense happiness can be, it does not change the fact that there is no moral urgency found in the neutral absence of happiness, or in mild happiness that could be more intense. Nor does it change the fact that the presence of intense suffering is felt as intrinsically problematic, as experienced from the inside, whereas the notion that the absence of intense happiness carries a similarly problematic nature must be imposed from the outside — it is not intrinsic to the mere absence of happiness.

---

seem warranted from an impartial perspective that takes all sentient beings into account.
57 Knutsson, 2015b, "Modern and future torture".
58 Tomasik, 2011; Althaus & Gloor, 2016; Baumann, 2017e.

The prospect of more intense future happiness is also irrelevant according both to anti-hurt views and the asymmetrical views of population ethics reviewed in the first chapter. Similarly unaffected is the principle of sympathy for intense suffering — we should still give total priority to those who consider their suffering unbearable and unoutweighable, regardless of how intense others' happiness may be. And the same holds true of the general moral principle defended in the third chapter: that it is wrong to create happiness at the price of suffering. Most people who consider it wrong to torture one person for the happiness of many do not do so, I submit, because the happiness of the many is insufficiently intense. This also applies to the city of Omelas in particular: raising the happiness of the already happy inhabitants of Omelas even higher does not address the underlying objection that it is wrong to cause the unfortunate child to suffer for others' happiness.

This is not just theoretical. For the truth is that space colonization, even if done to maximize happiness, would entail significant risks of extreme suffering, and hence would contain, in expectation, a considerable amount of extreme suffering.[59] Consequently, if we do not think extreme suffering can be outweighed by happiness, we should not work to create happiness on a cosmic scale (though we should remain cooperative with those who do). As Brian Tomasik notes:

> Those who feel that Ursula K. Le Guin's city of Omelas should not exist ought also to reconsider their support of post-human space colonization. Omelas is actually a much better scenario than almost any actual outcome we can expect to see, so even those who welcome Omelas should exercise caution regarding what kinds of futures they're working to bring about.[60]

---

59 Again, it has been argued that a very bad scenario is in fact what is most likely to follow from space colonization, Deudney, 2020; Torres, 2018a; 2018b.
60 Tomasik, 2013f.

8.7 The view that it is more important to reduce suffering than to increase happiness plausibly derives from the prioritarian view, according to which it is more important to help beings the worse off they are, rather than the view that suffering per se *is more important than happiness.*

First, even if the view that it is more important to reduce suffering does, in the eyes of some people, derive purely from a prioritarian view, this does not change what the view says. That is, whether we think this view derives from a prioritarian intuition or from the intrinsic badness of suffering, the main content of the view stands just the same: it is more important to reduce suffering than to increase happiness.

Second, the notion that the moral asymmetry between happiness and suffering derives purely from prioritarian intuitions seems most implausible. For no matter how well or badly off a person may be, there is still something intrinsically bad about extreme suffering, and it still contains an urgency that increasing happiness does not. Indeed, if the moral asymmetry between happiness and suffering derived purely from a prioritarian view, and if one thought there is a moral symmetry between happiness and suffering otherwise, then it could be right to impose torturous suffering on someone who is otherwise well-off in order to increase the happiness (i.e. happiness that does not reduce suffering) of some individuals who are otherwise badly off, if only the amount of happiness is great enough.[61] Yet I doubt many people who hold a prioritarian view would accept this implication, which is to say that I doubt most prioritarians accept a moral symmetry between happiness and suffering *per se*.

Thus, although prioritarianism does lend considerable support to the view that suffering deserves unique priority, it is still unlikely to be the sole, or even main, explanation of the moral asymmetry between happiness and suffering.[62]

---

61 One may object that the extreme suffering will make the otherwise well-off person worst off in total, yet this is not the case if the benefactors of the resulting happiness have also experienced extreme suffering, and indeed experienced more extreme suffering, at some point in their lives (and again, we must make clear that the happiness gained would not in any way reduce suffering, in which case we would not be pitting suffering against happiness).

62 See also Mayerfeld, 1999, pp. 149-157 for a discussion of whether prioritarianism or the intrinsic badness of suffering provide the better account of the moral asymmetry be-

8.8 *A paradise without any suffering and full of happiness and meaning is surely better than absolute nothingness.*

This claim is consistent with most of the suffering-focused views explored in this book. For example, it is directly implied by the impure anti-hurt view, which says that happiness and suffering both matter, although the reduction of suffering is more important than any increase in happiness.[63] Indeed, even views that assign absolutely no value to happiness can still agree with this claim — for example, pluralist accounts of value according to which things other than experiential well-being also matter, such as living meaningful lives and accomplishing life goals.[64]

Some pure anti-hurt views would reject the claim, however. One way to defend this rejection may be to say that we only consider happiness to be better than nothing because we already exist, and because we want there to be happiness (and hence *we* may feel dissatisfied about its absence). Yet if we or this want of ours did not exist, there would be nothing suboptimal about the absence of happiness.[65] As mathematician and philosopher Piet Hein put it:

> The universe may
> be as great as they say.
> But it wouldn't be missed
> if it didn't exist.[66]

---

tween happiness and suffering. Mayerfeld expresses great sympathy toward both views, yet notes that his "confidence in the priority view is not quite as strong as it is in the intrinsic property view." Ibid., p. 154.
63 See section 2.3.
64 As highlighted by Lukas Gloor in his defense of tranquilism, Gloor, 2017. And again, pluralist views are also endorsed by the most prominent suffering-focused thinkers within academia, such as Jamie Mayerfeld and Clark Wolf (both of whom assign some value to happiness).
65 This view is consistent with Fehige's anti-frustrationist view as well as the perfectionist axiology explored in Contestabile, 2014. See also Anonymous, 2015, 2.2.2; Jules, 2019.
66 This stems from one of Hein's many collections of "grooks", yet I have failed to find where it was published originally. A large collection of his grooks were published posthumously in Hein, 2002.

8.9 *Most people would say that a mere pinprick can be outweighed by a large amount of happiness.*[67]

First, the sentiment expressed in this objection is perfectly consistent with maintaining that our overriding moral priority should be to minimize extreme suffering, not least since a pinprick is not remotely close to extreme suffering. It is also consistent with my core claim that the reduction of suffering deserves a foremost priority.

Second, we should be careful to clarify what is entailed by a pinprick in the context of this objection, as a pinprick may just lead to an aversive component in an overall agreeable experiential state, which is different from suffering as defined here: an overall bad experience.[68] Thus, views that say suffering cannot be outweighed by happiness need not say the same about pinpricks.[69]

Third, from the perspective of a consciousness-moment that *does* experience an overall bad experience (even if just mildly bad), there is indeed something bad and problematic about the suffering. And if the alternative to imposing such suffering is an entirely untroubled and problem-free state without any suffering whatsoever, it is not obvious why creating this suffering together with a lot of happiness is a better state of affairs.

---

67   See also section 3.4 (my reply below restates some of the points made in that section). Sometimes this objection is framed in terms of world destruction: pure negative utilitarianism would imply that we should destroy the world to avoid a pinprick. Yet it should be noted, again, that similarly unpalatable implications follow from other consequentialist views that take welfare to be the only thing that has moral value. For instance, as David Pearce points out (Pearce, 2017, "The Pinprick Argument"), classical utilitarianism would also, in theory, mandate the destruction of a world full of sentient beings to avoid even the smallest pain if it otherwise contained exactly net zero welfare. This too seems implausible to most people, and hence one should be careful to consider whether what one objects to (when objecting to negative utilitarianism, say) is the emphasis on reducing suffering over increasing happiness, or instead the notion that nothing besides welfare matters. For more discussion of the world destruction argument against negative utilitarianism, see Knutsson, 2019a.
68   A similar distinction has been drawn by Justin Klocksiem, who argues that any amount of genuine pain has greater disvalue than any amount of mere discomfort, Klocksiem, 2016.
69   Though similar to the impure anti-hurt view that acknowledges two lexically distinct values, one can also construct a view that prioritizes the reduction of aversive experiential components before increasing pure happiness (i.e. states of happiness that contain no aversive components). For instance, one may hold a three-level view according to which any amount of suffering has greater moral weight than any amount of aversive experiential components, which in turn have greater moral weight than any amount of pure happiness.

A relevant thing to keep in mind in this context is the distinction between interpersonal and intrapersonal tradeoffs. For if we consider the interpersonal case in particular, it is not clear that most people or "common sense" would say that the imposition of even mild suffering for the purpose of creating happiness is permissible, much less morally required (provided, again, that the alternative is an entirely untroubled state).

Indeed, imposing such suffering on someone for the sake of others' happiness would be forbidden by Parfit's compensation principle: one person's burdens cannot be compensated by benefits to another person who is already well-off, which seems quite commonsensical (as noted earlier, Parfit considered this principle "clearly true").[70] And we obtain a similar conclusion by applying the common-sense principle defended by Seana Shiffrin in the context of what we are allowed to do to others for their own sakes; that principle being that it is permissible to harm someone in order to prevent greater harm for them, even without their consent, yet never permissible to harm someone (without their consent) to provide them a pure benefit.[71] Thus, if we accept and combine these two common-sense principles, it follows that it is not morally permissible to impose even the mildest suffering on another person without their consent in order to create a pure benefit such as happiness (i.e. happiness that does not in turn reduce suffering or other harms).

Lastly, in practice, the creation of large amounts of happiness all but surely would compensate for mild suffering, even according to pure negative utilitarianism, since creating large amounts of happiness in already existing beings likely means they will suffer considerably less than they otherwise would.[72] Which is to say that happiness that has no effect on suffering hardly exists in the real world. And this is probably a strong confounding factor when we seek to appraise the intrinsic value (as opposed to the instrumental value) of happiness versus the intrinsic disvalue of suffering.[73]

---

70   Parfit, 1984, p. 337; Wolf, 1997, I.
71   Shiffrin, 1999.
72   Kant similarly defended an indirect duty to secure happiness on deontological grounds: "To secure one's own happiness is a duty, at least indirectly; for discontent with one's condition, under a pressure of many anxieties and amidst unsatisfied wants, might easily become a great temptation to transgression of duty." Kant, 1785, "First Section".
73   As noted in the second chapter, a defender of pure anti-hurt views may also argue that this is why we consider it worthwhile to go through pinprick-level suffering to obtain happiness in the intrapersonal case: if we do not obtain happiness, we tend to suffer (and notice in this

8.10 *The claim that extreme suffering is worse than any amount of mild suffering seems strange and implausible. For if we have a state of extreme suffering that occurs for a certain duration, it seems that a slightly less intense state of suffering extended for a much longer duration would be worse. This is presumably true at all levels of suffering: for a given duration of any intensity of suffering, some slightly less intense suffering extended for a sufficiently long duration would be worse. In this way, we can construct a sequence in which intense suffering is gradually exchanged for longer durations of less intense suffering, and in which we eventually get a vast duration of mild suffering that is worse than a short duration of extreme suffering. And since mild suffering can always be outweighed by happiness, it follows that extreme suffering can be outweighed by happiness.*[74]

The last premise in this objection — that mild suffering can always be outweighed by happiness — is what I argued against in the previous objection based on common-sense principles, as well as in previous chapters.[75] So the last step in this argument cannot readily be granted, nor can it readily be considered more commonsensical than its rejection.[76]

---

regard that words like "unhappy" and "unpleasant" refer to negative states, not neutral ones). What we tend to call a neutral state often entails subtle yet significant boredom and frustration, which can be removed by pleasure. The following quote from Benatar may help explain the seeming contradiction in how everyday discomforts can both be significant and overlooked at the same time: "Because of Pollyannaism we overlook the bad (and especially the relatively mildly bad). Adaptation also plays a role. People are *so* used to the discomforts of daily life that they overlook them entirely, even though they are so pervasive. Finally, since these discomforts are experienced by everybody else too, they do not serve to differentiate the quality of one's own life from the quality of the lives of others. The result is that normal discomforts are not detected on the radar of subjective assessment of well-being." Benatar, 2006, p. 72.

74 This objection does not distinguish between inter- and intrapersonal tradeoffs, which one may consider relevant as well. For instance, one may think that it is morally acceptable to undergo extreme suffering oneself to avoid experiencing a large duration of mild suffering, yet not consider it permissible to impose extreme suffering on someone else to prevent a longer duration of mild suffering for oneself or others.

75 See the third chapter and section 1.4.

76 Indeed, for a great number of people in the East, the commonsensical view is arguably that suffering cannot be outweighed by happiness: "There are nearly 1.5 billion Buddhists and Hindus [actually there are more], and while Buddhism is less explicit and less consequentialist than negative utilitarianism, the basic (though not uniform) Buddhist view on how pleasure and suffering are being valued is very similar to negative utilitarianism; Hinduism contains some similar views." Anonymous, 2015, 2.2.14.

As for the first step, there are many things to be said. First, even if it seems "strange" to say that extreme suffering is more important to prevent than any amount of mild suffering, perhaps primarily because we can make this seemingly plausible sequence argument against it, this does not imply that the alternative will not *also* seem strange — the alternative being the claim that there *is* some number of mild states of suffering that, collectively, would be more important to prevent than extreme suffering, such as a full day of brazen-bull torture. Indeed, to many people, this latter claim will appear significantly *more* strange and implausible, even if the sequence argument in its favor also seems somewhat plausible.

Yet how can one respond to this sequence argument? One way to respond is to argue that there indeed is a discontinuous step where suffering becomes worse than all lesser forms of suffering, such as at the point where one can no longer consent to it.[77] As mentioned earlier, however, one actually does not need to accept such an abrupt point of discontinuity to defend value lexicality between mild and intense suffering.[78] Here is Simon Knutsson outlining a rough sketch of one of the many alternative approaches one may favor instead:

> [O]ne can, for example, hold that there are different orders or levels of suffering and that the separation between them is not sharp [in the sense that it kicks in between two very similar intensity levels of suffering]. There are different versions of such non-sharp distinctions, but here is just a simple example to illustrate. Say that someone claims that there are bald and non-bald humans, must that person hold that there is some sharp line such that if one adds a single hair, a person would go from bald to non-bald? This is a typical illustration of vague terms such as 'bald,' and non-sharp differences between levels of value have been described both in terms of vagueness and in other ways ...[79]

---

77 This particular view was defended at greater length in the fourth chapter and in Tomasik, 2015a, "Consent-based negative utilitarianism?"
78 Arrhenius & Rabinowicz, 2015, 12.5, 12.7; Knutsson, 2019b; Vinding, 2020a.
79 Knutsson, 2016e. See Knutsson, 2019b for a more elaborate and technical argument based on many-valued logic.

Indeed, one can reasonably maintain that no amount of mild suffering carries greater significance than extreme suffering while being largely agnostic about the details: maybe there is a discontinuous step,[80] maybe there are ranges and vagueness in the way described by Knutsson,[81] maybe the disvalue of aggregates of mild suffering levels off asymptotically,[82] or maybe something else entirely accounts for this superiority in value.[83] The fact that we may not have a single, universally accepted account of the structure of this value lexicality at a very fine-grained level does not render it implausible — any more than the fact that we cannot explain the details of how biological life emerged via crude mechanical processes provides a compelling reason to doubt that it in fact did.

Finally, it is worth noting that, at least relative to the moral intuitions of many people,[84] the position we take in relation to the objection above will be largely inconsequential either way, since it does not alter the conclusion that we should prioritize the reduction of extreme suffering over the creation of happiness in practice. As Brian Tomasik notes:

> [W]e don't need to know whether there exists a theoretical amount of happiness that can outweigh torture to know that our moral priority should be on reducing extreme suffering rather than trying to create new happy beings.[85]

---

80 As defended in the fourth chapter. A similar view is defended in Klocksiem, 2016.
81 Knutsson, 2016e, "Thresholds"; 2019b.
82 Carlson, 2000; Arrhenius & Rabinowicz, 2015, 12.7.
83 In particular, one may assign different credences to different theories, or "structures" of lexicality that have been proposed, *cf.* Knutsson, 2016g, "The structure of lexicality". For example, one may assign some credence to the account outlined in Arrhenius & Rabinowicz, 2015, 12.5; some credence to the account outlined in ibid., 12.7; some credence to the account defended in Knutsson, 2019b; etc. Together, these credences should then add up to the total credence one has in the general lexicality thesis.
84 *Cf.* Future of Life Institute, 2017.
85 Tomasik, 2015d. See also Tomasik, 2013b, "Practical implications aren't much affected by the choice". This even applies when we consider our potential to create an astronomically large future paradise, since any endeavor to create such a paradise would entail vast amounts of extreme suffering in expectation as well, Tomasik, 2011; 2013f.

Chapter 8

8.11 *The view that it is more important to prevent some amount of extreme suffering than any amount of mild suffering seems implausible because it implies we should just ignore all mild suffering in practice.*

Although this implication seems intuitive, it does not in fact follow, for various reasons. First, there are considerations about instrumental effects: if we ignore mild suffering in practice, we will probably be more likely, through self-conditioning, to fail to reduce extreme suffering in the future.[86] Second, there are considerations pertaining to empirical uncertainty: we often cannot know whether other beings experience extreme versus non-extreme suffering (this is especially true of beings such as fish and insects, as well as disembodied brains).[87] Indeed, there is a small yet non-negligible risk that those who seem to experience "merely" mild suffering in fact experience extreme suffering, implying that reducing what *seems* to be mild suffering also deserves priority in practice on views that assign lexical weight to extreme suffering.

Third, even ignoring the two previous considerations, it is by no means unthinkable that there might be cases in practice where one has no idea whether an action that prevents mild suffering has a positive or negative influence on the amount of extreme suffering there will be (though the previous considerations suggest the effect will generally be positive). In such cases, the lexical view will indeed require us to prevent the mild suffering, as this is still better than reducing no suffering.[88]

---

86 *Cf.* Salamon & Rayhawk, 2009. This mirrors Kant's worry about harming non-human animals: even though he excluded non-human animals from the "Kingdom of Ends", he still thought it was wrong to harm them because it in turn made people more likely to harm people. (For a defense of a Kantian view that does not disregard non-human animals in this way, see Korsgaard, 2018.)
87 For more on disembodied brains, see section 11.4.
88 One may object that the expected value of our actions with respect to extreme suffering would never be exactly zero. This is true, of course, at least on reflection. Yet we often need to act before we can meaningfully perform any expected value calculations, and in such cases the immediate evaluation may well be exactly neutral (unlike on reflection, where various considerations will quickly lead the expected value to diverge from zero; yes, one may say we have crude intuitions that can point in some direction, yet translating such intuitions into an actionable expected value may also be infeasible in many cases). Beyond that, one may reasonably defend an epistemic or decision-theoretic threshold view according to which sufficiently small credences should be rounded off to zero, one

Lastly, the actions that seem most promising for the reduction of extreme suffering, such as working to prevent very bad outcomes on an astronomical scale, are probably also among the better actions we can take to reduce less intense suffering. This is another sense in which views that give supreme weight to extreme suffering do not lead us to ignore less intense suffering in practice.[89]

8.12 *It seems implausible to assign supreme moral disvalue to just a single second of the most extreme suffering.*

First, one can maintain that some amount of extreme suffering has lexically greater moral disvalue than everything else without assigning such moral disvalue to a single second of extreme suffering. For example, Jamie Mayerfeld argues that it is more plausible that such lexical disvalue only obtains above a certain intensity *and* duration of suffering.[90]

Second, our intuitions about short durations of extreme suffering may not be reliable. After all, it is probably difficult for us to imagine that the most extreme suffering could last for only a second. We probably feel that we could bear a single second of any kind of suffering and keep our heads above the water. Yet this betrays the premise we are assuming: for the consciousness-moments experiencing the worst forms of suffering, there is nothing bearable about this suffering. Nor is there any comfort or relief to be found in its short duration (which may, subjectively, *feel like* an eternity).[91] From the perspective of such consciousness-moments, the suffering in question is indeed supremely bad and unbearable.

An exercise that may be helpful in controlling for unreliable intuitions in this regard, especially if one holds that the moral disvalue of an

---

rationale for which may be to avoid absurd conclusions in expected value calculations (this is related to the issue of fanaticism discussed in Bostrom, 2011b, 4.3).
89 Though to be sure, we should not expect the practical implications of the respective aims of minimizing extreme suffering and minimizing mild suffering to be perfectly convergent, *cf.* section 13.4.
90 Mayerfeld, 1999, pp. 179-180.
91 If there were any comfort to be found in its short duration, this would contradict the underlying premise, as the suffering in question would then not be among the very worst states of suffering.

experience scales linearly with its duration, is to multiply the duration of the experiences in our proposed moral tradeoff by a given constant. For example, if one suggests that a single second of the most extreme suffering is less morally significant than some larger duration of mild headaches or great bliss, one may multiply the durations of all these experiences by a billion, upon which the extreme suffering in question will last more than 30 years. And it may then seem more intuitive to say that extreme suffering cannot be morally outweighed by a (correspondingly) larger duration of mild suffering or bliss, even if one finds it intuitive that the moral disvalue of an experience should scale linearly with its duration.

A similar exercise that may help control for unreliable intuitions, especially if one holds the distribution of experiences across time and space to be morally irrelevant, is to take the sum of experiential states one may claim to have greater moral significance than extreme suffering — say, an enormous amount of mild headaches or states of sublime bliss — and then distribute this sum to many different beings in chunks that each last only a single second. When framed in this way, we may find it more plausible to say that a single second of extreme suffering has greater moral importance than any amount of single-second chunks of mild suffering or sublime bliss. More generally, this framing may help us realize that our intuitions assign little value to short-lived experiences in general, which in turn suggests that our tendency to intuitively assign limited moral significance to short durations of extreme suffering should not be taken to say much about extreme suffering in particular.

Lastly, it is worth reiterating that, even if we think a single second of the most extreme suffering is more morally significant than any amount of mild suffering, we should still, in practice, work to reduce what appears to be milder suffering because of empirical uncertainty and instrumental effects.

8.13 *What about the importance of creating lives that are meaningful and virtuous? Is this not also important, and indeed potentially more important than reducing suffering?*

First, the claim that there is intrinsic value in meaningful and virtuous lives is wholly compatible with my core claim that the reduction of suffering deserves a foremost priority. Second, if we pit the creation of meaningful and virtuous lives against the reduction of extreme suffering, I would still argue that the latter should take priority: adding meaningful and virtuous lives to the world does not justify adding extreme suffering to it. Indeed, I would argue that the highest meaning we can pursue in life is to alleviate and prevent extreme suffering for sentient beings. Likewise, it seems plausible to think that a life is virtuous roughly to the extent that it is congruent with the aim of reducing suffering, which Breyer argues is in fact the view of virtue found in the Pāli tradition of Buddhism:

> Why ... might Pāli Buddhists think that virtue and prosperity are good? I want to argue that virtue and worldly prosperity are derivatively good in a very specific sense: they contribute to and are sometimes constitutive of *the cessation of suffering*.[92]

Lastly, just as happiness can reduce suffering and thereby have great instrumental value, meaning and purpose can also help keep suffering at bay and make it more bearable — they can serve as a bulwark against despair. As Nietzsche wrote: "If you have your *why* for life, you can get by with almost any *how*."[93] We should be careful not to let this distort our view of the value of meaning and purpose: their ability to reduce suffering

---

92 Breyer, 2015, p. 541. Note too that Aristotle, who is arguably the philosopher most strongly associated with virtue ethics, viewed virtue as a means to what he considered the highest good, eudaimonia ("happiness"; "flourishing"), which entails the avoidance of suffering (indeed, recall that Aristotle's starting point in his discussion about the value of pleasure was the badness of pain, Aristotle, 350 BC, Book 7, chap. 13). Relatedly, a virtue ethical case for giving significant consideration to the potential suffering of small beings, such as insects, is found in Knutsson & Munthe, 2017. Knutsson and Munthe's argument lends further support to a complementarity, rather than a conflict, between virtue and concern for suffering, even in the context of substantial uncertainty about the sentience of other beings.
93 Nietzsche, 1889, p. 6.

should not lead us to consider them positive goods that can justify the creation of more suffering.

8.14 *What about spiritual experiences and the attainment of spiritual or contemplative insights?*

Such experiences and insights arguably do not carry moral urgency, or at least no urgency that is comparable to the urgency of alleviating and preventing extreme suffering. Adding more spiritual insight to the world cannot justify adding more extreme suffering to it, as most prominent contemplatives and contemplative traditions themselves would probably agree.[94] After all, most contemplative traditions and figures consider the cessation of suffering to be among the core goals, if not *the* core goal, of spiritual practice and insight.[95] The goal is not to find something positive, some novel experience that "outweighs" suffering, but rather to attain *moksha* or *nirvana* — the *release* from suffering — by giving up the longing for pleasure and the identification with an egoic self that always craves and longs for more.[96]

In the words of meditation teacher Joseph Goldstein:

> [O]ne of the things we discover through this simple introspection and observation is to see what patterns of thought and emotion create suffering, for ourselves and others, and how to be free of that suffering. And that's really the bottom line of why to [engage in introspective practice]: it's a way of coming out of suffering.[97]

---

[94] And thus, if we are consequentialists who do not accept a strong commission-omission distinction, it would also follow that we cannot justify prioritizing the attainment of spiritual insight (for its own sake) at the opportunity cost of reducing extreme suffering (though it may well be justified on instrumental grounds — if it enables us to better reduce extreme suffering).

[95] For a review of the importance of reducing suffering in Buddhism in particular, see Keown, 1992, pp. 175-176 ("The goal of diminishing *dukkha* [including all mental and physical suffering] is common to all forms of Buddhism" p. 176); Goodman, 2009; Contestabile, 2010; 2014; Breyer, 2015.

[96] Contestabile, 2010; 2014.

[97] Harris, 2014b.

So again, as in the case of happiness and meaning, spiritual practices and insights may well help reduce suffering, and thus have great instrumental value (on top of any intrinsic value they may have). Yet we should be careful not to confuse this instrumental value for an intrinsic value that can justify the creation of extreme suffering.

Relatedly, it is sometimes claimed that suffering is an illusion, and that spiritual practice enables us to see through this illusion. This claim probably stems from the fact that it is often possible to focus one's attention and reframe one's experience in such a way that suffering disappears. Yet such a reframing itself constitutes a change of one's experience, and it would be a great mistake to think that suffering does not exist or is illusory merely because one can sometimes get rid of it or reduce it by mental means.

8.15 *It would likely have dangerous consequences if people accepted the views presented here. These views may well lead to more suffering rather than less.*

There is indeed a risk that some people will draw naive and misguided implications from the views presented here — both when it comes to the broad claim that the reduction of suffering deserves a foremost priority as well as the stronger claim that we should minimize extreme suffering. Yet this does not, of course, remotely suggest that these views are wrong. More than that, risks of this kind exist for all moral views, especially consequentialist ones: some people may derive false implications based on misguided beliefs about the world. And it is not clear that the views presented here pose a unique risk in this regard, especially relative to the aim of reducing suffering. Indeed, the acceptance of moral views that do *not* explicitly give great importance to suffering probably entails a much greater risk of catastrophic outcomes that involve a lot of suffering.

Thus, the fact that there is a risk that people may take suffering-focused views the wrong way does not imply that we should endorse other moral views instead, nor that we should emphasize the reduction of suffering any less. Rather, it implies that we should be careful to debunk the naive and false

Chapter 8

implications that people may be tempted to derive from suffering-focused views (as I shall seek to do at greater length in the second part of this book).

8.16 *Most people do not agree that life is mostly suffering. The view defended here merely seems to be depression presented as a moral truth.*

First, the claim that "life is mostly suffering" can itself be understood to mean many things, such as "most consciousness-moments on the planet are moments of suffering", or "most people would say that their lives are dominated by suffering". One need not accept any of these particular claims in order to maintain that the reduction of suffering deserves unique moral priority. Nor need one be depressed in the least to hold this view. One can think one's life is wonderful and be perfectly satisfied with it and yet still think the reduction of suffering deserves unrivaled priority. After all, the view that the torture-level suffering of one individual cannot be morally justified by the creation of "greater" happiness for others seems widely held, and it would be strange to suggest that one must be depressed to agree with it.

Similarly, even if most people report their life satisfaction to be quite high, this does not imply that those people's life satisfaction in any sense outweighs the suffering experienced by those who are worst off. Indeed, a high self-reported life satisfaction does not even imply that the person giving the report would say that their life has been "net good" or worthwhile, all things considered. For example, Dax Cowart, the young airplane pilot who was severely burned, eventually reported that he had a "very good quality of life", in spite of his assessment that no amount of happiness could ever outweigh the suffering he had experienced.[98] (To say that his suffering could not be outweighed by any happiness is obviously not to say that he could never be happy again.)[99]

---

98 Engel, 1983.
99 For an essay on how we mostly fail to appreciate how bad things in fact are, even for many people who seem to do well from the outside, see Alexander, 2015. Also, surveys of life satisfaction almost never allow a negative evaluation of life (e.g. the available options

Beyond that, we should also, in the context of this objection, recall the many biases reviewed in the previous chapter that color our evaluations. For example, a signaling bias to display strength and happiness while hiding suffering, as well as various positivity biases that make our memories and life evaluations more optimistic in hindsight.

Lastly, we should keep in mind that humans are not the only beings who suffer. If only we dared to contemplate the lives of the billions of non-human beings whom humanity exploits and kills under the horrific conditions of factory farming, we would be given pause in proclaiming that life is not mostly suffering. For these billions of beings at humanity's mercy, life indeed is mostly suffering — in every sense of the term.[100]

8.17 *Very few people have held the views presented here. Does this not speak against these views?*

The fact that a view is not widely held is not a strong reason to reject it, especially not if most people plausibly hold various compounding biases against the view in question. Besides, the claim that very few have held the views presented here is simply not true. Indeed, even if we only consider variations of negative utilitarianism in particular, quite a number of supporters can in fact be cited among academic philosophers, as Simon Knutsson points out:

---

may be to rate it from 1 to 10), and hence such surveys are already biased toward a positive conclusion in the way they are phrased, Vinding, 2018j.

100 Again, for some insight into the actual and indisputably horrendous conditions on factory farms, see mercyforanimals.org/investigations. For similar insights into the conditions faced by animals in nature, see Horta, 2010a; 2015; Iglesias, 2018.

Chapter 8

> [Negative utilitarianism] has been supported by mainstream philosophers: Gustaf Arrhenius and Krister Bykvist say that they "reveal" themselves "as members of the negative utilitarian family." J. W. N. Watkins describes himself as "sort of negative utilitarian." Clark Wolf defends what he calls "negative critical level utilitarianism" for social and population choices. The principle says that "population choices should be guided by an aim to minimize suffering and deprivation." Thomas Metzinger proposes the "principle of negative utilitarianism." Ingemar Hedenius held a view similar to negative utilitarianism. According to his form of consequentialism, some sufferings cannot be counterbalanced by goods. Joseph Mendola proposes a modification of utilitarianism that "resembles ... negative utilitarianism." His principle prescribes that "we are to look to the worst possible outcomes in evaluating actions and institutions" and "to ameliorate the condition of the worst-off moment of phenomenal experience in the world."[101]

Another academic who expressed support for negative utilitarianism was linguist and philosopher Henry Hiz:

> Utilitarianism failed, but what is sometimes called 'negative utilitarianism' avoids many of the shortcomings of classical utilitarianism. It is a good candidate for an ethics that expresses the Enlightenment tradition.[102]

Furthermore, scholars of Buddhism Damien Keown, Charles Goodman, and Daniel Breyer have all argued that there are significant similarities between prominent strands of Buddhist ethics and negative utilitarianism.[103]

---

101 Knutsson, 2016e. Other academics who have defended variants of negative utilitarianism include H. B. Acton (Acton & Watkins, 1963; Mathison, 2018, 2.5.1), A. D. M. Walker (Walker, 1974), Christoph Fehige (Fehige, 1998), Fabian Fricke (Fricke, 2002), and Roger Chao (Chao, 2012).
102 Hiz, 1992, p. 423. He also wrote: "For ethics, there is only suffering and the effective ways of alleviating it." Ibid., p. 429.
103 Keown, 1992, chap. 7; Goodman, 2009, pp. 101-102; Breyer, 2015.

If we go beyond negative utilitarianism, and consider the more general claim that suffering deserves unique moral priority, the list of supporters grows further.[104] And even more common is the view that it is more important to reduce suffering than to increase happiness. As noted in the "Negative Utilitarianism FAQ":

> The intuition that the badness of suffering doesn't compare to the supposed badness of inanimate matter (as non-pleasure) seems very common, and the same goes for the view that contentment is what matters, not pleasure-intensity.[105]

Indeed, as mentioned before, the Future of Life Institute's survey found "minimizing suffering" to be the most favored ideal aim of a future civilization.[106] So arguably, the truth is the opposite of what the objection states: the core claim argued for here — that reducing suffering deserves unique moral priority — is among the most widely shared moral views of all, despite the many biases that lead us to resist it.[107]

8.18 *How can we consider the reduction of suffering a foremost priority when it is impossible to measure suffering in the first place?*

We certainly can measure suffering. In fact, there are many ways to obtain information about others' suffering, such as self-reports (in the case of humans), seemingly pain-induced bodily movements and grimaces, self-harming and suicidal behavior, levels of stress hormones in the blood, and

---

104 We have seen many examples of philosophers whose views support this claim, including Epicurus, Arthur Schopenhauer, Karl Popper, Richard Ryder, and Jamie Mayerfeld. More supporters of strongly suffering-focused views are mentioned in Anonymous, 2015, 2.2.14; Knutsson, 2016e, "The purported lack of support for negative utilitarianism".
105 Anonymous, 2015, 2.2.14.
106 Future of Life Institute, 2017.
107 Though this is not to say that it is common for people to act in accordance with this value; it is sadly not, in part because of the many biases reviewed in the previous chapter. One of our great challenges is to close this enormous gap between our ideals and our behavior. More on this in chapter 12.

brain scans.[108] Yes, it is true that we often cannot measure suffering with great precision, yet this does not imply that we cannot reduce it. Consider, by analogy, the concrete form of suffering that is depression: the fact that we cannot measure depression with the same razor-sharp precision as we can measure, say, the mass of a rock does not mean that we cannot take reasonable, evidence-based measures to reduce depression. The same goes for suffering in general.

Furthermore, we often do not even need rough measures of suffering (beyond those we intuitively make) to be able to navigate toward the reduction of suffering. For instance, no advanced measurement effort is really needed to conclude that atrocities like the Holocaust should be prevented in any endeavor to reduce suffering, and the same can be said of most other sources and cases of extreme suffering — factory farming, North Korean torture chambers, sadistic crime, etc.

8.19 *The focus on reducing suffering advocated here overlooks the vital functions that pain and suffering serve.*

Suffering undeniably does serve various useful functions. It can help us maintain our physical safety, it can provoke important changes in our lives, it can foster learning and maturation, etc.[109] Even given negative utilitarian views that consider the reduction of suffering the sole moral aim, suffering can have enormous utility, not least in that it can help us understand the moral significance of suffering.

Yet the crucial question we must ask in response to this objection is whether the many functions served by suffering themselves are worth the creation of *more* suffering, in the aggregate. In particular, we must ask whether they can justify bringing more *extreme* suffering into the world, suffering of the kind endured by Dax Cowart, Junko Furuta, and Ahmad Qabazard. I have argued they cannot. On my account, the only

---

108 For more ways to measure suffering, see Daoust, 2015, "Preparatory Notes for an Algometry". A more elaborate discussion of this subject is found in Mayerfeld, 1999, chap. 3.
109 Arguments for the utility of suffering (or in many cases just aversive experiential components) can be found in Bastian, 2018; Bloom, 2019.

suffering that deserves the label "necessary" is that which in turn leads to less (extreme) suffering in the aggregate.

Moreover, it is clear that much suffering serves absolutely no function and entails no silver lining whatsoever, such as the suffering endured by countless individuals every second who are eaten alive while fully conscious and unable to escape, or the suffering entailed by debilitating chronic pain. The world contains vast amounts of such useless suffering, and we should all be able to agree that this suffering is worth preventing.

Finally, the conviction that one's suffering is helpful can itself render that suffering much less bad and more bearable.[110] For this reason, we should be careful not to draw sweeping conclusions about the acceptability of pain and suffering from the comparatively privileged vantage point of bearable and useful pain and suffering.

8.20 *Should we not maintain some humility on questions concerning ethics? After all, our knowledge of the world is rather limited.*

I agree that intellectual humility is important, and that we should continually subject our convictions to doubt and scrutiny. This also holds true in the realm of normative ethics in particular, whether we are moral realists or not. For if we are moral realists, we should doubt whether our views of ethics faithfully track the purported moral truth (and if our views of other factual questions are any guide, we will almost surely be wrong and ignorant about more than just small details). If, on the other hand, we think ethics only exists relative to some other, less strong ideal, such as "that which we find most reasonable given perfect reflection and information", we should still maintain some uncertainty as to whether our present views truly conform to this ideal.

Even so, epistemic humility by no means implies that we cannot be functionally certain about various conclusions. For example, our considerable

---

[110] A similar point seems to apply to physical pain in particular, at least according to the gate control theory of pain advanced by Ronald Melzack and Patrick Wall, Melzack & Wall, 1982; Mayerfeld, 1999, p. 27.

uncertainty in the realm of physics does not imply that we should have much doubt in the claim that, say, Earth is approximately spherical. And the claim that suffering carries uniquely significant disvalue and moral weight is, I submit, a claim with roughly the same status on any plausible conception of ethics.

Beyond that, intellectual humility and uncertainty can cut both ways: we may be overestimating the horror and moral importance of suffering, yet we may also be grossly *under*estimating it, even as we think nothing else is more important. For instance, even if we hold suffering-focused views, the outlook and the priorities we have most of the time may still be clouded by the biases reviewed in the previous chapter. (I would say this is true of myself.)

More generally, if we conclude that we have good reason to accept one set of moral views over others, intellectual humility does not alter the relative status of these views. We should still give most weight to the views we have the most reason to accept, and be most guided by these views in our actions. Thus, in light of the arguments I have presented in this first part of the book, I would argue that a healthy amount of intellectual humility does not alter the core conclusion I have sought to establish here: that we should give special priority to the reduction of suffering.

Having provided a case for this claim, let us now move on to the all-important practical question.

Part II

How Can We Best Reduce Suffering?

9

Uncertainty Is Big

To briefly recapitulate: the main claim I have defended in the first part of the book is that we should make the reduction of suffering a foremost priority. Beyond that, I have also defended more particular views according to which we should minimize extreme suffering. These strict suffering-minimizing views clearly imply the more general claim that reducing suffering should be a foremost priority, yet the reverse does not hold true. That is, one can accept that the reduction of suffering deserves special priority without agreeing with strict suffering-minimizing views.

My aim in this second part will be to derive some of the main practical implications of these views. These will be (what I take to be) the practical implications of both the strict suffering-minimizing views as well as the more general view that suffering deserves a foremost priority in practice. For although strict suffering-minimizing views surely can diverge significantly from other views that also consider the reduction of suffering a foremost priority, it is still reasonable to expect all suffering-focused views to have similar practical implications in most regards.

Chapter 9

9.1 Uncertainty: Our Inescapable Predicament

A crucial point is that uncertainty about how we can best reduce suffering is bound to be great.[1] The world is vast while our brains and knowledge base are relatively small. Indeed, even our knowledge of the present state of the world is highly limited, and much more uncertain still are the future states that would result from some hypothetical course of action.[2] Consequently, when trying to reduce suffering, we are bound to act on very rough estimates that will always be subject to reasonable doubts.

This is a fundamental fact about our circumstance. And though it may seem discouraging, it is in fact a key insight with many important implications. First of all, it implies that we should approach the question of how we can best reduce suffering with great humility. That is, we should maintain an open mind about what the answers to the question might be, and continually be open to new data that might update and improve our current beliefs. In doing so, we should remain mindful of the countless biases that tend to distort our thinking, such as confirmation bias, conformity bias, and the availability heuristic.[3]

This then leads to the next point, namely that we should not only be open-minded, but indeed actively and systematically seek out new data and knowledge that can inform our approach to reducing suffering. This should be a priority for a variety of reasons. First, the universality of confirmation bias suggests that we will not seek out new information and alternative perspectives that challenge our existing beliefs as much as we should, even if we are sincerely dedicated to reducing suffering.

Second, we should actively seek new information, broadly construed, for the simple reason that information is the only thing on which good estimates can be based. And the more (relevant) information we incorporate

---

[1] Tomasik, 2013m; Baumann, 2017d.
[2] Beyond these mundane sources of uncertainty — i.e. limited knowledge about the present and future states of the world *within* a common-sense framework based on standard physics — there are also fundamental uncertainties concerning the nature of the world and our place within it, and these add even more uncertainty to questions of optimal action, Baumann, 2017d.
[3] Plous, 1993; Kahneman, 2011. The availability heuristic refers to our tendency to estimate the likelihood of events based on how readily available they are in memory rather than on objective data.

in our estimates, the better we should expect them to be. Indeed, it is conceivable that a single novel consideration or piece of information could change our estimates of the optimal course of action quite radically, which further underscores the importance of seeking out such new information and considerations to improve our current estimates.[4]

Thus, one could say that a whole new research project is needed, a new science even: the science of reducing suffering. For how we can best reduce suffering is ultimately a scientific question — i.e. a question to which we can approach answers via empirical examination. And given that explorations of this question have been quite rare so far, it seems likely that there is much low-hanging fruit to pluck for a new research project focused on this question. I shall say more about this research project in chapter 16.

9.2 Beware Underestimating Uncertainty

The point I have made above concerning the inevitability of substantial uncertainty may seem trivial, and in many ways it surely is. Yet an additional reason to emphasize it is that we probably tend to underestimate it just the same. One obvious reason to believe this is our well-documented overconfidence bias: we tend to significantly overestimate the accuracy of our judgments.[5] And this bias is probably only magnified when it comes to large-scale endeavors such as "reduce suffering for all sentient beings", as our brains did not evolve to think about such extensive undertakings and the especially significant uncertainties that pertain to them.

Instead, in relation to our actions, our minds tend to hunger for concreteness. That is, we seem to prefer palpable goals and tasks that we can take clear steps toward accomplishing. Yet to say that it is an open question how we can best reduce suffering, and that there is bound to be substantial uncertainty about it, is in many ways antithetical to this preference. It is deeply annoying. Also because work on concrete tasks that yield more tangible results, such as reducing poverty in some particular country, gives

---

4   Tomasik, 2013m; Bostrom, 2014b.
5   Plous, 1993, pp. 219-220.

us something we can show others and ourselves to prove that we actually make progress and that we really "do something".

For these reasons, when it comes to large-scale questions of this kind, we probably have a strong bias to settle prematurely on some given answer — "we should probably focus primarily on X to best reduce suffering" — and to then overstate our confidence in this answer to ourselves and others afterwards.[6] To keep on investigating the big picture in a way that remains honest about the extent of our uncertainties along all dimensions can easily feel emotionally taxing. (Indeed, psychologists routinely use statements like "I understand" and "I see" to put people in a good mood, and statements like "I don't understand" and "I'm lost" to put them in a bad mood.)[7]

In the face of such exhausting explorations, settling on something more concrete may provide us psychological relief. Yet we should be skeptical of such relieving settlings and inclinations to rationalize them. In particular, given this putative bias to settle for some concrete path, as well as our tendency to rationalize our past choices,[8] we should probably subject any proposed "optimal concrete thing to focus on to reduce suffering" to extra scrutiny, especially if it is asserted with great confidence.

Another reason to expect us to be biased toward pursuing some concrete action is that it makes evolutionary sense if the urgency of suffering compels us toward direct action rather than general reflection and exploration. Urgent problems have not, historically, been of an intangible large-scale kind. Rather, they were more akin to here-and-now events, such as a predator ambushing a fellow group member — events that called for immediate action rather than reflection. Yet such an inclination to throw reflection and deeper exploration to the wind in the face of the urgency of suffering is not conducive to reducing suffering in the world of today.[9]

---

6   This claim of mine is not only based on speculative extrapolations of how I expect the human mind to behave in light of my own introspection and knowledge of general psychology, but also on more direct observations of self-identified effective altruists who tend to endorse rather general goals, yet who still seem unjustifiably sure about which specific actions are optimal relative to these goals.
7   Kagan, 2013, p. 258.
8   Lodge & Taber, 2013.
9   Robin Hanson makes a similar point about influencing the future in general, and argues that those who wish to influence the future should first make it a priority to understand the most likely future scenarios, and then try to steer accordingly, Hanson, 2014a.

After all, we can do much worse than doing nothing, even when we sincerely try to reduce suffering, and this is especially true if we have not reflected carefully about the consequences of our actions.[10]

Recent psychological studies also suggest that we are prone to not take uncertainty sufficiently into account at the level of our decisions. For example, in a study where people were asked to consider two competing hypotheses, both of which were plausible, yet where one was more plausible than the other, people would wholly ignore the less plausible hypothesis when making predictions and further inferences, even though they acknowledged that the less plausible hypothesis deserved some weight.[11] This finding is especially relevant for the endeavor of reducing suffering, in which there is no shortage of plausible hypotheses (concerning optimal paths to impact, say) that we may irrationally disregard in favor of our preferred hypothesis.

Given that we have such tendencies to underestimate and disregard our uncertainty, we should also expect to underestimate the importance of foundational exploration, and to be biased toward abandoning such exploration prematurely. This seems true to me: most people aiming to reduce suffering tend to underestimate the importance of foundational research into how we can best reduce suffering — what I tentatively consider one of the best things, if not *the* best thing, we can do to reduce suffering in expectation.

9.3 Be Prudent

Another, somewhat unexpected implication that follows from our inescapably substantial uncertainty is that we should avoid ill-considered radicalism, and instead adopt a prudent approach in most respects. Merely contemplating the fact that uncertainty is bound to be great lends support to this claim. "If you are highly uncertain about which action is best, then don't rush to do something radical" seems a reasonable rule of thumb.

---

10   For some ways in which people trying to do good can end up making things worse, see Wiblin & Lempel, 2018.
11   Johnson et al., 2019.

Indeed, for virtually any action we may propose to reduce suffering, a long list of plausible considerations for and against can be given, and just a slightly different weighting of this list of considerations — or the addition of a new consideration — can readily imply that a seemingly optimal action is in fact suboptimal, or even extremely bad.[12]

This high sensitivity to the weight we place on different considerations implies that we should be reluctant to pursue radical actions based on naive analyses — extraordinary measures require more than weak justification. Not least because "the action is considered overly radical by most people" itself counts as a *prima facie* reason against pursuing the action in question. For if something is considered too radical by most people, there may well be a good reason behind this assessment that our current perspective fails to fully appreciate (exceptions abound, of course). And even if most people's conviction that a given action is too radical is poorly justified, the mere fact that most people perceive it as such still counts as a reason against pursuing it. Why? Because if someone comes across as too radical, others will be less inclined to cooperate with them, which in turn limits that person's impact. (I shall say more in favor of cooperation in the following chapter.)

This is also a reason to favor moderation in general: most people are most comfortable with people who do not stand out too much in too many ways, such as by having extremely weird clothes, hairstyles, and ideas. Indeed, the psychological literature on "idiosyncrasy credits" suggests that people will be inclined to distance themselves from a person who deviates significantly from the norm in many regards, which suggests that we may reduce suffering more effectively by limiting such deviation.[13]

These may be consoling points for those seeking to reduce suffering, not least since one may naively suppose that reducing suffering will require us to relinquish all moderation and conformity to common norms. That is, one may feel a strong pull from one's ideals to do something extreme in order to reduce suffering — "whatever it takes, social conventions be

---
12 Tomasik, 2013m; Bostrom, 2014b.
13 Hollander, 2006. The same general point is made in Hanson, 2012. Others have described a concept similar to idiosyncrasy credits in less formal yet more descriptive terms, namely in terms of a limited amount of "weirdness points" that one should spend with care, Hurford, 2014.

damned!" — while social pressures may pull strongly in the opposite direction. It can then be a relief to know that various considerations suggest that extreme actions are most likely not endorsed by these ideals either, and that a fuller extrapolation of ideals aimed toward reducing suffering may well, in practice, imply that we would do best by conforming to standard norms in most regards.[14] If there are things we should be extreme about, these are probably things like being extremely well-considered, wise, and prudent — the polar opposites of extremism by any common definition.[15]

To be clear, the points above should not be taken to imply that the optimal course of action for reducing suffering will not entail significant sacrifices and deviations from the norm. It surely will. The point is just that balance is important, and that we have stronger reasons to be prudent in our endeavor to reduce suffering than a naive analysis might suggest.

9.4 The Silver Bullet Delusion

It may be tempting to assume that what we are seeking is some singular answer that, if only we could find it, would lead us to reduce suffering most effectively. The One Insight to Rule Them All. I have certainly held such an implicit assumption myself. Yet this is almost certainly mistaken. There is no single, simple answer to the question of how we can best reduce suffering.

This is not to say that there are no crucial insights, as there undoubtedly are. But the point is that there are probably many such crucial insights, and that these need to be supported by countless smaller ones. Consider science by analogy. Every scientific field surely has foundational insights, and discovering these is no doubt of great significance. Yet all fields have *many* such core insights, as well as many smaller, supporting observations that account for the details. And we should expect the insights necessary for reducing suffering to be even more numerous and varied in nature than

---

14   Though it may be less of a relief if one prefers to signal that one is different and uniquely sincere about one's chosen cause, Hanson, 2012.
15   Similar points are made in Caviola, 2017.

the sum of theories found within any given scientific field (not least because reducing suffering is aided by knowledge from virtually all scientific fields).

Uncovering these insights is more akin to learning a language than to finding a super-equation — a gradual and continuous learning process rather than a single, momentous step. Indeed, both at the level of our actions and our insights, it is important to realize that success is a matter of degrees rather than all or nothing. As Jamie Mayerfeld notes in relation to our actions in general:

> We do not comply fully with the duty to relieve suffering until we achieve the maximum reduction, but if we achieve something less than this, we have partly complied with the duty to relieve suffering. Compliance admits of degree. Furthermore, though nothing less than full compliance is required of us, there is nothing significant about taking the final step into full compliance, as distinct from intermediate steps that lead from lesser to greater though not yet maximum compliance.[16]

The same can be said about insightfulness: it admits of degrees, and every new insight counts for something. Appreciating this makes the difference between whether we meet new information with an attitude of "if this does not seem of the greatest importance, I will drop it and move on" versus the more open and curious attitude of "what small yet perhaps significant insight might I be able to learn from this?" If successfully reducing suffering is indeed a continuous quest of accumulating and applying many different insights, failing to adopt this latter attitude may be costly.[17]

---

16 Mayerfeld, 1999, p. 119. A similar point is made in Norcross, 2006, as well as in Tomasik, 2015e, which argues that it is best to think about reducing suffering along the lines of "a point counter in a video game, where you aim to accumulate as many points as you can within the bounds of reason. There's no binary 'right' and 'wrong'. You just do the best you can."
17 The same point is made at greater length in Tomasik, 2013k.

9.5 Optimizing on Many Levels

Not only are there many different levels on which we should seek important insights, from physics to sociology,[18] but there are also many distinct levels on which we must apply our many insights, ranging from the individual level to various social and political levels. Indeed, a successful endeavor to reduce suffering will require every aspiring suffering reducer to make efforts on many of these distinct levels. (Again, this point may seem trivial, but it is still worth stressing lest we take a simplistic approach to reducing suffering.)

At the personal level, we need to invest in our own health and wellbeing, as well as in our abilities, if we are to contribute competently to the cause. More than that, we also need to continually remind ourselves of the importance of suffering, in healthy and sustainable ways, as our minds otherwise tend to creep back into the homeostatic equilibrium they evolved to be in — caught up in relatively petty thoughts and pursuits.

We might here find inspiration in ancient traditions, such as Buddhism, in which practices aimed to remind us of the reality and importance of suffering have been cultivated over millennia. Such practices include "loving-kindness meditation" and "compassion meditation", in which one wishes others happiness and relief from suffering. Research suggests that these meditation practices not only increase compassionate responses to suffering,[19] but that they also help to increase life satisfaction and reduce depressive symptoms for the practitioner,[20] as well as to foster better coping mechanisms and increased positive affect in the face of suffering.[21]

---

18 And here I do not mean to imply we should only seek knowledge at the level of concepts. After all, the intrinsic badness of suffering is arguably preconceptual. Exploration of psychedelic substances and introspective practices may well be important too (e.g. to reflect deeper and to refine our epistemology).
19 Condon et al., 2013.
20 Fredrickson et al., 2008.
21 Klimecki et al., 2013. Likewise, affirmations may also have their place, even if they seem superstitious. After all, thinking or saying out loud an expression like "I endeavor to reduce suffering" is an action in the world with a real causal impact trickling throughout one's brain as a whole, and it is thus not unthinkable that an affirmation like this can help bring one's moment-to-moment attention into better alignment with one's deepest values, even if just marginally.

More generally, both individually and collectively, we need to develop a stronger "suffering object permanence" (object permanence refers to the ability to know that some object still exists even when one cannot see it). For it is as though we forget that suffering exists when we are not confronted with it directly. And one may argue this is only healthy — after all, would we not be traumatized otherwise? Yet it is important to distinguish between 1) being aware of the reality of suffering and having sympathy for it, and 2) suffering ourselves. Even as these two are related, they are by no means coterminous. As Mayerfeld notes:

> Sympathy is sometimes defined as the suffering we experience as a result of contemplating the suffering of other people and animals. If this were what sympathy meant, there would be even less of it—much less of it—than the small amount actually found! But suffering in the onlooker is by no means a necessary condition of sympathy. In fact, sympathy usually exists without it. Sympathy just means the sincere desire to see another person's or animal's suffering removed. … One can have the superficial verbalized knowledge that another person is suffering; one can trust, on the basis of previous perception, that such suffering is a horrible evil; and one can therefore have a sincere abiding desire for the removal of that suffering. It is thus possible to feel sympathy while skirting genuine awareness.[22]

Such abstract, painless recognition of the reality of suffering combined with a strong dedication toward its alleviation may well be the optimal state of mind to adopt for reducing suffering.[23]

---

22 Mayerfeld, 1999, p. 105. Psychologists draw a similar distinction between (affective) empathy and compassion, where the former is the ability to feel what others feel, which often overwhelms and paralyzes us, whereas the latter, compassion, entails more positive affect and a strong drive to help others. See Bloom & Davidson, 2015; Bloom, 2016.
23 And one can work toward this state of mind from both opposing extremes: either if one has virtually no awareness of suffering, or if one has an intensely painful awareness of suffering, in which case practices of compartmentalizing and abstracting may be helpful — to have the string of symbols, "suffering", as an amnesia-inducing placeholder for the traumatic real thing. A similar point about compartmentalization is made in Ben Kuhn's essay "To stressed-out altruists", Kuhn, 2013.

Things we should prioritize at the social level include the cultivation of good interpersonal relationships and the establishment of healthy communities that consider the reduction of suffering a foremost priority. Ideally, we should then, through these communities, create a political movement aimed toward reducing suffering — at every level of policy — in cooperative and considerate ways. Less ideally, in terms of what is realistic for everyone at the political level in the short term, we should support political actions that, on the margin, reduce suffering and push us toward greater concern and compassion for suffering in the future.

9.6 Reducing Suffering Does Not Change Everything

A lot is already known concerning all the levels mentioned above, and this established knowledge is worth drawing on to the extent possible. There is no need to reinvent the wheel, which ties into the more general point that, in many ways, the goal of reducing suffering does not change everything. For example, basic facts about how things work and how to succeed in different areas remain the same. How to optimize personal productivity and health, how to navigate well in one's relationships and in the social world at large, how to create political change — none of this really changes.

Another way in which the aim of reducing suffering does not change everything is that most people already agree that suffering is bad and worth preventing, even if they do not act accordingly (though, to be sure, no one acts in perfect accordance; it is really a matter of degree for all of us). In other words, humanity's current values are quite far from 180 degrees opposed to the goal of reducing suffering — they are perhaps more like 30 degrees off.

As horrible as human behavior often is, the reality is that we could do much worse than we currently do, which implies that we should have at least some bar of standards and caution when it comes to novel ideas concerning "obviously better" ways of doing things. More than that, it implies that there may be much more to lose than to gain with respect to changes in humanity's values. This is another reason to go to great lengths to not be perceived as overly radical or off-putting by others: pushing people and future values away from suffering-focused values may be many times more negative than drawing them closer would be positive.

9.7 Adhering to Firm Principles

Another way in which reducing suffering does not change everything is when it comes to basic moral principles and virtues. For it would indeed be simplistic to think that a single principle like "minimize extreme suffering" can be a sufficient guiding principle in practice, even if we believe it captures our highest moral aim in theory. Rather, successfully reducing suffering will require us to adhere to a multitude of principles and virtues, such as honesty, non-aggression, and law-abidingness.[24] There are many strong reasons for this.

For one, adherence to principles of non-aggression, honesty, and respect is crucial for building trust, which is in turn critical for being able to cooperate with others and for gaining support for one's endeavors.[25] Indeed, as pointed out by Schubert et al., there are reasons to think that people engaged in a community that seeks to improve the world should strive to be extra considerate:

> [B]eing considerate can improve the level of trust and collaborativeness among members of the community. It can also improve the reputation of the community. Conversely, failing to be considerate can harm the community, both internally and in its reputation.[26]

A related consideration in favor of rule-following in the context of cooperation is that psychological studies have found that most people find non-consequentialists (i.e. people who adhere to firm principles rather than optimize on a case-by-case basis) to be more moral, more trustworthy, and better cooperation partners than consequentialists.[27] These are findings

---

24 Provided the laws we are supposed to abide by are reasonably just, of course.
25 In relation to the benefits of honesty in particular, see Harris, 2011; Tomasik, 2013j.
26 Schubert et al., 2017. The authors here write about the so-called effective altruism community in particular, yet their point applies more generally.
27 Everett et al., 2016; Everett et al., 2018.

that any consequentialist should take into consideration, and they suggest that adherence to firm principles will often be the best way to create good outcomes in dealings with humans.

Another reason for adhering to a multitude of disparate principles and virtues — including kindness and compassion — is that they can stimulate actions and cognitive styles that a single, purely cerebral principle like "reduce suffering" cannot. After all, we are not deductive machines that can start at some single intellectual principle and then deduce the optimal path forward. Deep principles and intuitions provided to us by our culture, as well as by our nature, will often be better than anything we can derive from first principles in the purely cerebral departments of our minds. For example, our ability to be kind and empathetic derives far more from our nature and culture at large than from our abstract moral principles, and we would do a very poor job indeed if we always insisted on navigating by our cerebral principles over these time-tested virtues. In a complex world with many challenges, we should not expect a single principle to be sufficient for navigating every situation.

None of this is to say that we should not think from first principles. Indeed, such thinking is all too neglected in efforts to reduce suffering. The point is just that we need to combine such thinking with the many other moral "tools" and faculties at our disposal. We should view first-principles thinking as a captain of a team of players rather than as a lone super player.

Considerations of self-serving biases provide another reason to stick to firm rules. As Jamie Mayerfeld notes:

> An agent who regarded [sound moral principles] as mere rules of thumb would ignore them whenever she calculated that compliance wasn't necessary to minimize the cumulative badness of suffering. The problem is that it might also be in her own interest to violate these principles, and self-interest could distort her calculations, even when she calculated sincerely. She could thus acquire a pattern of violating the principles even when compliance with them really was necessary to prevent the worst cumulative suffering. To avoid this, we would want her to feel strongly inhibited from violating the principles. Inhibitions of this kind can insulate agents from the effect of biased calculations.[28]

And as Mayerfeld goes on to write, this point also applies, perhaps even more strongly, to communities and political groups at large where ingroup biases may lead judgments astray.[29]

Adherence to set rules and virtues is also important for the simple reason that we do not, and cannot, deliberate over each and every small decision. Indeed, most of the choices we make during the day are performed on autopilot, implying that we hardly have any alternative but to find good rules to follow when we are in this default-mode, as the only alternatives are no rules or bad rules.

Yet even when it comes to small choices we *could* deliberate over, it is arguably still better to adhere to fixed principles and virtues so as to spend our limited resources optimally. By adhering to such principles in small day-to-day choices rather than deliberating arduously, we free up our cognitive resources and time to focus on more important problems on a larger scale.

Abiding by common-sense principles and virtues also saves resources in that it guards against costs and risks to one's reputation and resources in general. After all, the point of our law and norm enforcement mechanisms is to make adherence less costly than non-adherence. Similarly, observance of accepted norms and virtues can also help us save resources by enabling us to be more transparent and less worried, in turn freeing up more cognitive

---

28 Mayerfeld, 1999, p. 121.
29 Ibid.

resources in this way as well. As an apocryphal Mark Twain quote on honesty goes: "If you tell the truth, you don't have to remember anything."

Another reason to act on simple principles and virtues is that it often simply leads to better decisions than do more advanced deliberative models and decision-procedures. This is a surprising yet solid conclusion in the study of bounded rationality: less is often more. As cognitive scientist Henry Brighton and psychologist Gerd Gigerenzer note:

> In contrast to the widely held view that less processing reduces accuracy, the study of heuristics shows that less information, computation, and time can in fact improve accuracy.[30]

Finally, we should adhere to firm principles because, even disregarding most of the considerations above, we have strong reasons to think that a significant degree of rule-following is the best way to produce good long-term outcomes on a collective level. As James Wood Bailey shows in *Utilitarianism, Institutions, and Justice*, various game-theoretic models suggest that a collective observance of strict rules tends to bring about significantly better consequences for virtually everyone compared to other strategies.[31]

Which exact set of firm principles and virtues we should ideally adopt stands as an open question for us to explore. Yet there is good reason to think that it will at least encompass many of the most widely accepted moral principles and virtues, including honesty, fairness, and kindness.[32]

This point may provide some relief in the face of our great uncertainty about how to best reduce suffering. The fact that we have so many good reasons to follow common-sense moral principles and virtues seems to give us something we can fall back on with at least some confidence: if nothing else, we can at least strive to be curious, honest, kind, cooperative, etc.

---

30 Brighton & Gigerenzer, 2012, abstract.
31 Bailey, 1997.
32 Mayerfeld provides more discussion of the reasons to adhere to strict principles in Mayerfeld, 1999, pp. 120-125, pp. 196-205.

9.8 Introducing Key Concepts

Before we conclude this chapter and dive deeper into the question of how we can best reduce suffering, we still need to introduce a few key concepts. These concepts apply to virtually everything related to the reduction of suffering, and are worth always keeping in mind in examinations of the issue.

9.8.1 Marginal Influence

Each of us, as individuals, only exerts a limited influence on the world — a modest effect on the margin. In a world with more than seven billion people who each try to shape the world in their own ways, and eventually with many future agents who will try to do the same, we should not expect our own actions to shape the large-scale direction of the future all that much (compared to a counterfactual scenario where we exert no influence). We often forget how big the world is, but one instance where we probably do realize it is when we cast our vote in a national election: a single vote is obviously unlikely to change much in the bigger picture. Yet the same holds true about our actions in the world in general.[33]

Crucially, however, this claim should not be confused with the claim that we can have at most a small or insignificant influence in an absolute sense, which is surely not the case. Indeed, each of us probably has the potential to spare many thousands of lives from extreme suffering.[34] This may seem in tension with the claim above, but this is only because our intuitions are not well-calibrated to think about large-scale outcomes: in our ancestral environment, a large absolute impact no doubt did constitute a great influence on the trajectory of one's tribe. Yet this no longer applies when one's "tribe" is the entire world. To be sure, it is not that it is impossible that one could influence the large-scale trajectory of civilization — it is just extremely unlikely.[35]

Marginal thinking is also relevant with respect to which particular areas we should support with our resources. If the value of additional

---
33 More elaboration on this point can be found in Tomasik, 2013c; Hanson, 2014a.
34 See section 15.2.
35 Tomasik, 2013c.

resources in a given area faces strongly diminishing returns, it may be better to direct our marginal resources toward other areas that are more neglected.

9.8.2 Expected Value Thinking

The concept of expected value is employed in a wide range of fields related to optimal decision-making. Indeed, in many contexts, optimal decision-making is thought to consist entirely in maximizing expected value. The concept is perhaps best explained in terms of betting options: if we are trying to maximize the amount of money we win from a set of available betting options, then we must consider *both* the probability and the prize money entailed by each option. In particular, to find the expected value of a given option, we must multiply these two factors.

To take a concrete example: say that option A gives us a 50 percent probability of winning a prize of $10,000, which means that option A has an expected value of 0.5 times $10,000 (= $5,000), while option B gives us a one percent chance of winning a prize of a million dollars, which yields an expected value of 0.01 times a million dollars (= $10,000). Thus, although the probability of winning the prize is much smaller with option B, we should still bet on that over option A to maximize the expected reward. This illustrates the general point that even highly unlikely outcomes can still be the most important ones to focus on according to the expected value framework, provided they are sufficiently (dis)valuable.

The expected value framework can be applied to virtually all decisions where we can make reasonable estimates of probabilities and the value or disvalue of different outcomes (though with some important qualifications).[36] And if we take seriously the point that small-probability events can potentially be the best thing to focus on given this framework, we see that our being unlikely to effect large-scale changes does not in fact imply that we should not focus on such large-scale influence. Careful analysis could, for example, suggest that the way to reduce the most

---

36 Some of these qualifications are reviewed in Karnofsky, 2011; 2014. For a brief case for trying to maximize expected value in the context of reducing suffering, which means minimizing expected suffering, see Tomasik, 2007.

suffering in expectation is to steer our future away from *a priori* unlikely futures that are very bad and that everyone can agree we should avoid.

9.8.3 The Importance of the Long-Term Future

If we accept that suffering matters equally regardless of where and when it is experienced — as I maintain we should[37] — it follows that the long-term future matters far more than common sense suggests. Why? Because we have good reason to believe that the vast majority of suffering we can reduce will lie beyond the next few decades that tend to occupy all our moral and political attention. The immediate implication of which is that the impact our actions have on the long-term future may well be the most important thing about them.[38]

This carries many important implications, some of which we shall explore in the following chapters. Yet it is worth highlighting here how the significance of the long-term future lends additional support to many of the points mentioned above. For one, it gives us even more reasons to be prudent, as it highlights the importance of considering not just the immediate effects of our actions, but also the secondary and tertiary effects. Beyond that, it reinforces the point about epistemic humility stressed above: the consequences of our actions are difficult enough to predict over just the next decade, yet they become much harder still to foresee when we consider spans of time that are orders of magnitude greater. This further strengthens the case for prioritizing foundational research and deep reflection.

Unfortunately, our intuitions are poorly equipped to grasp the importance of the long-term future. In fields ranging from biology to economics, we find strong reasons to expect humans to engage in temporal discounting (i.e. to consider things less valuable the further into the future they might occur).

---

37 A brief defense of this view is found in Effective Altruism Foundation, 2016. A more elaborate case for an impartial view is defended in Vinding, 2017b.
38 The moral importance of the long-term future is explored in depth in Beckstead, 2013, though not from a suffering-focused perspective.

In economic terms, we may reasonably prefer having a certain good today rather than in twenty years, as we may not be around by then. And in biological terms, we should expect our "selfish genes" to "care less" about any particular descendant the further away in time they are, as our genes get more diluted. These reasons can make sense of strong temporal discounting at the level of our intuitions. Yet they are not good reasons to discount the intrinsic disvalue of future suffering. In other words, there is a strong divergence between our immediate intuitions and impartial concern for suffering as time progresses. Consequently, we appear to have good reason to make an effort to continually remind ourselves of the importance of the long-term future. No matter how much we think we have internalized this point, our brains will still not be long-term futurists at the core.

It is worth noting, however, that the case for focusing on the long-term future can also be overstated, and that various counter-considerations dampen it at least modestly. One such counter-consideration is that there is a non-trivial probability that humanity, including its potential machine descendants, will go extinct in the future, and when evaluated from the present, this probability only increases the further into the future we look. And it turns out that even modest values of this extinction probability imply that the vast majority of suffering we can reduce, in expectation, does not lie all that far into the future. For example, an annual extinction probability of 0.1 percent[39] would imply that virtually all the suffering we can influence is found within the next 1,000-10,000 years.[40] Furthermore, it is probably easier to reduce suffering reliably in the near-term future compared to the long-term future, as the difficulty of predicting the consequences of our actions grows considerably with time. There are several more counter-considerations of this kind.[41]

These considerations do not undermine the importance of the long-term future, which should arguably still dominate our priorities significantly. Yet they do at least dampen naive versions of the long-term

---

39 An annual extinction probability of 0.1 percent would imply less than a ten percent probability of extinction by the end of this century. For comparison, one informal survey of experts landed on an estimate of human extinction that was roughly twice as high: 19 percent probability of extinction before 2100, Sandberg & Bostrom, 2008.
40 Vinding, 2017e.
41 For reviews of some of these, see Tomasik, 2015c; Baumann, 2017a; 2019b.

thesis, and show that we also have strong reasons to prioritize reducing suffering in the short term.

What I have argued for in this chapter — humility, prudence, rule-following, etc. — may seem in stark tension with one of the main claims I defended in the first part of the book, namely that we are always confronted with an acutely urgent opportunity to reduce suffering. This claim about urgency sounds strong and motivating whereas what I have said in this chapter may feel weaker and much less motivating. Where did all the urgency go? But the truth is that it went nowhere. The tension only exists at the level of our psychology, where we commit an "urgency fallacy" of sorts. For the fact that we have a truly urgent opportunity to reduce suffering in no way implies that we know how to best take advantage of this opportunity.

Again, it is understandable if this is deeply confusing at an intuitive level, given that feelings of urgency were mostly tied to palpable actions in our evolutionary past. Yet if we are to reduce suffering effectively, we must step beyond this confusion and learn to maturely integrate these two important insights: we are confronted both by great urgency *and* great uncertainty. Consequently, what we urgently need to do is to learn more about how we can reduce suffering so that the estimates guiding our actions are as refined as possible.

10

We Should Be Cooperative

"We are all in this together."

— Common expression of solidarity

We live in a world where people disagree profoundly about many things, including about what our priorities should be. This will remain true for the foreseeable future, and hence we have good reason to learn to cooperate with people with whom we disagree.

10.1 Cooperation: A Positive-Sum Prospect

A simple reason why cooperation is desirable is that it often allows better outcomes in expectation for all parties involved. Consider a simple example where two basketball teams have each been granted a respective half of a local gym hall. Both teams wish to use the full hall to practice properly, as half-court practice is suboptimal. This leaves the teams with two options: 1) they can each try to gain more of the gym hall for themselves by encroaching on the other team's space, or 2) the two teams can make a cooperative agreement to share the entire hall between them by practicing at different times. Both teams find the latter option clearly superior, as it enables them to get what they want without sacrificing anything of significance.

Another example whose relevance in the moral sphere may be more obvious is that of two moral agents who intend to push for opposing sides on some moral or political issue, yet who agree to instead further a shared goal. For example, a Republican who wants to donate $1,000 to the Republican Party and a Democrat who wants to donate the same amount to the Democratic Party may agree that it would be better if they each donated their money to a charity they both consider worth supporting.[1] Each person may consider a $1,000 donation to the charity less good than a $1,000 donation to their own party, yet they may consider the combined bargain that is $2,000 to a favored charity and $1,000 less to the other party to be much better still, in which case they both win by cooperating.

Trade of this kind has been referred to as "moral trade", and the wins produced can be thought of as "gains from moral trade" (by analogy to gains from trade in economics). A wide variety of moral views can, in theory, see gains from such moral trades.[2] Moreover, gains of this kind are also potentially wide-ranging in that there is no limit, in principle, to the number of agents with different values who can come together in this way to agree on positive-sum decisions. In cases where such improvements are possible, it would be a great shame for everyone involved if the respective agents choose not to cooperate.

10.2 Why Do We Not Cooperate?

If cooperation can yield significantly better outcomes in expectation, we should wonder why people do not cooperate more. A few plausible reasons can be given.

First, we may fail to cooperate because of crude human nature. Our brains are deeply tribal, and so we may be naturally reluctant to even consider cooperating with perceived outgroups (and disagreeing on values is arguably a strong catalyst for outgroup perception). Beyond that, we also

---

[1] This example is also mentioned in Ord, 2015.
[2] Ibid.

like to signal that we are loyal to our own group, which likely biases us further away from cooperating with "outgroups".[3] For instance, when a Democrat and a Republican make an agreement that results in no money donated to their respective political parties, this may be perceived as a betrayal by their political peers. In this way, our drive to signal loyalty can keep us in a suboptimal tug of war when we could cease to "tug" against one another and instead go in directions that benefit all parties.[4]

Another reason we may fail to cooperate is simply a lack of trust, which is a vital precondition for cooperation.[5] For example, the two basketball teams in the example above would never agree to share the gym hall if they thought the other team would keep on showing up to claim their own half. Such a lack of trust may be justified, of course, especially if one lives in a society where people rarely honor agreements, or if the particular agent one would ideally like to cooperate with has not held true to their promises in the past. These justified reasons to withhold trust highlight the importance of promoting trust and observance of shared rules, as failures in these regards may well result in big losses for everyone.

Lastly, one may refuse to engage in moral trade because a fuller analysis would in fact often recommend against it. For example, as mentioned in the previous chapter, people generally find consequentialists less trustworthy and less worth cooperating with, which may also have important implications for moral trade in particular.[6] It suggests that moral trade, although cooperative in itself, may reduce one's potential to cooperate in the future because of the impression it makes on third-party observers (e.g. the impression that one is willing to sell out on one's moral principles).

This reservation does not necessarily count as a decisive reason against engaging in moral trade — especially when the potential gains are great — yet it does at least give us reason to be somewhat cautious about it.[7] Similar considerations about people's perceptions also suggest that we should hesitate to dismiss the loyalty signaling cited above as just being

---

3   Simler & Hanson, 2018.
4   A similar point is made in Hanson, 2007; 2019.
5   Ord, 2015, pp. 132-134.
6   Everett et al., 2016; Everett et al., 2018.
7   Additional caveats in relation to moral trade can be found in Ord, 2015, pp. 137-138.

primitive human nature that we should ignore. For even if loyalty signaling is just primitive human nature, it remains a fact that most people do care about it, and failing to take this into consideration could well prove costly to one's ability to cooperate with others in the future.

Note, however, that none of these caveats about moral trade in particular speak against cooperation in general. Indeed, the underlying reason that animates these reservations about moral trade is that it may harm one's ability to cooperate in a more general sense. After all, moral trade is but one of many ways in which disagreeing moral agents can gain by cooperating. Another form of cooperation, one that need not have anything to do with compromises between conflicting values, is cooperation between different agents toward aims that they do agree on.

This kind of cooperation is especially relevant for suffering reduction, since the aim to reduce suffering is already among the most widely shared moral aims.[8] In effect, those who share the goal of reducing suffering will have a lot to lose by competing fiercely on issues they disagree on compared to if they spend their resources working toward their common goal. For not only does competition over other things count as an opportunity cost to the advancement of this common goal, it also constitutes a risk to the entire project of cooperation. Sometimes all it takes for cooperation to break down among humans is a single conflict.

This leads to a tentative maxim for those seeking to reduce suffering: most people already agree that suffering deserves significant priority, and so we should work on finding ways to reduce suffering that most people are willing to support. Failing to do this could be highly suboptimal relative to the goal of reducing suffering. Unfortunately, tribal human nature makes it all too tempting to succumb to failures of this kind, as we too readily focus on what divides rather than what unites us.

---

8 For some support for this claim, see Future of Life Institute, 2017.

10.3 Additional Reasons to Cooperate

Many other reasons can be cited in favor of being cooperative. A significant theoretical reason comes from game theory, the study of strategic interaction between rational decision-makers. For example, in variations of the so-called iterated prisoner's dilemma, which approximates many real-world scenarios, simulations suggest that an agent seeking to maximize its own gains should generally adopt a cooperative strategy.[9]

Specifically, in simulations of simple iterated games, political scientist Robert Axelrod found the winning strategy to be: cooperate from the outset, keep on cooperating as long as others cooperate, and defect if others defect.[10] And in more complex games that introduce noise, such as random mistakes or unclear feedback about what is going on, it turns out that an even more generous strategy, in which one cooperates in ten percent of the cases where one should defect in the simpler games, tends to win out in the long run.[11] This strategy may be thought of as giving one's cooperation partners the benefit of the doubt, and, in the words of Axelrod, its upside is that it "prevents a single error from echoing indefinitely" — i.e. it prevents mistakes from ruining all future cooperation for good.[12]

One can also give reasons for cooperating that are less abstract. For example, that common sense strongly endorses cooperation, and that human nature in many ways is set up to reward cooperation (and punish defection).[13] More than that, being cooperative and kind also generally makes one more likable, which in turn makes others more willing to listen to and sympathize with one's views, including one's moral views in particular. For example, animal rights activists who show a kind and cooperative attitude toward their listeners are probably more likely to have people listen with an open mind.

---

9   Axelrod, 1984; 1997.
10 Axelrod, 1984, chap. 2. For some examples and discussions of possible exceptions, see Press & Dyson, 2012a; 2012b. Press and Dyson discovered "zero-determinant strategies" (ZD strategies) that can beat the tit-for-tat strategy in a stochastic iterated prisoner's dilemma. However, ZD strategies actually allow even more gainful cooperation between agents (provided both agents know of ZD strategies), as they make it possible to ensure maximum rewards for both parties, Press & Dyson, 2012b. However, there is reason to be skeptical that these abstract results have great real-world relevance, ibid.
11 Axelrod, 1997, pp. 34-35.
12 Ibid., p. 34.
13 Henrich & Henrich, 2007; Tomasello, 2009.

In this way, cooperation is not only crucial for win-win decisions between competing value systems, but also when it comes to not turning people away from values that they would in fact agree with if only they reflected more deeply, or if only those who endorsed these values seemed more kind and worth associating with. This point is especially true in relation to aggression and violence in particular. That is, we should go to great lengths to avoid hostile behavior, not least since it tends to alienate potential supporters. A strict adherence to principles of non-aggression and "do no harm" is generally advisable.

Here is how Brian Tomasik sums up the importance of being cooperative and promoting compromise:

> I think advancing compromise is among the most important projects that we who want to reduce suffering can undertake. A future without compromise could be many times worse than a future with it. This is also true for other value systems as well, especially those that are risk-averse. Thus, advancing compromise is a win-win(-win-win-win-...) project that many of us may want to work on together. It seems like a robustly positive undertaking, squares with common sense, and is even resilient to changes in our moral outlook.[14]

10.4 Cooperating with Empirical Disagreements

As noted above, cooperation is not only important in the context of value disagreements. Another respect in which it is crucial is in the context of empirical disagreements. For people who agree fully about the importance of reducing suffering will inevitably still have disagreements on various factual questions, including questions about which future scenarios are most likely, and these disagreements can readily imply different practical priorities. If those aiming to reduce suffering are to be effective, then they must manage to cooperate in the face of such disagreements.

---

14 Tomasik, 2013g. Additional reasons for being cooperative are listed in Tomasik, 2014d.

It may be tempting to understate the significance of empirical disagreements. After all, if two parties agree on fundamental values, disagreements on other issues should be relatively minor and easy to tolerate. Sadly, this view turns out to be naive. Indeed, some of the most divisive disputes are found among people who are in close agreement on goals, yet who disagree about other things, such as optimal strategies or key empirical claims. Obvious examples include political allies and scientists. The latter are a particularly good example in this context, since scientists all share the aim of discovering the truth (at least ideally) and their disagreements are purely empirical (again, at least in the ideal). Nonetheless, it is quite common to see scientists end up in bitter disputes that impede cooperation and scientific progress; a famous example is the dispute between Robert Hooke and Isaac Newton.

The reason disputes like this happen despite the convergent ideal aims of the people involved is hardly a deep mystery, since the ideal motives people state are obviously not their only motives — for instance, personal prestige and group psychology also tend to motivate us strongly. And the point here is that those who share the ideal aim of reducing suffering face the same challenge. Empirical disagreements should be acknowledged for the readily flammable substance they are among those who are value-aligned. After all, empirical beliefs, beyond just tracking reality, also serve as a loyalty signal to our peers.[15] And so it may well feel like a betrayal — to the more primitive parts of our minds, that is — when someone who is otherwise an ally disagrees with us on empirical matters.

So how should we conduct ourselves in the face of empirical disagreements? Striving for compromise again seems the right response, on two fronts. First, at the level of the empirical beliefs themselves, it seems that two truth-seeking agents who end up with different beliefs should seek to update their beliefs in each others' direction.[16] After all, the fact that another reasonable

---

15 Hanson, 1997; Simler, 2016. For example, as Kevin Simler suggests, someone on the political left may be seen as stepping out of line if they do not believe in anthropogenic climate change, whereas someone on the right may be seen as stepping out of line if they do believe climate change is real and caused mostly by human activity, although these are purely empirical beliefs.

16 This is related to Aumann's agreement theorem, which says that two rational agents with the same knowledge cannot agree to disagree. A problem, of course, is that agents in the real world can never fully share all their knowledge and intuitions.

person believes something should be considered (at least) weak evidence that the given belief is correct. If one gives no weight to someone else's belief and full weight to one's own prior belief, then this requires an explanation, such as that the other person has less information or reasons incorrectly.[17] Second, beyond seeking to converge on beliefs, it is also necessary to cooperate and make compromises in the face of divergent empirical beliefs. For even if people sincerely strive to update their beliefs, some empirical disagreements will still persist. This leaves no alternative but to learn to tolerate empirical differences and to seek a pragmatic path forward that involves compromises where necessary (while continually being open to updates and belief convergence).

10.5 How to Promote Cooperation?

A general propensity toward cooperation in society is useful for all the specific forms of cooperation mentioned above, which then raises the question of how we can best promote such a general willingness to cooperate. One way may be to increase interpersonal trust, which is probably best done via institutions — ranging from informal norms to formal public institutions — that help make people worth trusting in the first place.[18] Beneficial informal norms include honesty and integrity, as well as norms against intolerance, aggression, and tribalism, whereas important things to promote at the level of our formal institutions include transparency, fairness, and stability. There is also evidence that less income inequality leads to more interpersonal trust.[19] Other ways to foster cooperation may include general education about how cooperation is a surprisingly effective strategy in countless game-theoretic scenarios, especially in the long term.[20]

---

17 Hanson, 2001.
18 There appears to be a mutual relationship between trust and institutions in that they seem to grow and fall together: greater trust makes better institutions possible and *vice versa*. See Sønderskov & Dinesen, 2014.
19 Ortiz-Ospina & Roser, 2019; Wilkinson & Pickett, 2009. This is also what one would expect in light of humanity's egalitarian origins, Boehm, 1999.
20 More suggestions on how we can promote cooperation are found in Tomasik, 2013n.

Given that cooperation might well be among the best tools we have for avoiding the very worst futures — i.e. future outcomes with vast amounts of suffering that everyone wants to avoid — we seem to have good reason to work toward a future that is generally more cooperative.[21] As Brian Tomasik writes:

> Probably the strongest reason [to promote cooperation] is that cooperation puts our descendants in a better position, both in terms of social institutions and moral values, to be able to tackle issues that we have no hope of addressing today. It's quite plausible that most of the suffering in the future will come from something that we can't even anticipate now. We should aim to empower our descendants to handle unknown unknowns, by advancing positive social technology — including institutions for peace and compromise — relatively faster than scientific technology.[22]

That said, the promotion of cooperation on a large scale is unlikely to be a particularly tractable endeavor, which renders it doubtful that large-scale cooperation is the *main* thing we should push for with our marginal resources. By contrast, the task of embedding cooperation deeply into our own approach to reducing suffering is quite tractable. And not only would this be beneficial in terms of win-win relations with outsiders, but also in terms of the large gains it can secure within the community of people seeking to reduce suffering. The promotion of such "local" cooperation should be a top priority.

---

21 *Cf.* the tragedy of the commons scenarios, which are best avoided via cooperative agreements that enable agents to collectively steer away from the tragic outcomes that would otherwise emerge by default. A concrete example may be arms races between conflicting groups: everyone may prefer to avoid arms races, yet if cooperation fails, each agent may see no alternative but to spend resources on destructive technology rather than spending it on something constructive and positive-sum. Another example, one that is perhaps more salient to us today, is the increasing political polarization we currently witness, where each individual seems to win points in the ingroup by distancing themselves from the other side, which may be considered a win to that individual within their group, yet the net result is an environment of polarization that makes everyone worse off.
22 Tomasik, 2014a.

11

Non-Human Animals and Expansion of the Moral Circle

Contemporary discussions and efforts pertaining to the reduction of suffering tend to be conducted from a thoroughly anthropocentric perspective. Yet if our aim is to reduce suffering effectively, this narrow focus cannot be defended. We must prioritize the suffering of *all* sentient beings.[1]

Imagine, by analogy, if virtually all our efforts to alleviate suffering were focused on people of just one nationality — Norwegians, say. This would obviously be an ineffective and unjustifiable focus. And yet the prevailing moral focus on humans to the exclusion of all other sentient beings is really no better. Indeed, the ratio of Norwegians to all humans is considerably larger than the ratio of humans to all sentient beings. Most sentient beings — more than 99.99 percent even if we just count vertebrates[2] — are non-human, and this fact should be strongly reflected in our approach to reducing suffering.

---

[1] Much of my work to date has focused on the subject of this chapter, and hence I will not here restate an elaborate case for the moral importance of non-human animals and of expanding our moral circle. I have provided more elaborate treatments of these subjects in Vinding, 2014a; 2014b; 2015a; 2016a.

[2] Tomasik, 2009d. Indeed, it is likely that the number of fish alone is 10^{15} at any given moment, implying that if we consider just the set of all humans and fish alive at any one time, fish constitute more than 99.999 percent of these beings. (In relation to the ability of fish to suffer, see again Braithwaite, 2010; Brown, 2015; Balcombe, 2016; Jabr, 2018.) And yet vertebrates are in turn vastly outnumbered by invertebrates, who are thousands of times

11.1 Rejecting Speciesism

The argument against discounting the suffering of non-human beings is simple: an individual's species membership is not relevant to their intrinsic moral value — only their sentience is. Hence speciesism, discrimination against beings based on their species membership, is unjustifiable.[3] We should give equal priority to equal interests in general, and to equal suffering in particular. Indeed, it is the *rejection* of the principle of equal consideration of equal interests that requires justification, since such a rejection faces the burden of identifying a morally relevant criterion that can justify this discrimination.

The claim that species membership itself constitutes such a criterion is question-begging; it would be no different from a racist who claims that one ethnic group of humans is inherently more morally important than all others. To justify treating beings differently, one must point to a morally relevant difference between them. And in this regard, efforts to justify discrimination against non-human animals run into the "argument from species overlap" (also known as the "argument from marginal cases"): whatever purportedly relevant difference we can point to between humans and non-human animals, such as differences in cognitive abilities, can also be found among humans. That is, many humans do not possess the cognitive abilities (or the ability to take moral responsibility, or "special social relationships", etc.) that supposedly constitute the morally distinguishing feature that justifies discrimination against non-human animals. And yet we rightly do not accept discrimination against humans based on these differences. On the contrary, we realize that, if anything, we have *greater* obligations to assist such disadvantaged humans — the complete opposite of what we take these differences to imply in the case of non-human individuals.

In this way, the argument from species overlap suggests that the reasons we generally give for discriminating against non-human animals are not in fact reasons we ourselves consider valid.[4] In the case of humans, we realize that

---

more numerous than fish (Tomasik, 2009d), and there is indeed no justification for not also granting them consideration, as they may well suffer. For more on this subject, see Tomasik, 2009a; 2015b; Elwood, 2011; Knutsson, 2016c; Tye, 2016; Singer, 2016; Birch, 2017.
3   For a more elaborate case for this conclusion, see Horta, 2010b; Ryder, 2011; Animal Ethics, 2012; Vinding, 2015a. The term "speciesism" was coined by Richard Ryder.
4   For a deeper exploration of the argument from species overlap, see Horta, 2014.

sentience alone is sufficient to warrant full moral consideration. And there is really no excuse for not extending this realization to all sentient beings.[5]

11.2 Wild-Animal Suffering

The implications of rejecting anthropocentrism in relation to our efforts to reduce suffering are far-reaching and difficult to summarize in a short space.[6] But an obvious yet widely overlooked implication worth highlighting is that we should seek to reduce the suffering of *all* sentient beings — including those who live in nature. Sadly, this point tends to be overlooked even by self-identified animal rights activists. Yet when it comes to humans, we realize that not actively harming other individuals is far from morally sufficient. We should also actively help alleviate harms when possible. For example, we realize that we should help people who are struck by ills such as famine and natural disaster, regardless of whether we ourselves have played any role in causing these ills. And just as an individual's race is no valid reason not to extend such help, neither is an individual's species membership.

In other words, we ought to alleviate the suffering of non-human animals when it is in our power to do so, even if the suffering is not caused by ourselves, such as when it occurs in nature for natural reasons.[7] Indeed, the suffering of wild animals constitutes the vast majority of suffering on Earth today by virtually any measure, due both to the vast numbers of wild animals[8] and the fact that a large fraction of them suffer in horrendous ways, such as by being eaten alive, starving to death, and being infected by parasites.[9]

So what can we do about such suffering? This is admittedly a difficult question to answer in detail, especially since very few people have explored it at this point. Some answers have been proposed, however. In

---

[5] Horta, 2010b; Vinding, 2015a.
[6] A more elaborate examination of the implications can be found in Vinding, 2015a, part II.
[7] More arguments for this conclusion can be found in Tomasik, 2009b; Pearce, 2009; 2012; Horta, 2010a; 2015; 2017a; 2017b; Mannino & Donnelly, 2014; Vinding, 2015a.
[8] Tomasik, 2009d.
[9] Tomasik, 2009b; Pearce, 2009; Horta, 2010a; 2015; 2017a; 2017b; Iglesias, 2018.

the short term, there are interventions such as vaccinating against diseases, as well as small-scale interventions that help visibly afflicted individuals.[10] Beyond that, at a more comprehensive level, David Pearce defends what he calls "compassionate biology", which entails using advanced technology to create a "pan-species welfare state".[11]

Yet even if we had no proposed answers, this would not give us reason to dismiss the issue. Consider, by analogy, the case of human poverty: the mere fact that this is a difficult problem to solve does not mean that we should give up and do nothing. On the contrary, it implies that we should do more research and think harder about how we might alleviate the problem of human poverty. So too with the problem of suffering in nature: it is unclear what we can do at the level of direct interventions at this point, which suggests that, rather than give up, we should do more research. Another thing we can do is to make the case that wild-animal suffering is a serious problem that merits priority, and to promote concern for non-human individuals in general — especially for numerous and yet neglected beings such as fish and insects.[12] So there is in fact much we can do about this problem, even today.[13]

---

10 For examples of such interventions that have already been done, see Animal Ethics, 2014; Horta, 2019.
11 Pearce, 2016. For a discussion of other proposed answers, see Vinding, 2019.
12 Again, for resources on the sentience and moral relevance of fish, see Braithwaite, 2010; Balcombe, 2016; Jabr, 2018. For resources on the sentience and moral relevance of invertebrates, see Tomasik, 2009a; 2015b; Elwood, 2011; Knutsson, 2016c; Tye, 2016; Singer, 2016; Birch, 2017. One may reasonably question whether invertebrates such as insects can suffer intensely (e.g. whether they can experience extreme suffering of the kind described in the fourth and fifth chapter). However, on an expected value framework, one need only assign a modest probability to the possibility that they can — say, one percent — in order for the intense suffering of invertebrates to dominate that of vertebrates in expectation, due to the vast numbers of invertebrates. And as many of the sources quoted above suggest, we have reason to have more than just a one percent credence in this possibility.
13 See Animal Ethics, 2013.

11.3 Ending the Exploitation of Non-Human Animals

Another important implication is that we should end society's exploitation of non-human animals.[14] That is, we should work toward a society in which non-human animals are not considered mere property, and in which we do not exploit and kill them for frivolous reasons such as palate pleasure — as we currently do by the billions every year.[15] Likewise, at the individual level, we should abstain from consuming animal products to the extent possible. This is important for various reasons. For one, it is obviously important so as to reduce the suffering we directly cause to non-human animals today, as well as to remove support from various industries and institutions that actively impede greater moral concern for non-human animals at the societal level. However, it is also important for more subtle yet no less significant reasons, namely to purify our own minds of the biasing influence exerted by the consumption of "animal products".[16] And there are good reasons to think that this biasing influence is strong indeed.

First, it seems highly plausible that we evolved to display a strong moral apathy toward the beings whom we have learned to see as food, as there was probably strong selection pressure against displaying even mild sympathy and moral concern for such beings in our evolutionary past (it would likely make a prehistoric human a worse hunter, cook, and consumer of limited resources). Psychological studies bear out this apathy hypothesis: not only do we appear to show apathy toward the beings we consider food, but we even seem to deny that they have minds in the first place.[17] And this insidious influence on our perception of the beings we eat is unlikely to be limited to just the beings we eat themselves, but will likely trickle out and skew our moral perception of non-human individuals

---

14 This conclusion is defended at greater length in Vinding, 2014a; 2014b; 2015a.
15 For more elaborate arguments for this conclusion, see Francione, 2000; 2008; Vinding, 2015a.
16 In scare quotes because the things I refer to here are "animal products" in the same sense that severed human body parts and forcefully obtained human breast milk would be "human products". That is, it is a grotesque euphemism. However, it is also important to note that, in the world of today, grotesque euphemisms and worse should sadly often be used, even casually, so as to communicate effectively with people who will only be turned off by words that track reality more faithfully.
17 Bastian et al., 2012.

in general. For example, if one consumes the body parts of non-human animals on a regular basis, this probably makes one more resistant toward arguments that suggest speciesism is wrong.

Another way to appreciate the influence that the consumption of "animal products" has on us is to consider how it would influence our minds to consume the body parts of certain humans. For example, if a Dutch person regularly ate the flesh of German people (and never Dutch people), would this person really be an apt candidate for the board of an organization that works for better treatment of Germans? Is it at all plausible that this person's ability to reason about Germans, in moral terms, is left wholly uncompromised? It seems not. Yet why should we think the situation is significantly different in the case of non-human beings?

Indeed, there seems to be a tendency among utilitarian-minded people to think that there is nothing uniquely important about the steps we can take toward not eating non-human animals and "products" of their exploitation relative to other things we can do for them, such as doing activism or making charitable donations. While there is a grain of truth to this view — the importance of activism and donations surely is immense and universally underestimated — it also contains a large grain of falsehood. This is clear when we consider the equivalent human case mentioned above, where we are not tempted to say that there is nothing special about the step from "eating humans" to "not eating humans". As is viscerally clear in this case, it is more than plausible that we lose concern for the kinds of beings we eat, and hence that eating a certain group of beings risks influencing us in deeply undesirable ways. This is a deep *psychological* point, and it is all too readily missed in naive consequentialist calculations, such as calculations that focus only on body counts of beings exploited and killed. (Indeed, this point is often missed even among those who stress the importance of avoiding naive consequentialism.)

And while some utilitarian-minded thinkers may manage to be significantly less influenced in this way, it should still be noted that most people probably cannot do the same, and hence such utilitarian-minded thinkers may well underestimate the psychological significance the consumption of "animal products" has for most people.[18] Moreover, even if one has a unique ability to *reduce* the biasing influence that the consumption of "animal products" has on one's own mind, it seems unlikely that one can come close to eliminating it entirely — again, compare the difficulty of remaining unbiased toward a group of humans despite consuming their flesh and other "products" of their exploitation. Finally, there are also considerations of self-serving biases that suggest that our convenient evaluations of the (un)importance of a principled approach cannot be trusted.[19] In sum, utilitarian-minded thinkers often grossly underestimate the importance of not consuming "animal products".[20]

These arguments for the importance of personal consumption notwithstanding, a strong case can be made that the main focus of our broader efforts to create positive change for non-human animals should be to change institutions — not individual consumer behavior. In other words, there is good reason to think that our chief priority should be to influence societal norms, politics, and laws, and that we should phrase our aims in these terms rather than in terms of, say, changing people's diets.[21]

An important reason for this is that people are much less resistant to institutional change, partly because it is less about them personally. In fact, not only are people less resistant to institutional change, but they even express surprisingly strong support for it. For example, a survey from 2017 suggests that almost half of the US population supports a ban on factory farming and slaughterhouses — i.e. a surprisingly high level of support for radical institutional change. In contrast, when the issue is raised in the context of personal consumption, people express a strong support for the status quo.[22]

Another reason it may be promising to focus on institutional change, in particular in the realm of politics, is that, in a democracy, radical reforms

---

18   This is also a reason for utilitarian-minded thinkers to abstain from such consumption, since it would be hypocritical to advocate for others to follow a norm that one does not follow oneself.
19   See Mayerfeld's point about self-serving biases mentioned in section 9.7.
20   See also Vinding, 2014b; Sebo, 2019. This point is worth stressing here because the readers of this book are likely to be at least somewhat utilitarian-minded.
21   Reese, 2016; 2018, chap. 7; 2020; Vinding, 2016c.
22   Sentience Institute, 2017; Reese, 2020. The results of this survey were replicated in Norwood & Murray, 2018.

and bans can in principle be achieved when just slightly more than half of the population supports them. This consideration, combined with the finding that almost half of the US population already seems to show some support for radical legislative changes, hints at the enormous potential that lies in strategies and advocacy focused on institutional change.[23]

11.4 Expanding Moral Consideration Beyond (Live) Animals

The importance of expanding our circle of moral concern goes much further than what we have covered above. For beyond the sentient beings inhabiting Earth today, there is also a potential for enormous amounts of suffering to emerge in new kinds of minds that may exist in the future. In fact, we need not even go to the future to get a sense of the risks this possibility entails. Recently, scientists have been able to partially revive the brains of dead pigs, reactivating their cerebral metabolism by keeping them in an isolated chamber.[24] Reportedly, the pigs did not regain consciousness, yet it seems difficult to rule out the possibility that some fleeting experiential states emerged, and this should be considered a serious risk given the potential of such states to entail intense suffering. At any rate, the fact that technologies of this kind already exist and are likely to be developed further should lead us to take seriously the prospect of disembodied minds that can suffer.

Indeed, disembodied minds pose a unique challenge to our moral sentiments, in that they have no accompanying face, body movements, or screams to which we can relate. There is just a mind-brain that may be undergoing suffering far more severe than any scream could ever convey. Combine this with the possibility that disembodied minds — in the form of "artificial" sentience realized in future hardware[25] — could be by far the

---

23 Mannino, 2016. Such a strategy is already being pursued in Switzerland, where the organization Sentience Politics has managed to collect enough signatures to bring about a public vote on whether factory farming should be banned. For more on the importance of politics in relation to non-human animals, see Animal Ethics, 2017b; Garner & O'Sullivan, 2016; André, 2019.
24 Vrselja et al., 2019.
25 Ziesche & Yampolskiy, 2019a; 2019b.

most numerous minds in the future, and we begin to see how important it is that we make an effort to appreciate the moral significance of such future minds.[26]

On an expected value framework, greater future concern for such "silent" minds could turn out to be orders of magnitude more important than greater concern for presently existing beings. For this to be plausible, one would only need to assume a modest probability that vulnerable minds of this kind will exist in astronomical numbers in the future. And given that humans, in a race for purely economic gains, have created the still growing institution of factory farming that imposes horrific suffering upon billions of sentient beings every year, it is by no means guaranteed that our descendants will not eventually create similar suffering on an astronomical scale for similar reasons.

What the minds of the future will be like is, of course, highly uncertain, which in turn renders it difficult to say how we can best reduce the suffering that may emerge in such minds. It might well be that the best we can do today is to raise concern for the presently existing beings whom we neglect in moral terms — an approach that also has the advantage of pertaining to beings who are both actual and relatable.

On the other hand, focusing primarily on presently existing beings could also turn out to be suboptimal. For example, it could be that people are significantly more open toward the moral inclusion of future beings. One reason this might be the case is that most people are behaviorally invested in practices that harm presently existing non-human individuals, and they may fear social disapproval if they stop such behavior and start speaking up for these individuals. In contrast, it may feel less threatening to people's identities to support advocacy and measures that help future beings.[27]

---

26 For instance, if our descendants colonize space and fill it with minds, it seems likely that disembodied minds will be the most effective way to do so.

27 This should not be taken as an excuse for our current atrocities against sentient beings. The point is merely that we must focus on that which best reduces suffering for sentient beings, and the fact that people are less personally and socially invested in harming future beings, as well as the fact that there will be many more future beings than there are present beings, do in combination count as a considerable reason to focus primarily on future beings in our efforts to reduce suffering (a reason that may, of course, be counterbalanced by other reasons).

In the absence of clear answers to the questions raised by these considerations, it seems to me wise to opt for a middle road that relates both to beings of today and of the future. Specifically, to invoke the relatability of presently existing non-human individuals while also emphasizing arguments about the importance of reducing suffering in all beings, regardless of their temporal location and external traits.

11.5 Biases

There are quite a few relevant biases to be aware of in relation to our circle of moral consideration. These biases are important to understand for two principal reasons: 1) to see how we ourselves may be biased against prioritizing non-human beings, which will hopefully enable us to better correct for these biases, and 2) to understand the psychology of other people so that we can adjust our focus accordingly and navigate more effectively toward the goal of reducing suffering.

An especially relevant bias is our "speciesist bias". As a recent study found, we humans tend to "value individuals of certain species less than others even when beliefs about intelligence and sentience are accounted for."[28] And this bias probably affects all of us, regardless of how sincere we are about reducing suffering. For both biological and cultural reasons that are difficult to transcend, we tend to care much less about beings who are not human. At the biological level, it is wholly unsurprising that we are hardwired to care disproportionally about our own kin and kind. And the reasons for our anthropocentrism are no less obvious at the cultural level. For example, our laws and culture at large fail to promulgate concern for non-human beings to any considerable extent, and indeed do not punish most misdeeds against them, such as frivolously killing and eating them. More generally, just about everywhere one turns in society, one is met by intense propaganda against non-human individuals — in supermarkets where their body parts are on sale, in our conversations where

---

28 Caviola et al., 2019.

their names are used pejoratively, and in nature where they are "objects of conservation".[29]

Again, it is difficult to appreciate the extent to which these things blind us to the moral importance of non-human beings, not to mention the continual effort that is required to reduce their biasing influence. For even if we adamantly reject speciesism at the level of our explicit beliefs, we are still deeply anthropocentric at the level of our attitudes and sentiments, which probably in large part determine our moral motivation and focus.

Our speciesist bias is also worth keeping in mind in order to see reality more clearly and to avoid undue cynicism. For in a world where the suffering of non-human animals is often met with indifference, and sometimes even amusement, we should remember that it is not the case that most people have no empathy or concern for suffering, but rather that these capacities are heavily muted relative to the suffering of non-human beings. More than that, we should remember that most people actually do display concern for non-human animals at the level of their stated beliefs. For instance, a 1996 poll conducted in the United States found that 67 percent of people reported agreement with the statement that a "[non-human] animal's right to live free of suffering is just as important as a [human] person's right to live free of suffering".[30] Thus, the challenge arguably lies more in bringing people's attitudes and behaviors in line with their stated beliefs than it lies in revolutionizing their convictions about the moral importance of non-human beings.

Other biases that are important to control for include two biases we have mentioned before, namely our scope neglect and our perpetrator bias. Scope neglect, the tendency of our moral sentiments to give insufficient weight to large numbers, is obviously relevant given that the number of non-human animals is so overwhelmingly large — both on factory farms and in nature. And we should expect our scope neglect to be even more significant still in relation to risks of non-human individuals suffering in astronomical numbers in the future.

---

29 See Vinding, 2015a, "The Conservationist Delusion".
30 Deseret News, 1996 (38 percent agreed strongly, while 29 percent agreed somewhat). Similar findings are reported in Sentience Institute, 2017; Norwood & Murray, 2018.

Perpetrator bias is likewise important to control for at all these three levels.[31] At the level of humanity's systematic exploitation and abuse of non-human animals, we find no single perpetrator we can point toward, but rather many partly complicit agents — the farmer, the slaughterhouse worker, the customer. This division of maleficence blinds us to the atrocities committed by this institution as a whole.

Far stronger still is our perpetrator bias in the context of suffering in nature for natural reasons: here there are absolutely no agents we can identify as culpable perpetrators and who can fire up our moral sentiments — just an enormous amount of suffering that human psychology evolved to ignore.[32] (And this is, I believe, the great blindspot of most vegans: the absence of a perpetrator leads them to neglect the suffering of the majority of the beings they claim to care about.)[33] Lastly, we should expect our perpetrator bias to be strong in relation to risks of astronomical suffering, as the greatest such risks are not due to any single evil agent but rather, like the moral catastrophe of factory farming today, due to failures of a more distributed and systemic kind.[34]

A final bias worth highlighting here is that people display a significant bias against vegetarians and especially vegans. For instance, a recent study conducted in the United States found that people on average evaluate vegans more negatively than other minority groups such as atheists and homosexuals.[35] The study also found that vegans themselves reported experiencing negative judgements from others, and to have had friends

---

31 For more on (what I call) the perpetrator bias, see Tomasik, 2013i; Davidow, 2013. See also section 7.7.
32 Davidow, 2013.
33 Another bias that is relevant is underestimating the moral importance of small beings relative to larger beings, Vinding, 2015a, "A Short Note on Insects". For example, ants have significantly more neurons than lobsters, yet people generally seem to display greater moral concern for lobsters than for ants. This consideration is relevant because small beings constitute the vast majority of non-human beings, both among vertebrates (most of whom are small fish) and invertebrates.
34 Even in scenarios in which the majority of future suffering is caused by a single evil agent, the emergence of such a powerful agent would itself be the result of systemic failures — still the product of factors our perpetrator-biased minds are not naturally geared to appreciate and take seriously.
35 MacInnis & Hodson, 2017. See also Horta, 2018.

and family members contact them less, and in some cases even no longer contact them at all, after they revealed they were vegan.[36]

This bias against vegans is first of all relevant because it likely skews our appraisals of veganism itself, and disinclines us from adhering to it.[37] Yet the bias also constitutes an important psychological fact about how people may react to various messages. Indeed, such biased attitudes against vegans are a significant hurdle to many otherwise straightforward endeavors to reduce suffering. It is therefore important that we take such biases into account in our evaluations of optimal strategies for reducing suffering.

11.6 Caveats

If our core goal is to reduce suffering, we should be careful not to simply assume that expanding humanity's moral circle — or any other intuitively related and appealing goal — is necessarily perfectly convergent with our core aim. Indeed, the three goals "minimize suffering", "expand humanity's moral circle", and "minimize human consumption of 'animal products'" are not identical. And even though these goals are surely related, one should be skeptical that the actions best suited to address one of them also happen to be best suited for the others. That would be a remarkable coincidence.[38]

In fact, it is not difficult to point to ways in which expanding humanity's moral circle could end up increasing future suffering.[39] For example, many people hold moral views according to which the extreme suffering of one individual can be outweighed by goods enjoyed by others. Some people even consider factory farms good for the beings who live on them,[40] and

---

36 MacInnis & Hodson, 2017.
37 The existence of such an effect is supported by a study that found fear of stigmatization to be a likely barrier preventing "dietary shifts toward a plant-based diet", Markowski & Roxburgh, 2019.
38 *Cf.* Lewis, 2016.
39 For more on this point, see Tomasik, 2015d; Vinding, 2018h.
40 This is a version of the "logic of the larder" ("raising and killing other beings is good for them, as they would not have existed otherwise"). For an example where it is applied in the context of factory farming, see Hanson, 2002. Curiously, as pointed out by naturalist Henry S. Salt (Salt, 1914, "Logic of the Larder"), this argument is never used to argue that it would be good to raise and kill humans, although it would seem just as (in)valid in that context.

many more consider the sentient condition in nature to be "net positive", despite the enormous amount of extreme suffering it entails. Given the popularity of such optimistic views, a wider circle of moral concern could well increase future suffering by leading people to prioritize bringing more beings, and hence more suffering, into the world. This consideration suggests that it may be better and more robust to focus on raising humanity's concern for suffering, or at any rate to emphasize that the most.

Another way in which work to expand humanity's moral circle may be suboptimal is if it imposes significant opportunity costs relative to other crucial tasks we could pursue to reduce suffering. That is, there may be other endeavors that are more important to focus on, such as promoting concern for suffering. Or it may be that work to expand humanity's moral circle comes with too high signaling costs — if it, for psychological reasons, makes other people less sympathetic and more hostile to one's persona and cause in general. This is a risk worth considering before investing most of one's resources into advocating for veganism or expansion of humanity's moral circle: these things could, given most people's biases, be costly to other projects that are crucial to the reduction of suffering, many of which we may not even have thought of yet.[41]

Expanding humanity's moral circle probably remains among the more promising endeavors we can support. Yet the caveats above do at least give us reason to doubt that generic work to expand humanity's moral circle is what we should devote *most* of our resources to.

---

41 Where does this leave my argument above against consuming "animal products"? It leaves it quite intact, as my argument did not pertain primarily to activism. That is, one can be vegan and reap the benefits of a less morally biased mind without necessarily devoting a significant fraction of one's resources to vegan advocacy.

12

Promoting Concern for Suffering

The promotion of greater concern for suffering appears a particularly good strategy to reduce suffering. In this chapter, I shall present some of the reasons why it seems promising and explore how it can best be done.

12.1 Why It Seems Promising[1]

Actions that promote concern for suffering appear uniquely robust. There are few pursuits we can expect to be positive across a wide range of possible future scenarios — as noted in the previous chapter, even expansion of humanity's moral circle entails a significant risk of increasing suffering in some scenarios. Yet greater concern for suffering does seem positive in expectation in almost all future scenarios. This is no coincidence, as concern for suffering is oriented more directly toward the reduction of suffering than anything else.

Indeed, as Brian Tomasik argues, other interventions have a greater risk of being useless, or even negative, whereas the promotion of concern for suffering can build a uniquely flexible resource:

---

[1] This section draws heavily on Tomasik, 2015d.

Pushing for a particular object-level policy stance, such as opposing climate change, runs the risk that you'd change your mind about the policy with further information. For example, maybe it turns out that climate change is actually net beneficial with respect to wild-animal and future suffering. In that case, your previous advocacy would have been worse than wasted. In contrast, if you work to advance broader ethical principles, such as the priority of reducing extreme suffering, then you create a more flexible resource, since as further information comes in, people who share that viewpoint can change what they work on. Future generations will have much better insight into problems of the future than we have today, so imparting a concern for suffering to future generations will often more reliably conduce to good outcomes than will promoting some particular, ideology-independent policy.[2]

The promotion of greater concern for suffering has the advantage of making people more likely to join the endeavor to reduce suffering at the most fundamental level — the level of core values — from which they can help figure out the best ways to reduce suffering. A movement of people oriented toward this goal seems the best kind of movement we can create. Not least since everything else is in a sense downstream from our core values: they are ultimately what determine our practical priorities, which renders them uniquely consequential.[3]

Another reason to prioritize the promotion of concern for suffering is that society's values seem somewhat more contingent than many other things we could focus on advancing, such as technological and scientific progress, and hence we may expect to make a greater marginal difference by increasing concern for suffering.[4] Beyond that, the promotion of concern

---

[2] Tomasik, 2015d.
[3] More elaboration on these points is found in Vinding, 2017a, "The Tree of Ought — A (Cause) Prioritization Framework", "Reasons to Focus on Values as Our Main Cause".
[4] For a case for the limited contingency of technological and scientific advances, see Kelly, 2010. Kelly demonstrates that scientific discoveries and technological inventions were often made independently, almost simultaneously. By contrast, religious leaders and philosophers seem to have exerted a more contingent influence throughout history. For example, different religions differ quite strongly on values, and in relation to political philosophy, it is unclear whether we would have seen communist revolutions had it not been for the writings of Karl Marx.

for suffering also appears more neglected, in terms of resources devoted to it, than most other specific projects and mainstream causes one could pursue, such as scientific progress or moral circle expansion.

Finally, another significant reason to promote concern for suffering is that many of those who currently focus on reducing suffering seem to have adopted dangerously naive views and approaches — neglecting, for instance, the importance of being cooperative. And it is plausible that one of the best ways to influence these people in more cooperative and effective directions is by defending the moral views these people hold, and to then present a more sophisticated and balanced picture of these views' implications. If nothing else, this may at least reduce the risk that people aiming to reduce suffering will harm the cause due to naive ideas.

12.2 What Promoting Concern for Suffering Means

Promoting concern for suffering can mean many things and take many forms. For one, it can mean presenting arguments in favor of giving special priority to the reduction of suffering, as I have done in the first part of this book. Yet it can also consist in producing educational documentaries that help raise people's concern for suffering,[5] or in promoting practices that raise people's compassion and emotional attunement to suffering, such as compassion meditation or so-called compassion cultivation training.[6]

Another sense in which one can promote concern for suffering is by bringing the concern people show for suffering at the level of their behavior into congruence with the concern they have at the level of their ideals. For example, as mentioned earlier, a large survey found that a plurality of people — roughly a third — believe that minimizing suffering should be the main aim of future civilization.[7] Yet it is hardly the case that a third of people work to reduce suffering in a dedicated and effective way. There can be many reasons for this, of course, some of which we already explored

---
5   For a short such documentary, see Leighton, 2015.
6   See The Center for Compassion and Altruism Research and Education: ccare.stanford.edu.
7   Future of Life Institute, 2017.

in the chapter on biases: we may not be aware of our potential to reduce suffering, we may be suppressing the reality of suffering in our day-to-day lives, we may be too caught up in our own pursuit of pleasure, etc. In this way, promoting concern for suffering need not primarily be about changing people's values, but can just as well be a matter of helping people bring their actions into alignment with the core values they already hold.

12.3 Is It Uncooperative?

The main argument against promoting concern for suffering is that it is uncooperative: advancing one's own values is a zero-sum activity that just steals resources from other, opposing value systems. Thus, the heuristic that we should be cooperative suggests that we should focus on other, more positive-sum projects instead.[8]

This argument is problematic, for many reasons. One problem is that it rests on a crude toy model of cooperation between abstract value systems. A more realistic and sophisticated view of cooperation will instead focus on cooperation between actual moral agents[9] — a much more complicated and nuanced view that must factor in the myriad diverse norms, values, and interests that animate individuals in the real world, of which their abstract moral values are but a subset.[10]

For the truth is that the values people hold are many and complex, and they go far beyond moral values in a narrow sense. For example, people also tend to observe tacit norms tied to their communities and cultures, and such norms will often prize the open-ended exploration of different

---

8   A fuller version of an argument along these lines is found in Christiano, 2013; a brief version is outlined in Tomasik, 2015d. Christiano's argument is against "moral advocacy" in general while the argument Tomasik outlines is about concern for suffering in particular. Christiano does not explicitly define what he means by moral advocacy, yet this lack of definition is not relevant to what I write in this section, as my main aim here is not to examine Christiano's arguments but rather to examine the particular argument I just stated in the text (which is roughly the one Tomasik outlines).
9   By "actual moral agents" I do not mean to exclude future moral agents. I simply mean moral agents that are or will (potentially) be actual — as opposed to crude, abstract agents.
10 Which is to say that the toy model of cooperation between abstract values is incorporated in this more multidimensional model to the extent it is relevant.

moral views and perspectives. Beyond such community values, reflective moral agents also hold various epistemic values, at least tacitly (after all, without epistemic norms, one cannot meaningfully do any moral reflection in the first place). And these epistemic values are also often friendly toward the advancement of many different moral views, as they tend to include an ideal of openness and impartiality toward novel views and arguments.

Indeed, one can argue that we all, as reflective moral agents, have a genuine interest in being exposed to the strongest arguments for any given moral view so that we can reflect and make up our minds in a well-informed manner, implying that those who are advancing views with which we disagree are in fact in some sense acting in our interest.[11] Such a natural interest in being exposed to arguments is among the core tenets of the tradition of liberalism and the Enlightenment more broadly. As John Stuart Mill wrote in *On Liberty*:

> [T]he peculiar evil of silencing the expression of an opinion is, that it is robbing the human race; posterity as well as the existing generation; those who dissent from the opinion, still more than those who hold it. If the opinion is right, they are deprived of the opportunity of exchanging error for truth: if wrong, they lose, what is almost as great a benefit, the clearer perception and livelier impression of truth, produced by its collision with error.[12]

Not only is it cooperative to disseminate the strongest case for one's moral views, but it is in fact, on Mill's conception of liberalism, uncooperative *not* to do so, as that would rob others of a great benefit — whether these others will agree with the view or not. In other words, arguing for a particular moral view is a cooperative contribution that adds to the

---

11   Indeed, Christiano says something similar about his own preferences and reflection: "My preferences are loosely defined by reference to what I would judge good upon reflection." Christiano, 2013. Yet engaging with the arguments that others have proposed in favor of a set of values is arguably among the best ways to find out what one would "judge good upon reflection", implying that the dissemination of such arguments is a good thing relative to such reflective preferences.
12   Mill, 1859, chap. 2. It may be objected that no one argues that suffering-focused views should be forcefully silenced, which is true. Yet Mill's point applies just the same to silently withholding one's own opinion for supposedly cooperative reasons.

common good by potentially advancing everyone's views. And so to the extent the toy model above recommends against stating and disseminating the strongest case for one's values, it is worth asking whether that model should weigh heavier than the widely endorsed and elaborately defended values of liberalism and the Enlightenment more generally.

That these traditions hold such a view of the importance of getting every argument out in the open is no coincidence: it stems from the underlying claim that there can be truly better or worse reasons for accepting a given view, including a moral view in particular. And this is indeed another thing I would criticize in the toy model above — it seems to tacitly assume that our values are ultimately arbitrary, as though we cannot come to truly better views through collective reflection and examination. Such a claim about the complete arbitrariness of values seems highly implausible.[13] For instance, humanity has seen countless value changes over the last few centuries that have happened partly due to moral arguments, including the abolition of (legal) slavery, and few people would claim that these changes have been wholly arbitrary and without merit in any real sense. Many of these changes in humanity's values can be considered beneficial relative to the reflected values of most of us, and it seems reasonable to expect future moral examinations and discussions to be able to effect more such changes.

For these reasons, it seems unlikely that defending and discussing values in public constitutes a zero-sum game. And this seems especially true of defending greater concern for suffering, since most people can probably agree, on reflection, that we should have greater concern for extreme suffering and do more to alleviate and prevent it.

Additionally, it is worth highlighting how the *manner* in which a moral view is advanced can also be positively cooperative. For example, one can advance a set of moral values in a way that directly promotes cooperation. In particular, promoting suffering-focused values can be highly cooperative if it makes otherwise imprudent agents more cooperative and less naive.

---

13 Note that this claim is not predicated on moral realism: one can think we have truly better reasons to hold one moral view over another without being a moral realist. For example, many moral anti-realists will probably agree that we have good reason not to hold inconsistent moral views.

The discussion above pertains mainly to the promotion of concern for suffering via arguments for certain moral values. Yet as pointed out in the previous section, there are many other promising ways to promote concern for suffering, and these are not uncooperative either — quite the contrary. For example, there is the promotion of greater compassion through various practices, which is different from advancing arguments in that it is not a matter of changing cerebral beliefs, but rather a matter of changing people's emotional attentiveness to suffering. One may then wonder whether such training of people's emotions is uncooperative, yet this seems implausible since compassion is considered a virtue in most societies and cultures, and promoting something that is widely considered positive and worth promoting is hardly uncooperative either.[14]

Another important way to promote greater concern for suffering that does not involve arguing for or changing moral values is to help people bring their views and actions in line with the values they themselves endorse upon reflection. For the truth is that we all have some level of disconnect between our deepest ideals and our actual behavior. And given that people's deeper values generally do entail a significant concern for suffering, helping to reduce this disconnect seems a good and cooperative way to increase concern for suffering in practice (such as by reducing the degree to which we suppress the reality of suffering, and by making us aware of our opportunity to reduce it). If being cooperative means respecting other people's preferences, then there is hardly anything more cooperative than this.

Moreover, this way of promoting concern for suffering could well be the most promising of all given the magnitude of the disconnect there seems to be, in society as a whole, between the priority we give the reduction of suffering at the level of our values versus how many resources we devote toward this end in practice.[15] There may be a lot of low-hanging fruit to reap in translating this widely shared value into congruent actions.

Similarly, one may also lead others to give greater priority to suffering by presenting purely empirical arguments, such as by pointing out that there seems to be an asymmetry in the ease of realizing states of suffering

---

14   Lampert, 2005.
15   *Cf.* Future of Life Institute, 2017.

versus happiness, which can in turn imply that efforts to reduce suffering are generally a superior investment of resources. Such refinements of empirical beliefs can also change people's practical priorities without changing their values in the least.[16]

12.4 Is It Better Still to Focus on Technology?

Another objection against prioritizing the promotion of concern for suffering is that we may do even better by trying to influence emerging technologies.[17] The argument is roughly as follows: the vast majority of potential future suffering is probably due to irresponsible uses of technologies not yet invented, and hence trying to influence the formation and use of these technologies seems the most direct and effective way to reduce future suffering.[18]

This proposal to focus directly on future technologies is certainly worth exploring. Yet I see quite a few reasons to believe that the promotion of concern for suffering is a better strategy. One reason is that we do not presently know what the relevant future technologies will look like in much detail, and hence we cannot be sure that efforts to influence future technologies will be significantly more focused and direct than the promotion of concern for suffering. Indeed, in light of this uncertainty, there is a high risk that direct work to influence future technologies will be wasted. In contrast, as noted above, greater concern for suffering seems robustly positive almost regardless of the contingent details. (Given that we tend to greatly underestimate the extent of our uncertainty,[19] I believe we have a difficult time appreciating the force of this consideration and the value of such robustness.)

---

16 Likewise, knowledge of the various biases described in the seventh chapter can also lead one to give greater priority to suffering in practice without necessarily changing one's values. For example, a classical utilitarian may conclude that these biases probably lead most classical utilitarians to focus too little on suffering relative to what their moral values demand. No value change need be implied by this judgment.
17 Baumann, 2017c.
18 For a brief case for focusing on emerging technologies, see Effective Altruism Foundation, 2016.
19 See section 9.2.

Another problem with the argument in favor of focusing directly on future technology is that it seems to assume that the future will be determined by one or a few technologies on which we can exert a direct influence, as opposed to there being countless important technologies that each have a significant, yet not all-important impact on the world. The latter is arguably what we see today, and the question is then why we should expect it to be otherwise in the future.[20]

By analogy, consider factory farming: this is a clear example of a moral catastrophe made possible by modern technology. Yet there was no single technology that made factory farming possible. It required the confluence of many different technologies, such as big farms, big trucks, and big slaughterhouses, and it is doubtful that a focus on any one of these technologies would have been the best way to reduce the suffering caused by factory farming. Trying to make people connect with their own professed concern for non-human animals and the implications that follow from this concern would probably have been a better strategy — not least because this strategy would pertain to the whole institution of factory farming, including all the technologies involved.

In my view, this is likely also true of risks of astronomical suffering due to future technologies: increasing people's concern for suffering seems a more effective way to mitigate these risks, not least since there will probably be many crucial technologies and many people working to build these technologies.[21] Indeed, even if there were just one crucial technology to influence, it seems that one would still do better by increasing concern for suffering among the people developing it, again since such capacity-building seems uniquely robust, and since it likely taps into far greater technical expertise than that held by oneself or the few people currently focused on these "suffering risks".[22]

---

20 Some argue that artificial intelligence is likely to be such a crucial technology, Bostrom, 2014a; Gloor, 2016. Whether this is plausible is discussed in Hanson & Yudkowsky, 2013. One of the main arguments against the notion that a few AI systems will be all-important is that AI systems of the future are also, in light of recent trends in technological development, likely to be many and diverse — not a single, all-purpose "supersystem". For elaboration on this point, as well as more counterarguments, see Vinding, 2016b; 2017g; 2018i.
21 For another perspective, see Gloor, 2016, which I have critiqued in Vinding, 2018i.
22 There is also an important question of technology vs. values focus in relation to

12.5 How to Increase Concern for Suffering?

It stands as an open question how we can best promote greater concern for suffering. As noted above, there are various options, such as refining and disseminating arguments, familiarizing people with real-world cases of extreme suffering, increasing compassion through various techniques, and helping people close the gap between their ideals and their actions.[23] These different ways of promoting concern for suffering can be pursued through various media, such as writings, documentaries, and lectures.

Which of these methods and media are most effective is an empirical question. Investigations of this question should ideally inform our approach in practice, along with theoretical considerations about which approach seems most conducive to reducing future suffering all things considered. One such relevant consideration is that those who will contribute the most to the endeavor of reducing suffering — the researchers, influencers, and donors of tomorrow — are likely to be reached best through intellectual arguments, not least since a certain intellectual bent seems a prerequisite for developing an interest in reducing suffering *effectively*. This consideration suggests that our attempts to promote concern for suffering should have a strong intellectual component.[24]

---

factory farming in particular, namely whether we can best reduce the horrors of factory farming by investing in alternatives to "animal products" or by influencing people's values with arguments, Witwicki & Greig, 2018. It seems to me an open question which option is best for the sake of reducing factory farming, yet if one focuses on the expansion of humanity's moral circle more generally, i.e. if one includes wild animals and potential future minds in one's considerations, then the dissemination of arguments that pertain to all these beings (e.g. arguments against speciesism and for the moral importance of sentience) seems a better, more robust investment. And relative to the aim of reducing suffering, the promotion of concern for suffering seems even more robust and promising still.

23 This is by no means an exhaustive list. Another promising option may be to start a political party aimed toward reducing suffering, and which takes an empirical approach to politics, favoring the policies that seem to best reduce suffering all things considered. This is promising since political parties get much attention and can, if successful, exert a significant influence. Similarly, founding academic institutions and fields aimed toward the reduction of suffering also seems promising (see Daoust, 2012; 2015). Arguing for reductionist views of personal identity (empty/open individualism) may also be a promising strategy, Vinding, 2017b, "How Do We Reduce Suffering?"; Kaufman, 2018.

24 For more reasons to favor an intellectual approach, see Mannino, 2016.

Personal talents and skills are also relevant. For example, if one has a lot of knowledge and experience within a given field — e.g. psychology, philosophy, or politics — it may well be that relevant work within that field is the best one can do to increase humanity's understanding of and concern for suffering. Beyond that, the effectiveness of different methods and media will probably depend on the receiver, which suggests that we, as a collective, may do best by focusing on various strategies and media as opposed to just a single one.[25]

Finally, it is worth stressing once more that the greatest potential for increasing concern for suffering may well lie in connecting people with the concern for suffering they themselves already hold on some level, and to explore with them how they can best act in accordance with this concern. This means we should be especially careful not to antagonize people, as that risks losing this great potential, and to instead communicate in a measured way that most people will find appealing, and which makes them want to stand by rather than reject their own concern for suffering.

---

25 Speaking of receivers, it may also be worthwhile to focus the most on elite audiences, as elites may generally be more open to arguments and to changing their minds, and since they generally have more resources and can exert a disproportionate influence on the world, Mannino, 2016.

13

The Abolitionist Project

Suffering is mediated by certain physical states. And given that such states are subject to rigorous understanding and engineering, it is only natural to wonder whether the science of tomorrow will enable us to engineer suffering away for good — to make it impossible for sentient beings to experience any kind of mental or physical pain. This prospect has been explored most thoroughly by David Pearce, who coined the term "the abolitionist project", the project of abolishing suffering throughout the living world via technological means, which he argues is both technically feasible and morally urgent.[1]

13.1 A Theoretical Possibility: Convergent Arguments

Pearce is, as he himself stresses, not the first person to argue for this possibility. Medical doctor Lewis Mancini published a paper that outlined essentially the same idea in 1990.[2] In short, Mancini argued that various genetic conditions prove that it is possible to create painless yet functional sentient life. In his own words:

---

1   Pearce, 1995; 2017.
2   Mancini, 1990.

> A hypothesis is presented to the effect that everything adaptive which is achievable with a mind capable of experiencing varying degrees of both pleasure and pain (the human condition as we know it) could be achieved with a mind capable of experiencing only varying degrees of pleasure.[3]

This is precisely the same core idea that Pearce would defend five years later in his manifesto *The Hedonistic Imperative*.[4] Pearce was wholly unaware of Mancini's work at the time, which renders the degree of convergence all the more striking. Both predict it will become technically feasible to abolish pain and suffering, and they both explore genetic engineering and direct brain stimulation as viable and complementary options toward this end.[5]

Perhaps the most tangible and recent case in support of Mancini and Pearce's abolitionist project is that of genetic outlier Jo Cameron, a retired schoolteacher from Scotland. When Cameron reported no pain after what is normally an intensely painful operation, a group of doctors decided to examine her more closely. Cameron indeed proved to be an exceptional case in that she appears unable to feel pain.[6] And not only is Cameron unique in that she does not feel physical pain, but she also does not appear to feel mental pain — she reports never having felt anxious, stressed, or depressed.[7] Yet her inability to experience any such painful states has not prevented her from leading a normal and socially responsible life just the

---

3   Ibid., abstract.
4   Pearce, 1995.
5   Pearce also explores future designer drugs as a third option, Pearce, 2007. Both Pearce and Mancini agree that genetic engineering would, in Mancini's words, be "the definitive" technology in the long term, Mancini, 1990; Pearce, 2007. There does appear to be some disagreement on timescales, though. Mancini believes the abolition of suffering "will probably take thousands of years to implement" (Mancini, 1990, abstract), while Pearce expects it to be possible "over the next few centuries" (Pearce, 2007).
6   Other examples of people who cannot feel pain include the Marsili family (whose condition is now known as the Marsili syndrome), as well as some people with Riley-Day syndrome, Mancini, 1990. In terms of entire species, it seems that African mole-rats are insensitive to at least many kinds of pain, Eigenbrod et al., 2019.
7   Cameron's inability to feel both mental and physical pain appears to be due to mutations in both the FAAH gene and the FAAH-OUT gene, Habib et al., 2019.

same.[8] Indeed, Cameron is vegan and reportedly displays exceptional kindness and compassion.[9]

The case of Cameron merely hints at the prospect envisioned by Mancini and Pearce. Her case is but an early-stage proof of concept, presumably quite far from what could be achieved through future genetic engineering. Informed selection could further refine this already promising template thrown up by natural selection, in principle creating minds that are both incapable of suffering and super-humanly conscientious, intelligent, empathetic, etc. On Pearce's view, this rewriting of genomes to abolish suffering can and should be extended not just to humans, but to the entire living world, ultimately leading to the complete abolition of suffering.[10]

13.2 Practical Implications

Sentient life without suffering appears possible in principle. Yet the all-important question for us is what this implies in practice: what does it mean in terms of the actions we should take to best reduce suffering?

It may be tempting to think we should initially push for technologies that can make humans unable to suffer, not least since such a strategy that does not challenge people's anthropocentric values seems a realistic way to get a foot in the door. Yet there are many reasons to think this would not in fact be an optimal focus.

For one, Pearce himself describes humanity's values and ideas — not technological progress — as the key bottleneck to the realization of the abolitionist project.[11] If this is true, we should probably devote our marginal resources toward addressing this bottleneck directly. In particular: we should work to increase the priority and resources humanity devotes to the reduction of suffering.[12] As Pearce stresses: "Technical feasibility dif-

---

8 Ishak, 2019.
9 The Guardian, 2019.
10 Pearce, 2016; 2017, part III.
11 Pearce, 2007; 2016.
12 Note that this strategy would also funnel more resources into technologies that can reduce suffering, at least to the extent future agents influenced by this strategy will consider investments into such technologies a wise use of resources.

fers from sociological plausibility."[13] Which is to say that even if we grant that the complete abolition of suffering is technically feasible, this by no means implies that humanity will make it happen.

Indeed, some researchers, such as Brian Tomasik and Lukas Gloor, believe humanity is likely to vastly *increase* suffering in the future, even if we in principle could abolish it, as they think other aims are likely to override concern for suffering (as is the case today with factory farming).[14] Moreover, in expected value terms, future scenarios with large amounts of suffering merit greater priority than scenarios in which suffering is soon abolished, even if such catastrophic outcomes are much less likely.[15] This implies that significantly reducing the probability or badness of very bad future scenarios would have much greater expected value than, say, making the abolition of suffering on Earth happen one century from now rather than two.[16]

Thus, both when we consider issues of sociological plausibility and when we consider the expected disvalue of very bad outcomes, it seems significantly better to focus primarily on increasing the resources and priority humanity devotes to the reduction of suffering (for *all* future beings). Again, this is a uniquely robust strategy, and the fact that people of radically different empirical convictions, from David Pearce to Brian Tomasik, can agree that it is highly beneficial indeed lends it significant support.[17] It is a strategy that can lead more people to help us refine our views of how to best reduce suffering, which is probably optimal given how much we have yet to learn.

Another consideration against focusing primarily on technologies to abolish human suffering in the short term is that there is significant evidence that people who have experienced suffering are more sympathetic toward

---

13 Pearce, 2015.
14 Tomasik, 2011; 2013c; 2016d; Gloor, 2018.
15 Of course, if such catastrophic scenarios are sufficiently unlikely, they will not merit greater concern. However, since we cannot confidently rule out future scenarios that contain astronomical amounts of suffering, working to reduce the probability of such scenarios arguably is more important in expectation. We shall explore this subject deeper in the following chapter.
16 A similar point is made in Gloor, 2018.
17 Tomasik, 2015d; 2016d; Pearce, 2016; personal communication.

the suffering of others. For example, one study found that adults who reported having experienced childhood trauma had "elevated empathy levels compared to adults who did not experience a traumatic event" and that "the severity of the trauma correlated positively with various components of empathy."[18] Another study found that the experience of physical pain "motivated participants to be more sympathetic in their moral judgments", supporting the view that "pain can serve a positive psychosocial function."[19]

To be clear, the point here is not that human suffering is not worth preventing. Nor is the point that people cannot be empathetic without experiencing pain — the case of Jo Cameron alone disproves that claim. Rather, the point is that, in a world where we only have limited marginal influence, the evidence above does suggest that the abolition of human pain and suffering is not the main thing we should push for in the short term if our aim is to reduce suffering for all sentient beings.[20] Yes, it may well be possible to create minds that do not suffer and which are far more compassionate and determined to reduce suffering than any presently existing mind. Yet this does not contradict the claim that pushing for the abolition of suffering in humans is likely a suboptimal use of marginal resources at this point.

Indeed, in a world where humans are the only agents who can reduce — and increase — suffering in a systematic way, there is potentially a very great danger in making these uniquely powerful moral agents uniquely unable to experience suffering. It seems better to push for technologies and ideas that make us wiser, more compassionate, and in general better motivated and able to reduce suffering. This also holds true in the realm of human genetic

---

18 Greenberg et al., 2018. Similar findings are reported in Lim & DeSteno, 2016.
19 Xiao et al., 2015. For more discussion of the importance of experiencing suffering for caring about it, see Tomasik, 2014c. Of course, suffering can often have negative instrumental effects as well. For example, prolonged suffering, even if relatively mild, can lead people to become much less productive and less motivated to create positive change, and a complete and balanced perspective should also take this into account.
20 Again, this is by no means to say that we should ignore human suffering, even when it is merely mild. We have many good reasons not to, beyond just the intrinsic badness of the suffering in question. One of them is the reason mentioned in section 8.11: ignoring mild suffering, including human suffering in particular, likely conditions us slightly toward ignoring suffering in general.

engineering in particular: to the extent one should push for changes in this regard (and its controversial nature does cast some doubt on this), one should probably push primarily to boost traits such as compassion and prudence.[21]

Another reason not to use our limited resources to develop technologies that alleviate human suffering in the short term is that humans already devote a substantial amount of resources toward this aim.[22] By contrast, work to increase the priority humanity devotes to reducing the suffering of *all* sentient beings in the future is highly neglected.

13.3 Proportion Bias Revisited

In thinking about the abolitionist project, we should be especially mindful of our proportion bias: our tendency to care significantly more about helping 100 out of 100 individuals than about helping 100 out of 1,000, even though the absolute impact is the same.[23] For if we consider the abolition of suffering to be our main aim, we can easily come to think in rather binary terms: either we succeed and abolish suffering completely, or we fail to abolish it, and hence fail completely. Though perhaps intuitive, this is not a good way to think about the task of reducing suffering. After all, one would make a far bigger difference by preventing suffering from being multiplied by orders of magnitude beyond Earth than by abolishing all the suffering that would counterfactually have been on Earth alone.[24] Tacitly assuming that our aim should be to abolish suffering could bias us to focus on the latter — abolishing Earth-bound suffering. And yet we may well be able to reduce the greatest amount of suffering in expectation by trying to prevent catastrophic scenarios that contain astronomical amounts of suffering.[25]

This is why our focus should not primarily be to abolish suffering, but rather to reduce suffering as much as we can *in expectation*,[26] which would

---

21 A similar point is made in Tomasik, 2016d.
22 Tomasik, 2016d.
23 Fetherstonhaugh et al., 1997.
24 This point is also made in Gloor, 2018.
25 Tomasik, 2011; Gloor, 2018.
26 Within the bounds, that is, of whatever side-constraints one may wish to adopt, and given other factors one may wish to consider, *cf.* the general nature of suffering-focused eth-

at any rate entail the abolition of suffering in the best case.[27] Indeed, Pearce sometimes speaks of how, if we one day abolish suffering completely and "we are sure — absolutely sure — that we have done literally everything we can do to eradicate suffering elsewhere, perhaps we should forget about its very existence."[28] Yet if suffering warrants special moral concern, the truth is that we should never forget about its existence.[29] For even if we had abolished suffering throughout the living world, there would still be a risk that it might reemerge, and this risk would always be worth reducing.[30]

13.4 Other Pitfalls

Aiming for the complete abolition of suffering in humans could be risky in other ways as well. For example, if mild suffering makes moral agents more motivated and better able to reduce extreme suffering, then we should perhaps have more mild suffering (in moral agents) rather than less. After all, we know the future will contain a lot of suffering, and so the question is not whether there will be *any* suffering, but rather which path we can take that involves the *least* suffering. And it could well turn out that the path of least suffering will entail a lot of mild suffering and discontentment. Indeed, this point about discontentment is not based on pure speculation, as bad moods seem to have various instrumental benefits:

---

ics versus strictly suffering-minimizing views. My point here being that even though not all suffering-focused views are strictly suffering-minimizing views, virtually all suffering-focused views will still entail a significant degree of minimization in some sense. They will just differ on the specific constraints within which this minimization should be sought.
27 For a case for why we should focus on minimizing expected suffering, see Tomasik, 2007.
28 Pearce, 2008.
29 Indeed, in the ultimate theoretical limit, the moral aim of minimizing suffering would seem to require us to exploit all available resources in the universe to figure out and implement the best ways to reduce suffering in expectation.
30 We can be sure that this risk would always be there for solid theoretical reasons: the world is just far too complex for us to predict future outcomes with great precision, especially at the level of complex social systems, and hence we can never be absolutely certain that suffering will not reemerge. Thus, we should never lose sight of this risk.

Chapter 13

> There is … evidence that bad moods elicit more thorough and careful information processing than good moods (e.g., Clore, Schwarz, & Conway, 1994; Schwarz, 1990). These findings are consistent with Taylor's (1991) view that negative information stimulates a special set of processes designed to cope with threat. Yet even when a person is not threatened, bad moods seem to lead to greater processing. For example, Bless, Hamilton, and Mackie (1992) induced good and bad moods and then presented to participants information about someone else. They found that participants in good moods tended to cluster information and process it superficially, whereas people in bad moods processed it more carefully.[31]

It would be a remarkable coincidence if the actions that minimize mild discontentment in the world also happened to minimize extreme suffering, which highlights the importance of not conflating these aims.[32] We should keep our priorities straight and maintain a hard-nosed attitude. If Atlas carries his responsibility best in a discontented state, so be it.[33]

The abolition of suffering through technological means remains an idea very much worth exploring further. Yet, in thinking about where we should push the most at this point, it is important to keep expected value considerations in mind. In particular, we need to pay great attention to ways in which things might go very wrong.

---

31 Baumeister et al., 2001, p. 333. Again, the point here is not that one could not achieve similar benefits without bad moods in principle. Yet given limited resources and path dependencies, uncovering such alternative styles of cognition should probably not be a main priority, at least at this point.

32 *Cf.* Lewis, 2016. Similarly, it would be a remarkable coincidence if the genetic tweaks that enable moral agents like humans to best reduce suffering were also those that make these agents themselves maximally happy. These aims are not *a priori* identical.

33 We shall, however, see some reasons against this sentiment in chapter 17, not least reasons pertaining to social signaling: if we make reducing suffering seem like something that mostly induces discontent, this makes joining the cause seem less attractive. Indeed, as we shall see, there are good reasons to think that we can reduce suffering more effectively if we live genuinely fulfilled lives. Yet this does not contradict the claim that we should occasionally be willing to use bad moods to process things better and gain clearer perspectives, and that our ability to reduce suffering would likely be handicapped if we had no access to bad moods.

14

Reducing S-Risks

"An ounce of prevention is worth a pound of cure."

— Common saying

It is conceivable that future space colonization will create orders of magnitude more suffering than anything that could ever be contained on Earth. The risk that suffering might be realized on such a large scale has been called a "suffering risk" or "s-risk", and reducing such risks should be a priority on all views concerned about future suffering.[1]

14.1 Astronomical Negative Potential

The case for prioritizing s-risks rests on expected value calculations that factor in the enormous amount of suffering that could potentially be realized beyond Earth, which is more than ten million times greater than all the suffering that could exist on Earth in the future.[2] This magnitude is difficult to grasp intuitively, as our minds probably do not feel much of a difference between, say, the prospect of multiplying all suffering on

---

1 See Althaus & Gloor, 2016; Daniel, 2017; Baumann, 2017e; 2017f.
2 See the numbers in Bostrom, 2013, p. 18; 2014a, p. 103.

Earth ten thousand times versus ten million times, although the difference is crucial in terms of expected (dis)value. Consequently, we should be careful to control for our scope neglect when assessing the importance of reducing s-risks.

The other defining component of expected value calculations, besides magnitude, is the probability of the outcomes in question: how likely are outcomes with astronomical amounts of suffering? For if the probability of such outcomes were negligibly low — as we may dearly hope — then they would not merit priority. Unfortunately, it does not seem reasonable to consider this probability anything close to negligibly low, for various reasons.

First, the conditions that would have to obtain for an s-risk to be realized are not all that far-fetched. Roughly speaking, outcomes with astronomical suffering merely require that 1) large-scale space colonization will happen, and 2) this colonization will involve an insufficient concern for suffering. This combination of conditions can hardly be written off as having extremely low probability, especially given that serious projects aimed to colonize Mars already exist,[3] and that humanity currently displays a gross lack of concern for the suffering of sentient beings.

Second, s-risks are disjunctive — they can be realized in many different ways that bear little relation to each other.[4] Thus, as David Althaus and Lukas Gloor note:

> Even if the probability of any one specific scenario involving astronomical amounts of suffering ... is small, the probability that at least one scenario will occur may be fairly high. In this context, we should beware the disjunction fallacy ... according to which most people not only underestimate the probability of disjunctions of events, but they actually judge the disjunction as less likely than a single event comprising it.[5]

Third, there is ample historical precedent for humanity causing suffering on a large scale relative to its available resources, from systematic

---

3   Musk, 2018.
4   For a typology of different s-risks, see Baumann, 2018.
5   Althaus & Gloor, 2016.

genocides against fellow humans to the atrocity of factory farming. Indeed, an extension of some kind of factory farming into space is a concrete example of how an s-risk might materialize that neither history nor contemporary events allow us to dismiss out of hand.[6] More generally, *if* space colonization becomes feasible (which cannot be ruled out), and *if* technological progress makes it easy to create ever greater amounts of suffering (as seems to have been the case so far), then we cannot be at all confident that we will not create suffering on an astronomical scale in the future.[7]

To be clear, none of the arguments above rest on the claim that suffering on an astronomical scale is close to being the *most* likely outcome. As Tobias Baumann notes:

> To be concerned about s-risks, it is sufficient to believe that the probability of a bad outcome is not negligible, which is consistent with believing that a utopian future free of suffering is also quite possible.[8]

Indeed, as noted earlier, even if utopian outcomes in which suffering is soon abolished were most likely, these outcomes still contain comparatively little suffering in expectation, and hence they warrant far less priority (in terms of which scenarios we should work to improve or prevent) than do outcomes that contain astronomical amounts of suffering in expectation.

14.2 Space Expansion May Be Catastrophic by Default

Relative to views that place primary importance on reducing suffering, space colonization is probably very bad in expectation: a vastly greater potential to create suffering likely means vastly more suffering, including extreme

---

6   Other examples of how s-risks might be realized include the spread of wildlife into space, which may be valued by certain environmentalist groups, Tomasik, 2014e; Dello-Iacovo, 2016. For more concrete examples of s-risks, see Tomasik, 2011.
7   The same point is made in Baumann, 2017e, "S-risks are not extremely unlikely", from which the preceding section of mine has drawn heavily.
8   Baumann, 2017e. However, a case against considering such utopian outcomes most likely is found in Tomasik, 2017c.

suffering in particular.[9] Yet there are also reasons to believe space colonization would be bad on most other value systems. As mentioned in the introduction, author Phil Torres and political scientist Daniel Deudney have argued that the most likely outcomes of space colonization are catastrophic ones animated by perpetual conflict and insecurity.[10] In Deudney's words:

> Once large scale expansion into space gets started, it will be very difficult to stop. My overall point is that we should stop viewing these ambitious space expansionist schemes as desirable, even if they are not yet feasible. Instead we should see them as deeply undesirable, and be glad that they are not yet feasible. … Space expansion may indeed be inevitable, but we should view this prospect as among the darkest technological dystopias. Space expansion should be put on the list of catastrophic and existential threats to humanity, and not seen as a way [to] solve or escape from them.[11]

Deudney argues that expansion into space would significantly increase the probability of human extinction, which would imply that the avoidance of such expansion should be a priority for a wide variety of value systems, not just suffering-focused ones. For it is indeed perfectly possible for space expansion to both increase the probability of human extinction *and* increase future suffering in expectation — such as by vastly increasing the expected suffering in non-extinction scenarios, or by increasing the expected suffering in scenarios where humanity goes extinct.[12]

It is, of course, by no means certain that Torres and Deudney's analyses of space expansion are correct, yet they do at least merit closer study. We should think deeply about these matters before we make choices that irreversibly lead to bad outcomes.

---

9   Tomasik, 2013f. Also, from a short-term perspective, space colonization would entail a large opportunity cost in terms of foregone opportunities to reduce suffering on Earth.
10   Deudney, 2020; Torres, 2018a; 2018b.
11   Cabrera, 2016.
12   For example, human extinction could be brought about by AI systems, and such systems could in principle go on to cause suffering on an astronomical scale, Althaus & Gloor, 2016; Sotala & Gloor, 2017. If space expansion is indeed most likely to lead to global insecurity, as Deudney argues, then it might also increase such AI-driven s-risks, as insecurity likely increases the risk of AI arms races, Tomasik, 2013l.

14.3 The Astronomical Atrocity Problem

Space colonization would lead to an enormous amount of suffering in expectation, which in turn raises the moral problem of whether any positive good we could bring about through space expansion could ever outweigh or justify this (in expectation) vast amount of suffering.[13] I call this the "astronomical atrocity problem", and it was already raised in the introduction, where we asked whether the creation of extremely happy lives for, say, a population of 10^{32} people can justify the creation of lives full of extreme suffering for 10^{24} people.[14] Put bluntly, can *any* amount of positive goods outweigh billions of Holocausts of suffering?[15]

It is worth highlighting some of the many pitfalls that pertain to our thinking about this problem, such as subtle equivocations and false extrapolations. For instance, one may have a mildly aversive experience that one considers readily outweighed by happiness, and then conclude from this that astronomical amounts of extreme suffering can probably also be outweighed by greater amounts of extreme happiness. Yet such an extrapolation jumps over many crucial issues and arguments in need of addressing.

First, it overlooks the distinction between a mere aversive component of an experience and actual suffering: a bad overall experience.[16] Second, it overlooks the important distinction between mild suffering — i.e. a mildly bad overall experience — and extreme forms of suffering, which I and others have argued are of incomparable moral significance.[17] Third, it overlooks the difference between interpersonal and intrapersonal tradeoffs: many philosophers have defended the view that one person's happiness cannot outweigh or justify the suffering, much less the extreme suffering,

---

13   Note that the conclusion defended in the third chapter implies that we should ideally not colonize space, at least not for the sake of creating happiness.
14   As Brian Tomasik points out, this ratio of happiness to suffering appears wildly optimistic relative to the ratio we should realistically expect given future space expansion, Tomasik, 2013f; 2017c.
15   This was also referred to as the "problem of evil 2.0": how can we justify creating far more suffering than the sum total of suffering that has been endured on Earth so far? A similar allusion to the problem of evil is found in Tomasik, 2014e.
16   See the introductory section in the first chapter and Klocksiem, 2016.
17   See chapters four and five.

of someone else.[18] Fourth, it ignores widely endorsed asymmetrical views in population ethics that do not consider it important to bring happy lives into existence, yet which do consider it important to prevent miserable lives.[19] Fifth, it ignores the view that the value of positive goods has diminishing returns whereas the disvalue of suffering does not.[20] Sixth, it ignores the view that there exists a threshold of a certain intensity *and* duration of suffering such that, beyond this threshold, no amount of positive goods can outweigh it.[21]

These are all crucial issues to consider carefully in the context of this problem.[22] For example, if one believes the value of positive goods has weakly diminishing returns whereas the disvalue of suffering does not, the implication could well be that the prevention of suffering deserves supreme priority on an astronomical scale (even if this were not the case on a terrestrial scale). The same applies to threshold views that consider it impossible for a certain intensity and duration of suffering to be outweighed: if one thinks there is such a threshold at what corresponds to, say, the intense lifelong suffering of 10^{20} beings, then preventing such suffering ought to be the dominant priority.[23] In short, we should be careful about naive extrapolations and assumptions when thinking about astronomical stakes.

It should be noted, however, that one need not even find the astronomical atrocity problem particularly compelling in order to prioritize reducing s-risks, since some scenarios involving astronomical suffering are so bad that they are vastly dominated by suffering *on any measure*. Such hell scenarios would be worth avoiding on *all* value systems, and hence we should

---

18 See section 3.2.
19 See section 1.1.
20 See section 6.2.
21 Such a view is endorsed in Mayerfeld, 1999, pp. 179-180. This view is different from the one I defended in the fifth chapter in that the latter only pertains to intensity.
22 There are many other important arguments and positions to consider as well, such as the other views explored in the sixth chapter, as well as asymmetry arguments of the kind explored in the first chapter — e.g. the view that it is far worse to create a dystopia than it is to fail to create a utopia.
23 Note that views that assign diminishing returns to the value of positive goods can be roughly equivalent to such threshold views — if the value of positive goods levels off asymptotically, then there is also, on such views, a threshold of suffering that can never be counterbalanced by positive goods.

all be able to agree on reducing the risk of their realization — a risk that, at least according to some, is also non-negligible.[24]

Also worth emphasizing here is the importance of being strategic about the prospect of space colonization. For if space colonization is indeed unavoidable, it should ideally be done by agents who show significant concern for suffering. Consequently, efforts to dissuade relatively compassionate agents from space expansion in ways that make other, less compassionate agents more likely to dominate space would probably be harmful. Which is to say that a dogmatic opposition to space colonization could well be bad, possibly even astronomically bad.[25]

14.4 S-Risk Reduction: Neglected and Tractable

Expected value calculations about beings suffering in immense numbers beyond Earth are quite remote from what our brains are adapted to think and care about. It should therefore not be surprising that few resources have been devoted to reducing s-risks, even as reasoned arguments lend considerable support to such a priority. Indeed, many of the biases reviewed in the seventh chapter plausibly work against s-risk reduction, as does the "illusion of control": our well-documented tendency to overestimate the control we have over events.[26] This illusion may lead us to overestimate the probability that we can control the future in positive directions, and thus lead us to neglect the risk of very bad outcomes.

The low level of resources devoted thus far to s-risk reduction provides an additional reason to direct our marginal resources toward this endeavor. It suggests there is much low-hanging fruit ready to be picked, particularly in the form of information that provides critical guidance for how we can best reduce s-risks.[27]

---

24   Sotala & Gloor, 2017. Note too how the view of Deudney outlined in the previous section supports the claim that the probability of outcomes that are very bad (by virtually any standard) is non-trivial.
25   A similar point is made in Tomasik, 2011, "Why we should remain cooperative".
26   Thompson, 1999.
27   A similar point is made in Althaus & Gloor, 2016; Baumann, 2017e.

Chapter 14

Yet not only does s-risk reduction seem highly neglected, it also seems more tractable than comparable large-scale objectives, such as utopia creation. Put simply: the asymmetry in ease of realization suggests that it is more cost-effective (for a wide variety of value systems) to work to avoid dystopian outcomes than to create utopian ones.[28] As Althaus and Gloor write:

> Creating vast amounts of happiness in the future without also causing vast amounts of suffering in the process requires a great deal of control over future outcomes; it essentially requires hitting a bulls-eye in the space of all possible outcomes. … By contrast, steering our future trajectory *away* from broad classes of bad or very bad outcomes could arguably be easier.[29]

The neglectedness and (comparative) tractability of s-risk reduction renders it a plausible priority on many different value systems, not just suffering-focused ones.[30]

14.5 How Can We Reduce S-Risks?

An important step we can take to reduce risks of astronomical suffering at this point is to advance research on the issue. Such research inevitably entails great uncertainty, speculation even, which highlights the importance of approaching it with great sophistication. Advancing s-risk research requires one to think through many strange possibilities while avoiding the trap of unwarranted confidence in speculative hypotheses.[31] This is a difficult task. What we need is to build a research program on s-risks that embodies intellectual humility and deep scholarship.

Beyond research, it is also difficult to overstate the importance of cooperation, which is especially important in relation to s-risks. For again,

---

28   See section 1.3.
29   Althaus & Gloor, 2016.
30   The same point is made in ibid.
31   *Cf.* section 9.2.

everyone can agree that a large class of s-risks are extremely important to avoid, including the very worst ones, which means we should ideally act in ways that capitalize on this broad consensus — doing so could potentially channel vast resources into s-risk reduction. This would be much better than non-cooperative actions that risk curtailing future resources dedicated to s-risk reduction, and thus greatly increase future suffering in expectation.[32]

Another important point, especially in light of our vast uncertainty, is that we should opt for robust strategies. In particular, the promotion of concern for suffering, including suffering due to s-risks, seems uniquely robust and promising given the uncertainty we face.[33] It can help build a flexible capacity in the form of a community and resources dedicated to reducing s-risks — a capacity that can help us clarify which problems we should prioritize, and in turn contribute to solving these problems once we understand them better.

Such a mundane mission of capacity-building, cooperation, and research-promotion hardly seems like a particularly attractive thing to be affiliated with for our status-obsessed brains. Nor does it stir our emotions in a way remotely comparable to, say, the prospect of saving a single, identifiable victim from excruciating horror. Yet these facts about our immediate attitudes do not imply that this mission is not indeed the main mission we should be pursuing at this point to prevent the greatest amount of horrors we can. I suspect it is.[34]

---

32 Again, a similar point is made in Tomasik, 2011, "Why we should remain cooperative" as well as in Althaus & Gloor, 2016, "Concluding thoughts".
33 This strategy also has the benefit of being robust for reducing suffering in the near future as well as in scenarios that do not contain astronomical suffering.
34 For more suggestions about how we can best reduce s-risks, see Baumann, 2017c, "How can we avert s-risks?"

15

Donating to Reduce Suffering

Monetary donations can be a great way to reduce suffering. Whether it is the main thing one should focus on depends on how much money one expects to donate, what one might be able to do otherwise, and what other people are doing.

15.1 The Case for Prioritizing Monetary Donations

"Earning to give" is the pursuit of a high-earning career for the purpose of donating large amounts of money to charity. The perhaps most compelling argument in favor of earning to give has to do with replaceability: many people will apply for the limited jobs at non-profit organizations and within academia, and the good done by a given person who gets such a job must therefore be compared to the good that could have been done by the person who would otherwise have gotten the job. By contrast, if one earns to give, it is unlikely that someone who would otherwise have done the same job would donate a comparable amount. Thus, by earning to give, one can expand the pie of altruistic resources, and in turn increase the number of people doing direct work, such as activists and researchers.[1]

---

1   Tomasik, 2006b; Todd, 2017a.

However, there are many caveats to this naive case for prioritizing donations. For one, the difference between two people hired in academia may be significant — for instance, it would be much better if a philosophy department hired a person who focuses primarily on suffering reduction than if it hired someone who defends, say, environmental conservation. Beyond that, the difference between two people pursuing the same objectives in the same job can also be great. For example, just like donations can create more activists and researchers, so can good activism, and hence even a marginal difference between two different activists in the same job may correspond to the good done by a large donation — say, if activist A creates six new activists a year while activist B would create only four. A similar point applies to researchers: better researchers can help us gain more clarity about what we should prioritize, in effect rendering our future investments more efficient.

Two key questions to consider in relation to which path is optimal are 1) what are the main bottlenecks relative to suffering reduction? Is it more money, better research, or better outreach? And 2) where do you, with your unique talents and opportunities, have the greatest potential to contribute? The answers to these questions will depend on specifics that vary across different times and different people. For example, even if research is the crucial bottleneck now, it may be that money will be the crucial bottleneck in a couple of decades. Similarly, even if the main bottleneck for suffering reduction is money at the level of the broader community, it will still be true of many people that they can make the greatest difference by doing research, given their talents.

The caveats above notwithstanding, it will still be true of many people that they can best help the cause by focusing primarily on donations because of their comparative potential. And in any case, one need not earn to give in order to contribute meaningfully with monetary donations. As we shall now see, even a modest monetary contribution can make a big difference in expectation.[2]

---

2   For advice on earning to give, see Brian Tomasik's site, reducing-suffering.org, "Making money to reduce suffering".

15.2 Promising Ways to Donate

The organization Animal Charity Evaluators estimates that a thousand dollars donated to their most recommended charities can be expected to spare more than 4,000 beings from a life of horror on a factory farm.[3] This estimate should be taken with a considerable grain of salt, yet even if it is off by a full order of magnitude, it remains true that the difference we can make with just a modest donation is incomprehensibly great. Indeed, for the majority of us who enjoy a relatively safe and cozy existence, it is difficult to get a sense of the significance of sparing even a single life on a factory farm — a life where you are endlessly confined to a tiny space, where one or more of your body parts are cut off without anesthesia,[4] and where you die in terror and agony in a slaughterhouse. And we are even less able to understand the significance of sparing *many* such lives, not least given our scope neglect.

Such a donation to reduce the suffering of non-human animals exploited by humans is a promising way to reduce suffering, also since the secondary effects are likely quite positive: beyond directly sparing beings from terrible lives, it probably also marginally increases general concern for suffering and for non-human beings in the long term. However, in terms of such positive long-term consequences, other ways to donate appear even more promising.[5]

After all, working to increase concern for non-human animals exploited on farms in particular is probably not the best thing we can do to increase concern for *all* non-human beings, such as animals in the wild or other kinds of beings who may suffer in the future (even as it likely does have a positive effect in this regard).[6] Nor does such increased concern for non-human beings necessarily translate effectively into concern for suffering in particular, as opposed to other things one may value for other beings

---

[3] Animal Charity Evaluators, 2018. Similar estimates are found in Tomasik, 2012a.
[4] As noted earlier, it is common practice to "debeak" birds so they do not peck each other to death, and to cut off the tails of piglets so other pigs do not bite their tails. It is also common practice to cut off the testicles of male piglets without anesthesia, American Veterinary Medical Association, 2013.
[5] And again, the long-term consequences should arguably dominate our considerations strongly (see the previous chapter and section 9.8.3).
[6] Vinding, 2016c.

(even though, again, its effect on humanity's concern for suffering is likely positive).[7]

Thus, relative to the goal of reducing suffering, it is probably significantly better to invest in efforts aimed more directly toward this particular goal, such as efforts to increase concern for the suffering of all sentient beings, as well as efforts to research how we can reduce suffering most effectively. In other words, to invest in the creation of more flexible capacity focused on reducing suffering.

An organization that seeks to promote concern for suffering, including at the level of governance, is the Organisation for the Prevention of Intense Suffering (OPIS), while an organization that pursues research, including research on s-risk reduction, is the Center on Long-Term Risk (CLR).[8] Similar aims are pursued at the Center for Reducing Suffering (CRS), which does work on suffering-focused ethics, prioritization research, and s-risk reduction (I should note that I am a co-founder of CRS).

Whether these particular organizations are the best bets in these areas is not the point here. The point is rather that the areas they focus on likely are the best areas to invest in to reduce suffering, and supporting these organizations is one way to promote these areas.

15.3 Beware Naive Views on Donations

Once again, a few caveats and clarifications are in order. First, one should be careful not to understate the importance of investing, in various senses. For example, if one has a thousand dollars, and if one can invest this money in a business that will enable one to donate hundreds of thousands of dollars later, then investing in this business would likely be optimal.[9]

---

7   See section 11.6.
8   In the interest of full disclosure, I should note that the founder of OPIS, Jonathan Leighton, is a friend of mine, and that my work on this book has been partly funded by the parent organization of CLR. That I personally know the people behind the organizations cited here does not reflect cronyism. Rather, it reflects the fact that the group of people who have made it their foremost aim to reduce suffering for all sentient beings is rather small at this point in time. I should also note that CLR reports not being strongly funding-constrained, whereas OPIS presently *is* constrained strongly by funding.
9   For an essay on starting a startup to donate money, see Todd, 2014.

Chapter 15

Similarly important is self-investment: if you invest in your own education and skills, this can make you far more capable down the line, whether that means earning more or being a better researcher. The same applies to investments in one's own health and well-being. Indeed, among those who are most dedicated to reducing suffering, it is a common mistake to neglect personal needs so as to be able to donate to worthy causes in the short term. This is probably not optimal, as it overlooks how much of a potential asset one is oneself.

Another important caveat is that different actions aimed toward reducing suffering, including donations in particular, do not for the most part differ by several orders of magnitude in terms of how much suffering they reduce in expectation (when the resource investment is roughly equal). This point has been stressed at length by Brian Tomasik, who argues that uncertainty and second-order effects tend to limit the expected difference in impact between actions that at first sight seem to differ radically in expected value.[10] (However, it still remains true that some pursuits will be significantly better in expectation than others.)

Being aware of this can prevent us from making naive statements about vast differences in impact, and keep us realistic about the magnitude of the uncertainty before us — in all we do. No less importantly, it may help reduce any snobbery we might be tempted to entertain in relation to the actions that others are pursuing to reduce suffering, and help us appreciate such actions rather than lament them. Some donations toward the alleviation of suffering, even if directed toward suboptimal targets, will for the most part be better than none. In general, encouraging and nurturing the growth of a tiny will to reduce suffering is better than thwarting it.

---

10   Tomasik, 2014b. See also Baumann, 2017d.

16

Researching the Question

"An investment in knowledge pays the best interest."

— Apocryphally attributed to Benjamin Franklin

Reducing suffering effectively requires extensive research. Investing most of our resources in a course of action that further research would have revealed suboptimal is an all too realistic prospect, which highlights the importance of investing in research. Our level of knowledge largely determines how qualified our actions to reduce suffering will be.

16.1 A Hard-Nosed Research Project

Ideally, we should establish a formal research project with the same depth and status as, say, physics has today: a field of study focused solely on suffering reduction, pursued at every university worthy of the name, with the most promising students all over the world seeking to major in this field of suffering reduction.[1] Less ideally, given the limited amount of resources

---

[1] Author Robert Daoust has argued for the establishment of a similar research field, although he advocates for a study of suffering in general, not a project focused specifically on its reduction, Daoust, 2012; 2015. See also Siu, 1988.

and people currently devoted to the cause, we should seek to promote research that can help us answer the most basic questions concerning what our priorities should be.

A few notes are worth making on the nature of the research we should promote. First, the research needs to integrate knowledge from many different fields. It is not enough to merely focus on, say, the biology of suffering in particular, as extensive and important as this subject is. We must also draw on insights from physics — to get a sense of what will ultimately be possible for a future civilization, for example — as well as the social sciences, to get a sense of what is *likely* for a future civilization, and to understand how we can best steer clear of bad outcomes at the social and political level.

A wide knowledge of many fields seems necessary for forming a sophisticated view of what our priorities should be. And the fact that a single crucial consideration could change our priorities significantly further highlights the importance of combing through many different fields to uncover such crucial insights.[2]

This search for information should be done in a hierarchical and recursive manner. Hierarchical in that it should prioritize exploring the areas and questions that seem most relevant in light of all we know (while still allowing plenty of room for random search to uncover unexpected avenues of insight). And recursive in that the new discoveries we make should continually update our future research directions: if we discover something new that seems uniquely important, we should obviously revise our previous research plans so as to study this new thing closer.

Such recursion should be done with care, however, as one can easily get caught up in a recursive loop of speculative inferences animated by confirmation bias. It is therefore essential that we practice insistent skepticism toward any idea announcing itself in our minds as "clearly the most important thing to focus on", and that we maintain humility about the extent of our uncertainty and the difficulty of the question before us. As hinted earlier, there is a great risk that we commit prematurely to juvenile conjectures and trust untested models too strongly.[3]

---

[2] Tomasik, 2013m; Bostrom, 2014b.
[3] See section 9.2.

Relatedly, it is important that we promote research that embodies deep scholarship and is laser-focused on the question. Rather than succumbing to the human tendency of telling pretty stories and devising impressive theories that make us feel good and reflect well on us, our research should primarily be guided by a hard-nosed determination to acquire accurate views. This can be painful and demanding, yet unless we think our drive to impress others and comfort ourselves with wishful and fancy theories is more important than extreme suffering, this is what we must do.[4]

16.2 Open Research Questions

The following are probably among the questions that deserve the greatest priority.

16.2.1 Social Dynamics and Suffering

How can we best increase concern for suffering and motivate people to reduce it in cost-effective ways? How can we entrench concern for suffering at the level of our institutions and make its reduction a collective priority?[5] How can we promote a sound research project focused on suffering reduction?[6]

---

[4] This point applies to researchers themselves as well as to their patrons: both are likely biased toward comforting and impressive research.
[5] As noted, most people seem to already agree, at least on reflection, that suffering deserves priority. The main challenge is arguably to translate this concern "in theory" into concern in practice. OPIS is an example of an organization that focuses on entrenching concern for suffering at an institutional level.
[6] One way to study this may be to examine how existing research fields and intellectual movements have been established. See e.g. Sheikh et al., 2011; Vaughan, 2016; Vermeulen, 2017.

16.2.2 S-Risk Reduction

How might s-risks come about? Which s-risks are most important to address, and how can they best be mitigated?[7] How can we best increase the priority and resources devoted to s-risk reduction? And which ways of communicating about s-risks are safest relative to information hazards and the danger of inadvertently increasing s-risks?[8]

16.2.3 The Structure of Reality and Its Implications for Suffering

What implications do various theories about the structure of reality have for suffering reduction? For example, what do the most plausible models of the universe at large (e.g. of cosmic expansion and the probability of the emergence of sentient life elsewhere) imply for suffering reduction? Is the universe infinite, and if so, what are the implications?[9]

Our answers to this last group of questions are bound to be speculative, yet given the potential stakes, having just slightly more qualified answers could still be highly valuable. More generally, we should be realistic about how complete our knowledge of suffering reduction can be in light of the complexity involved. It may well be that we can at most get, say, 25 percent of the way toward having complete knowledge about optimal suffering reduction (not defined in any precise way; I am merely trying to convey a basic point). Yet this does not render the quest for such knowledge any less important. It is still crucial that we work to gain as much knowledge as we can.[10]

So far, very few people have done serious research on how we can best reduce suffering for all sentient beings. Yet such research is too important to be beholden to the quirks of a few people. We need contributions from

---

7   See s-risks.org.
8   Bostrom, 2011a; Wiblin & Lempel, 2018.
9   Tomasik, 2006c; Bostrom, 2011b; Oesterheld, 2017; Vinding, 2017f.
10 Yet when does one stop refining one's views and go out and act? I think this question rests on a false premise, as though it is either-or. We should always do both: update our views based on the latest research and then take action based on those findings.

many people with different talents and intuitions so as to even out distorting idiosyncrasies, and to reduce the gaping holes in the current state of suffering reduction research.

Getting more people to do such research is probably among the most urgently important things to do at this point. We can do this by becoming such researchers ourselves, by donating toward such research, or by disseminating the research done so far and encouraging people to critique and build on it.

17

The Importance of Self-Investment

The overwhelming horror of suffering can readily make one feel like dropping everything in one's hands so as to jump to the aid of the afflicted. This is an admirable sentiment, yet care must be taken to channel the underlying desire to help in the right directions. In particular, neglecting ourselves and being unconcerned about our appearance are among the last things we should do to reduce suffering.

17.1 Self-Care: A Top Priority

We can help others more effectively if we take good care of ourselves. This is just a psychological fact. It is a mistake to think about self-care in zero-sum terms — as though investing in one's own well-being is tantamount to stealing resources from the pursuit of helping others. Quite the opposite is true. After all, whatever good one can do in a state of self-neglect, one can probably do much better in a healthy and happy state, implying that, even from a purely altruistic perspective, it is more than worth investing in one's own health and happiness.

It may be natural for us to think that we must neglect ourselves to reduce suffering effectively, perhaps even to the point of painful self-sacrifice. One can speculate that this sentiment stems from a drive to signal that we are doing things for others,[1] or it may simply be because zero-sum thinking is intuitive. Yet whatever its origin, it is important that we transcend it. Painful self-sacrifice is generally not a recipe for effectiveness and success.[2] Indeed, it is probably ideal to mostly enjoy the efforts one makes to reduce suffering, both for optimal motivation in the moment and for long-term sustainability.

So even though we are in some sense always facing a condition of maximal urgency, having the *feeling* of urgency is probably not optimal for us in order to do what needs to be done, at least most of the time. A calmly motivated state animated by a cerebral understanding of the urgency of suffering, as well as a strong desire to alleviate it — i.e. compassion — is probably better.[3] And the good news, as noted earlier, is that compassion appears to be something we can in fact cultivate to a significant extent, and that such cultivation not only makes us more attentive to suffering, but also decreases the empathic distress we experience in the face of suffering.[4] Thus, increasing one's compassion appears a worthwhile investment benefiting both oneself and others.[5]

(A similarly positive result that contradicts zero-sum thinking and shows personal happiness to be compatible with efforts to reduce suffering is that doing things for others, including donating to charity, actually seems to make people happier.[6] Doing good for others versus doing good for ourselves really is a false dichotomy in many ways.)

Another important investment that is difficult to overestimate is good sleep, which research suggests is critical for our mental health.[7] And yet

---

1   Miller, 1996.
2   Leighton, 2017b.
3   For one, such a state appears more sustainable and compatible with rational thought than do intense feelings of urgency or empathy, Bloom, 2016. To be clear, the point Bloom makes is not that strong feelings of empathy do not have their place, but merely that they make us prone to burnout and bias if care is not taken, and that such feelings are often less desirable than common sense would suggest.
4   Fredrickson et al., 2008; Klimecki et al., 2013; Condon et al., 2013; Bloom & Davidson, 2015; Sözmen, 2016; Weng et al., 2018.
5   One can find good compassion meditations by searching for "compassion meditation" on YouTube.
6   Dunn et al., 2008; Dunn et al., 2011; Mogensen, 2011.
7   One study (Winsler et al., 2015) of more than 27,000 teenagers found that getting less than eight hours of sleep was associated with progressively worse mental health

Chapter 17

sleep is not the only form of rest we need. We also need leisure: relaxed downtime that keeps stress at bay and refuels motivation, and which enables us to live wholesome lives. After all, it is quite plausible that, to effectively reduce suffering, most people will need to have other goals and pursuits in life than just to reduce suffering. Being singularly focused on a goal like that is hardly congruent with human nature.[8] Thus, a standard amount of leisure and enjoyable activities is probably advisable.

One reason adequate rest is so important is to reduce mistakes that require many good actions to undo. There is a real risk that we will make such mistakes, and this risk increases significantly when we are stressed out or sleep deprived. In part for this reason, it seems better to function stably at 80 percent performance than to work at 99 percent with a high risk of crashing and burning out. Beyond minimizing the risk of crash-induced mistakes that can cause setbacks and damage one's reputation, consistent performance at 80 percent is also just more sustainable, and hence likely more productive in the long term. Doing 80 percent of what *seems* like a hundred percent may well be a hundred percent, all things considered.[9]

Another thing worth emphasizing is the surprising importance of self-compassion and self-forgiveness.[10] Intuitively, one might think self-forgiveness stands in opposition to productivity: toughness and unforgiving discipline must surely be the way. Yet it turns out the opposite is true. Self-forgiveness and self-compassion are key to self-discipline and productivity.[11] As psychologist Kelly McGonigal notes: "[S]elf-compassion—being supportive and kind to yourself, especially in the face of stress and failure—is associated with more motivation and better self-control."[12]

---

outcomes. Similar associations between sleep quality and mental health have been found in adults, Al-Khani et al., 2019.
8 Flanagan, 1991.
9 An analogy to health may be instructive here: being obsessive and striving for perfection in everything is generally less healthy than a more relaxed and balanced approach. See also Tomasik, 2010; 2015e.
10 Jonathan Leighton's "Guided Meditation for Activists" (Leighton, 2017a) was created specifically "to support self-forgiveness … especially for people aiming to reduce suffering in the world."
11 McGonigal, 2012, chap. 6.
12 Ibid., p. 148.

Conversely, those who are hardest on themselves for procrastinating are generally those who procrastinate the most.[13] This is not surprising when we consider how other people best motivate us: kind and encouraging people are usually more motivating in the long run compared to unkind and shaming ones. And the lesson here is simply that the same is true at the level of self-talk and self-motivation.

Thus, we have good reason to recognize with self-kindness that we are not perfect. We all make mistakes, and that is okay. Likewise, it is worth acknowledging to ourselves that it can in fact be quite difficult to be alive, and that we nonetheless tend to do quite well for a creature full of conflicting drives, and who evolved to live in a very different kind of world.[14]

17.2 Investing in Future Abilities and Influence

Crucial self-investments go beyond just investments in self-care. To become an effective force for good, we also need to invest in building the requisite skills and networks.

This includes learning a lot of information in the form of book knowledge, but it also includes learning how to communicate well, as well as building social skills. Such learning is often not best pursued in a formal setting. Yet formal education can still be important, not least due to the status it confers, which can in turn lead to greater influence.[15]

Investments that increase productivity are important too. This includes building habits conducive to productivity — reducing distractions and training one's self-control and concentration. It also means investing in a few high-quality things rather than many mediocre ones: a reliable computer, a good mattress, a comfortable chair, etc.

Another thing we must invest in to have a positive influence is to look presentable, as trivial as it may seem. It is simply a fact about human nature that we judge each other based on appearances, and partly for good reasons:

---

13 Ibid.
14 In relation to this point, I think there are many valuable insights in Soares, 2015-2016.
15 For more on the importance of education for reducing suffering, see Tomasik, 2013k.

our appearance signals our conscientiousness and our degree of connection with social reality. Not caring what one looks like and how one comes across is usually not a healthy sign, and it is unlikely to be a path toward respect and influence. By contrast, looking well-groomed, friendly, and well-adjusted makes one seem more likable and worth associating with.[16]

17.3 Avoiding Social Failure

If we are to be effective in motivating people to reduce suffering, we must be realistic about what in fact motivates people, and orient our strategy accordingly. For the truth is that people care greatly about signaling: we want to associate with things and people that make us seem cool and high-status, and to avoid associating with things that make us seem uncool and low-status.[17] Unfortunately, having suffering reduction as one's highest priority is not, it seems, cool or high-status in the eyes of most people.[18] It carries an undercurrent of negativity and bleakness that most of us would prefer not to be associated with. And even more damningly, it may be natural to suspect that the people who share this aim are mostly sad losers — people we would prefer not to be associated with.[19] As crude as this all sounds, these social concerns likely do represent a major obstacle to people's willingness to prioritize the reduction of suffering.[20]

The remedy to this PR problem is to be just the opposite, namely people whom others very much do want to associate with: friendly, well-adjusted, accomplished people who inspire others with deep compassion and integrity. To be clear, it is not that we should merely *appear* to be such people in order to attract others. Rather, the point is that we have good reasons pertaining to self-care and self-investment to actually *be* such

---

16 *Cf.* the halo effect, Nisbett & Wilson, 1977. For more on self-investment for altruistic impact, see Todd, 2017b.
17 Simler & Hanson, 2018.
18 To clarify: it is not cool or common to focus predominantly on reducing suffering *in practice*, yet at the level of *ideals*, it is very common, as the Future of Life Institute's survey shows.
19 See section 7.12.
20 To be clear, I am not pointing fingers here. Perceptions of other people's status influence all of us to a significant extent, whether we realize it or not.

well-adjusted, accomplished people, and the signaling consideration outlined above is just an additional reason that points in the same direction.

Another mode of social failure worth avoiding is to turn people off by making suffering reduction seem impossibly demanding. Just as it may be optimal to only require 80 percent performance from ourselves, it is probably also ideal to avoid making near-maximum demands on others. For example, one study of charitable giving found that people were willing to give more, and felt they had more reasons to give, when demands were low compared to when they were high.[21]

The same may well apply to efforts to reduce suffering in general: if such efforts appear to demand a very large commitment, people will probably not be motivated to join them, whereas if the effort required appears modest and compatible with personal fulfillment, the motivation to join will likely be higher. Thus, we have good reason to only make relatively modest demands for the most part, and even more good reasons to hold ourselves to merely human standards and to live fulfilling lives (lest we make reducing suffering seem unappealing). Movements and memes that become associated with strenuous demandingness are probably not durable.

A similar way we can risk turning people off is by coming across as too "saintly".[22] For it turns out that people have a tendency to put down and dislike other people who display strong moral motivation — what is known as "do-gooder derogation".[23] This suggests that it is best if those seeking to reduce suffering come across more as normal people than as saints. Again, it is not that those aiming to reduce suffering should be dishonest about their true moral convictions, but simply that there are pragmatic reasons to not display one's moral behavior too strongly. (At least to outsiders; it could perhaps serve a positive function relative to ingroup do-gooder competition.)

---

21 Bruder & Tanyi, 2014, "V. General Discussion". A plausible explanation for this pattern may be that people start to disengage and dismiss the issue at hand when they feel the demands become too personally costly, *cf.* Cameron & Payne, 2011.
22 A similar point is made in Hanson, 2015.
23 Minson & Monin, 2011.

By contrast, there is no reason to hide the positive feelings one feels when helping others,[24] as positive feelings about altruistic behavior not only make it seem more inviting to join these altruistic efforts, but they also, it turns out, lead people to evaluate these efforts as more praiseworthy. Conversely, when people report feeling bad about altruistic actions, such actions are seen as less praiseworthy.[25] This is another reason to ensure that we ourselves feel genuinely fulfilled in our efforts to reduce suffering.

Contrary to what one may naively think in the face of the immense horror and urgency of suffering, we do in fact have good reason to invest in ourselves, both in terms of self-care and skill-building. Such self-investment not only makes us much better off ourselves, but it also allows us to be more effective in our endeavor to create a world with less suffering. And no endeavor could be more important.

---

24 Again, studies suggest that giving to and helping others can make us happier, Dunn et al., 2008; Dunn et al., 2011; Mogensen, 2011.
25 Yudkin et al., 2018. A complication, however, is the phenomenon of tainted altruism: when people also pursue and attain selfish ends in their altruistic behavior, or when altruistic behavior is mostly motivated by self-interest, this tends to be evaluated as worse even than purely selfish behavior, Newman & Cain, 2014. Thus, while it seems good to be happy in altruistic endeavors (and to display it), it may be best to mostly separate self-interested pursuits from altruistic ones.

18

What You Can Do

A key impediment to realizing our enormous potential to reduce suffering is not knowing which concrete steps to take. Thus, in this final chapter, I will briefly list some concrete things everyone can do.

18.1 Join the Community

Getting in touch with people who share the goal of reducing suffering can help maintain and boost our motivation to reduce suffering. It can connect us with role models and mentors, and enable us to collectively refine our ideas about reducing suffering — others can correct our blindspots, and we can correct theirs.

Specifically, one can join Facebook groups such as "Negative Utilitarianism and Suffering-Focused Ethics" and "Reducing Wild-Animal Suffering", as well as subreddits like r/negativeutilitarians and r/wildanimalsuffering. One can also join local animal activist groups to take part in discussions and meet inspiring people (though such groups are often not primarily focused on reducing suffering).

18.2 Donate to the Cause

Consistent donations, even in small amounts, can be highly valuable. Not only can donations fund important work, but they can also help the donor form the habit and self-identity of being someone who contributes to the cause of reducing suffering.

Specific organizations I recommend supporting, in part because they have considerable funding gaps, include Animal Ethics, the Organisation for the Prevention of Intense Suffering (OPIS), and the Center for Reducing Suffering (CRS). (As noted earlier, the latter is a new organization that I have co-founded.) I especially recommend donating to organizations that focus *primarily* on reducing suffering, and which take *all* future suffering into account.

18.3 Learn More

Learning more about reducing suffering includes reading about directly related subjects, such as the psychology of empathy and compassion, and the philosophy of antispeciesism and wild-animal suffering. It means reading the works of suffering-focused thinkers such as Jonathan Leighton, Jamie Mayerfeld, David Pearce, Brian Tomasik, and Clark Wolf (the more the better; it is important to avoid the common pitfall of relying too strongly on any one person's views). Yet it is also paramount to learn more about the world in general — about physics, economics, psychology, etc. — as well as learning how to optimize personal productivity and health.

Learning more about such relevant subjects is a concrete task we can always pursue to become more qualified agents of change, and it is difficult to overstate its importance. As mentioned, our knowledge largely determines how effective we can be in creating a better world.

18.4 Inform Others About Suffering-Focused Ethics and Practice

This can mean talking about the issue with open-minded friends and students who might be interested and willing to contribute. It can also mean informing larger groups of people, such as by sharing links, writing articles, or making YouTube videos. After all, we live in a time where a single hyperlink can change a person's life completely.

18.5 Reflect on Your Career

In terms of our ability to make an impact, there is perhaps no decision more important than our choice of career. It is therefore worth investing significant resources into getting this decision right.

Examples of promising careers for reducing suffering include:

Earning to give: pursuing a high-earning job to donate a large fraction of the salary to effective organizations.

Suffering-focused outreach: this can mean doing the kind of work pursued by OPIS, which includes presenting blueprints for compassionate governance to influential institutions and educating the public in creative ways.

Researching how we can best reduce suffering: one can explore open research questions such as those presented in chapter 16, and do scholarly work on the ideas presented in the second part of this book, such as cooperation, non-human suffering, abolitionism, and s-risks.

Developing suffering-focused ethics: one could make an elaborate case for the importance of reducing s-risks, or one could explore and develop ideas like those presented in the first part of this book.

It is generally advisable to aim for a career that fits both one's talents and personal needs, as this enables one to contribute better and more sustainably.

I have argued that our opportunity to reduce suffering is the greatest, most important opportunity we have. Even if you disagree with many of the arguments presented here, I hope that I have at least convinced you that the reduction of suffering deserves special priority. I sincerely hope you will consider taking action to reduce suffering.

Recommended Websites

abolitionist.com
algosphere.org
animal-ethics.org
centerforreducingsuffering.org
ea-foundation.org
hedweb.com
longtermrisk.org
magnusvinding.com
preventsuffering.org
reducing-suffering.org
simonknutsson.com
s-risks.org
suffering-focused-ethics.surge.sh

Acknowledgments

I have many people to thank here. David Pearce encouraged me and gave me feedback throughout the entire writing process. David has probably influenced my views on ethics more than anyone else, and it is safe to say that this book would not have existed had it not been for his work. I can never thank him enough. Also crucial has been the support of Tobias Baumann, who has encouraged me and provided support by reading early drafts and commenting, as well as in other ways, for which I am very grateful. I am also deeply grateful to Alex Nil for his extensive feedback, and for providing financial support for many book projects of mine.

Brian Tomasik deserves deep thanks as well, both for voicing support for this project in its early stages and for his work. In terms of the inspiration Brian's work has provided for this book, the extent to which it is cited in the bibliography speaks for itself.

I am deeply grateful to David Althaus, Lara André, Fredi Bechtoldt, Olivier Bertrand, Guillaume Chauvat, Robert Daoust, Ben Davidow, Denis Drescher, Mads Gertz, Manu Herrán, Oscar Horta, Sille Juul Kjærbo, Simon Knutsson, Jonathan Leighton, Jamie Mayerfeld, Rupert McCallum, L. Reeves, Joachim Robert, and Sebastian Sudergaard Schmidt for reading an early draft and providing useful comments.

I also owe great thanks to the "suffering reducers" reading group, particularly Janique Behman, Guillaume Chauvat, and Alex Nil, who discussed my book and gave me useful inputs. I also owe great thanks to the people who participated in the "S-weekend" in Switzerland, not least Janique Behman and Jonathan Leighton, who organized it, and Dani Sieber, who hosted it. It gave me important insights and encouragement.

My thanks also go to Jamie Mayerfeld, Thomas Metzinger, Richard Ryder, and Clark Wolf. I thank them for their important work, which has influenced this book greatly, and for expressing support and encouragement.

Deep thanks also go to Cynthia Stewart for her tremendous effort in proofreading and commenting with heroic discipline and stamina. Cynthia's keen eye has improved the book in many ways.

I am grateful to Greg Colbourn for hosting me at the Athena Hotel in Blackpool. The idea to write this book was conceived while I stayed at the hotel and enjoyed Greg's hospitality.

My work on this book was supported by the Effective Altruism Foundation, though the views expressed herein do not necessarily reflect the views of EAF. I thank EAF for working tirelessly to reduce suffering, as well as for having supported me despite not agreeing with all the views I express.

Finally, I thank Sille for supporting me, and for caring so deeply about all suffering beings. I cannot express the depth of my appreciation for you in words.

Bibliography

Acton, H. & Watkins, J. (1963). Symposium: Negative Utilitarianism. *Proceedings of the Aristotelian Society, Supplementary Volumes*, 37, pp. 83-114.

Akerma, K. (2010). Theodicy shading off into Anthropodicy in Milton, Twain and Kant. Tabula Rasa, 41.

Akerma, K. (2014). Antinatalist Manifesto: On the Ethics of Antinatalism Challenging Human and Animal Procreation. Retrieved from:
http://akerma.de/Antinatalist%20Manifesto_Karim%20Akerma.pdf

Alexander, S. (2015). How Bad Are Things? Slate Star Codex. Retrieved from:
https://slatestarcodex.com/2015/12/24/how-bad-are-things/

Al-Khani, A. et al. (2019). A cross-sectional survey on sleep quality, mental health, and academic performance among medical students in Saudi Arabia. *BMC Research Notes*, 12, 665.

Alloy, L. & Abramson, L. (1988). Depressive Realism: Four Theoretical Perspectives. In Alloy, L. (ed.), *Cognitive Processes in Depression*. New York, NY, US: The Guilford Press.

Althaus, D. (2018). Descriptive Population Ethics and Its Relevance for Cause Prioritization. Retrieved from:
https://forum.effectivealtruism.org/posts/CmNBmSf6xtMyYhvcs/descriptive-population-ethics-and-its-relevance-for-cause

Althaus, D. & Gloor, L. (2016). Reducing Risks of Astronomical Suffering: A Neglected Priority. Retrieved from:
https://foundational-research.org/reducing-risks-of-astronomical-suffering-a-neglected-priority/

Altman, N. (1988/2017). *The Nonviolent Revolution: A Comprehensive Guide to Ahimsa – the Philosophy and Practice of Dynamic Harmlessness*. Brooklyn, New York: Gaupo Publishing.

Amato, J. (1990). *Victims and Values: A History and a Theory of Suffering*. New York: Greenwood Press.

American Veterinary Medical Association. (2013). Literature Review on the Welfare Implications of Swine Castration. Retrieved from:
https://www.avma.org/KB/Resources/LiteratureReviews/Documents/swine_castration_bgnd.pdf

Anderson, R. (2017). *Alleviating World Suffering: The Challenge of Negative Quality of Life*. Cham, Switzerland: Springer.

Andorno, R. & Baffone, C. (2014). Human Rights and the Moral Obligation to Alleviate Suffering. In Green, R. & Palpant, N. (eds.), *Suffering and Bioethics*. Oxford New York, NY: Oxford University Press.

André, L. (2019). The relevance of sentience: shaping nonanthropocentric politics (master's thesis). University of Minho.

Animal Charity Evaluators. (2018). Donation Impact. Retrieved from: *https://animalcharityevaluators.org/donation-advice/donation-impact/*

Animal Ethics. (2012/2016). Speciesism. Retrieved from: *http://www.animal-ethics.org/speciesism/*

Animal Ethics. (2013/2016). Working for a future with fewer harms to wild animals. Retrieved from: *http://www.animal-ethics.org/wild-animal-suffering-section/helping-animals-in-the-wild/working-for-a-future-with-fewer-harms-to-wild-animals/*

Animal Ethics. (2014). Helping animals in the wild. Retrieved from: *https://www.animal-ethics.org/wild-animal-suffering-section/helping-animals-in-the-wild/*

Animal Ethics. (2017a). Scope insensitivity: failing to appreciate the numbers of those who need our help. Retrieved from: *https://www.animal-ethics.org/scope-insensitivity-failing-to-appreciate-the-numbers-of-those-who-need-our-help/*

Animal Ethics. (2017b). Animals and politics. Retrieved from: *https://www.animal-ethics.org/animals-and-politics/*

Anonymous. (2012). 44 Days Of Hell – The Murder Of Junko Furuta. Retrieved from: *https://ripeace.wordpress.com/2012/09/14/the-murder-of-junko-furuta-44-days-of-hell/*

Anonymous. (2015). Negative Utilitarianism FAQ. Retrieved from: *https://www.utilitarianism.com/nu/nufaq.html*

Aristotle. (ca. 350 BC/2009). *The Nicomachean Ethics*. Oxford New York: Oxford University Press.

Arrhenius, G. (2000). Future generations: A challenge for moral theory (PhD thesis). Uppsala University. Retrieved from: *http://www.diva-portal.org/smash/get/diva2:170236/FULLTEXT01.pdf*

Arrhenius, G. & Rabinowicz, W. (2015). Value Superiority. In Hirose, I. & Olson, J. (eds.), *The Oxford Handbook of Value Theory*. Oxford: Oxford University Press.

Atasoy, S. et al. (2017). Harmonic brain modes: a unifying framework for linking space and time in brain dynamics. *The Neuroscientist*, 24(3), pp. 277-293.

Axelrod, R. (1984/2006). *The Evolution of Cooperation*. New York: Basic Books.

Axelrod, R. (1997). *The Complexity of Cooperation: Agent-Based Models of Competition and Collaboration*. Princeton, N.J: Princeton University Press.

Aydede, M. (2014). How to Unify Theories of Sensory Pleasure: An Adverbialist Proposal. *Review of Philosophy and Psychology*, 5, pp. 119-133.

Bailey, J. (1997). *Utilitarianism, Institutions, and Justice*. New York, N.Y: Oxford University Press.

Bain, D. & Brady, M. (2014). Pain, Pleasure, and Unpleasure. *Review of Philosophy and Psychology*, 5(1), pp. 1-14.

Baker, K. (2015). Pigs chopped in half with ceremonial machetes while they're still alive … so villagers can dip money in their blood for good luck: Vietnamese ceremony condemned by animal groups. The Daily Mail. Retrieved from: *https://www.dailymail.co.uk/news/article-2966668/Pigs-chopped-half-ceremonial-machetes-alive.html*

Balcombe, J. (2006/2007). *Pleasurable Kingdom: Animals and the Nature of Feeling Good.* Basingstoke: Macmillan.

Balcombe, J. (2016). *What a Fish Knows: The Inner Lives of Our Underwater Cousins.* New York: Scientific American/Farrar, Straus, and Giroux.

Bastardi, A. et al. (2011). Wishful Thinking: Belief, Desire, and the Motivated Evaluation of Scientific Evidence. *Psychological Science*, 22(6), pp. 731-732.

Bastian, B. et al. (2012). Don't Mind Meat? The Denial of Mind to Animals Used for Human Consumption. *Personality and Social Psychology Bulletin*, 38(2), pp. 247-256.

Bastian, B. (2018). *The Other Side Of Happiness: Embracing a More Fearless Approach to Living.* London: Allen Lane, an imprint of Penguin Books.

Baumann, T. (2017a). Should altruists prioritize the far future? Retrieved from: *http://prioritizationresearch.com/should-altruists-prioritize-the-far-future/*

Baumann, T. (2017b). Should altruists focus on artificial intelligence? Retrieved from: *http://prioritizationresearch.com/should-altruists-focus-on-artificial-intelligence/*

Baumann, T. (2017c). Arguments for and against moral advocacy. Retrieved from: *http://prioritizationresearch.com/arguments-for-and-against-moral-advocacy/*

Baumann, T. (2017d). Uncertainty smoothes out differences in impact. Retrieved from: *http://prioritizationresearch.com/uncertainty-smoothes-out-differences-in-impact/*

Baumann, T. (2017e). S-risks: An introduction. Retrieved from: *http://s-risks.org/intro/*

Baumann, T. (2017f). S-risk FAQ. Retrieved from: *http://s-risks.org/faq/*

Baumann, T. (2018). A typology of s-risks. Retrieved from: *http://s-risks.org/a-typology-of-s-risks/*

Baumann, T. (2019a). Risk factors for s-risks. Retrieved from: *http://s-risks.org/risk-factors-for-s-risks/*

Baumann, T. (2019b). Thoughts on longtermism. Retrieved from: *http://s-risks.org/thoughts-on-longtermism/*

Baumeister, R. et al. (2001). Bad is stronger than good. *Review of General Psychology*, 5, pp. 323-370.

Beckstead, N. (2013). On the Overwhelming Importance of the Far Future (PhD thesis). Rutgers University. Retrieved from: *https://rucore.libraries.rutgers.edu/rutgers-lib/40469/PDF/1/play/*

Benatar, D. (1997). Why It Is Better Never to Come into Existence. *American Philosophical Quarterly*, 34(3), pp. 345-355.

Benatar, D. (2006). *Better Never to Have Been: The Harm of Coming into Existence.* Oxford New York: Clarendon Press Oxford University Press.

Benatar, D. (2015). The Misanthropic Argument for Anti-natalism. In Hannan, S. et al. (eds.), *Permissible Progeny?: The Morality of Procreation and Parenting.* New York: Oxford University Press.

Benatar, D. (2017a). *The Human Predicament: A Candid Guide to Life's Biggest Questions.* New York: Oxford University Press.

Benatar, D. (2017b). Kids? Just Say No. Aeon Magazine. Retrieved from: *https://aeon.co/essays/having-children-is-not-life-affirming-its-immoral*

Benatar, D. & Wasserman, D. (2015). *Debating Procreation: Is It Wrong to Reproduce?* Oxford New York: Oxford University Press.

Bennett, J. (1995). *The Act Itself.* Oxford New York: Clarendon Press Oxford University Press.

Bentham, J. (1789/2007). *An Introduction to the Principles of Morals and Legislation*. Mineola, N.Y: Dover Publications.

Berridge, K. & Kringelbach, M. (2011). Building a neuroscience of pleasure and well-being. *Psychol Well Being*, 1(1), pp. 1-3.

Berridge, K. & Robinson, T. (2016). Liking, wanting, and the incentive-sensitization theory of addiction. *Am Psychol*, 71(8), pp. 670-679.

Bertrand, O. (2016). Reducing suffering or adding years of life? Effective altruism and divergences in value judgments and worldviews. Retrieved from: *https://www.academia.edu/26705132/Reducing_suffering_or_adding_years_of_life_Effective_altruism_and_divergences_in_value_judgments_and_worldviews*

Birch, J. (2017). Animal sentience and the precautionary principle. *Animal Sentience*, 16(1).

Blackburn, S. (2001/2003). *Ethics: A Very Short Introduction*. Oxford New York: Oxford University Press.

Bless, H., Hamilton, D., & Mackie, D. (1992). Mood effects on the organization of person information. *European Journal of Social Psychology*, 22, pp. 497-509.

Bloom, P. (2016). *Against Empathy: The Case for Rational Compassion*. New York, NY: Ecco, an imprint of HarperCollins Publishers.

Bloom, P. [UNSW] (2019). The Pleasures of Suffering. Retrieved from: *https://www.youtube.com/watch?v=_cbVUxiRY8A*

Bloom, P. & Davidson, R. [The Aspen Institute] (2015). Empathy, Is It All It's Cracked Up to Be? Retrieved from: *https://www.youtube.com/watch?v=CJ1SuKOchps*

Boehm, C. (1999/2001). *Hierarchy in the Forest: The Evolution of Egalitarian Behavior*. Cambridge, Mass: Harvard University Press.

Bollard, L. [Centre for Effective Altruism] (2018). Ending Factory Farming | EAG 2018 San Francisco. Retrieved from: *https://www.youtube.com/watch?v=WcAaWL0geRU*

Boltanski, L. (1999). *Distant Suffering: Morality, Media, and Politics*. Cambridge, U.K. New York: Cambridge University Press.

Bostrom, N. (2011a). Information Hazards: A Typology of Potential Harms from Knowledge. *Review of Contemporary Philosophy*, 10, pp. 44-79.

Bostrom, N. (2011b). Infinite Ethics. *Analysis and Metaphysics*, 10, pp. 9-59.

Bostrom, N. (2013). Existential Risk Prevention as Global Priority. *Global Policy*, 4(1), pp. 15-31.

Bostrom, N. (2014a). *Superintelligence: Paths, Dangers, Strategies*. Oxford, United Kingdom: Oxford University Press.

Bostrom, N. (2014b). Crucial Considerations and Wise Philanthropy (talk delivered at a conference on effective altruism held at All Souls College). Transcript retrieved from: *http://www.stafforini.com/blog/bostrom/*

Bothara, S. (1987/2009). *Ahimsa: The Science of Peace, as Developed by Jain Thinkers*. Jaipur, Prakrit Bharati Academy.

Braithwaite, V. (2010). *Do Fish Feel Pain?* Oxford New York: Oxford University Press.

Breyer, D. (2015). The Cessation of Suffering and Buddhist Axiology. *Journal of Buddhist Ethics*, 22, pp. 533-560.

Brighton, H. & Gigerenzer, G. (2012). Homo Heuristicus: Less-is-More Effects in Adaptive Cognition. *Malays J Med Sci*, 19(4), pp. 6-16.

Brown, C. (2015). Fish intelligence, sentience and ethics. *Anim Cogn*, 18(1), pp. 1-17.

Bruder, M. & Tanyi, A. (2014). Overdemanding Consequentialism? An Experimental Approach. *Utilitas*, 26(3), pp. 250-275.

Brülde, B. (2010). Happiness, Morality, and Politics. *Journal of Happiness Studies*, 11, pp. 567-583.

Burkeman, O. (2012). *The Antidote: Happiness for People Who Can't Stand Positive Thinking*. New York: Faber and Faber.

Busnot, D. (1714/2015). *History of the Reign of Muley Ismael, the Present King of Morocco*. New York: Ishi Press International.

Cabrera, J. (1996/2014). *A Critique of Affirmative Morality: A Reflection on Death, Birth and the Value of Life*. Brasília: Julio Cabrera Editions.

Cabrera, J. (2019). *Discomfort and Moral Impediment: The Human Situation, Radical Bioethics and Procreation*. Newcastle upon Tyne: Cambridge Scholars Publishing.

Cabrera, L. (2016). An Interview with Daniel Deudney. World Government Research Network. Retrieved from:
http://wgresearch.org/an-interview-with-daniel-h-deudney/

Cameron, C. & Payne, B. (2011). Escaping affect: how motivated emotion regulation creates insensitivity to mass suffering. *J Pers Soc Psychol*, 100(1), pp. 1-15.

Camus, A. (1947/1991). *The Plague*. New York: Vintage Books, a division of Random House, Inc.

Carey, R. (2015). *The Effective Altruism Handbook*. Centre for Effective Altruism, Oxford, Oxfordshire United Kingdom.

Carlson, E. (2000). Aggregating harms – Should we kill to avoid headaches? *Theoria*, 66(3), pp. 246-255.

Cassell, E. (1991/2004). *The Nature of Suffering and the Goals of Medicine*. New York: Oxford University Press.

Caviola, L. [Effective Altruism Global] (2017). Against Naive Effective Altruism | Lucius Caviola | EAGxBerlin 2017. Retrieved from:
https://www.youtube.com/watch?v=-2oRgxxafXk

Caviola, L. et al. (2019). The Moral Standing of Animals: Towards a Psychology of Speciesism. *Journal of Personality and Social Psychology*, 116(6), pp. 1011-1029.

Center on Long-Term Risk. (2016). Bibliography of Suffering-Focused Views. Retrieved from:
https://longtermrisk.org/bibliography-of-suffering-focused-views/

Chao, R. (2012). Negative Average Preference Utilitarianism. *Journal of Philosophy of Life*, 2(1), pp. 55-66.

Chouliaraki, L. (2006). *The Spectatorship of Suffering*. London Thousand Oaks, Calif: SAGE Publications.

Christiano, P. (2013). Against moral advocacy. Retrieved from:
https://rationalaltruist.com/2013/06/13/against-moral-advocacy/

Churchland, P. (2011). *Braintrust: What Neuroscience Tells Us about Morality*. Princeton, N.J: Princeton University Press.

Clore, G., Schwarz, N., & Conway, M. (1994). Affective causes and consequences of social information processing. In Wyer, R. & Srull, T. (eds.), *Handbook of social cognition*. Hillsdale, NJ: Erlbaum.

Cohen, S. (2001). *States of Denial: Knowing About Atrocities and Suffering*. Cambridge, UK Malden, MA: Polity Blackwell Publishers.

Colebrook, R. (2018). Toward a Science of Morals (PhD thesis). City University of New York. Second chapter retrieved from:

*https://www.academia.edu/36014561/
Does_Moral_Realism_Matter_The_Moral_Vindication_Argument*

Collins, C. & Kays, R. (2014). Patterns of Mortality in a Wild Population of White-Footed Mice. *Northeastern Naturalist*, 21(2), pp. 323-337.

Collins, R. (2004). *Visigothic Spain, 409-711*. Oxford, OX, UK Malden, MA, USA: Blackwell Pub.

Condon, P. et al. (2013). Meditation Increases Compassionate Responses to Suffering. *Psychological Science*, 24(10), pp. 2125-2127.

Contestabile, B. (2005/2018). Antinatalism and the Minimization of Suffering. Retrieved from:
http://www.socrethics.com/Folder2/NU.htm

Contestabile, B. (2010). On the Buddhist Truths and the Paradoxes in Population Ethics. *Contemporary Buddhism*, 11(1), pp. 103-113. Draft version retrieved from:
http://socrethics.com/Folder2/Paradoxes.htm

Contestabile, B. (2014). Negative Utilitarianism and Buddhist Intuition. *Contemporary Buddhism*, 15(2), pp. 298-311. Draft version retrieved from:
http://www.socrethics.com/Folder2/Buddhism.htm

Contestabile, B. (2016a). The Denial of the World from an Impartial View. *Contemporary Buddhism*, 17(1), pp. 49-61.

Contestabile, B. (2016b). Why I'm Not a Negative Utilitarian: A Review of Toby Ord's Essay. Retrieved from:
http://www.socrethics.com/Folder3/Negative-Utilitarianism-Review.htm

The Cowherds. (2015). *Moonpaths: Ethics and Emptiness*. New York, NY: Oxford University Press.

Crisp, R. (2003). Equality, Priority, and Compassion. *Ethics*, 113(4), pp. 745-763.

Daleiden, J. (1998). *The Science of Morality: The Individual, Community, and Future Generations*. Amherst, N.Y: Prometheus Books.

Daniel, M. (2017). S-risks: Why they are the worst existential risks, and how to prevent them (EAG Boston 2017). Retrieved from:
https://foundational-research.org/s-risks-talk-eag-boston-2017/

Daoust, R. (2012). The Study and Management of Pain Require a New Discipline about Suffering: Paper for the "Making Sense of Pain" Inter-Disciplinary.Net conference, Prague (19-20-21 May 2012). Retrieved from:
https://drive.google.com/file/d/0B0UU47Q_u9YmUF91TU5YU2FpZ1E/view

Daoust, R. (2015). Introduction to Algonomy. Retrieved from:
http://www.algosphere.org/intro/index.html

Darwin, C. (1872). *The Expression of Emotion in Man and Animals*. Oxford, England: Appleton.

Davidow, B. (2013). Why Most People Don't Care About Wild-Animal Suffering. Retrieved from:
http://reducing-suffering.org/why-most-people-dont-care-about-wild-animal-suffering/

Davis, G. (2013). Moral Realism and Anti-Realism Outside the West: A Meta-Ethical Turn in Buddhist Ethics. *Comparative Philosophy*, 4, pp. 24-53.

Dawkins, R. (1976/2006). *The Selfish Gene*. Oxford New York: Oxford University Press.

Dawkins, R. (2011). Richard Dawkins on vivisection: "But can they suffer?". Retrieved from:
http://boingboing.net/2011/06/30/richard-dawkins-on-v.html

Dello-Iacovo, M. (2016). On terraforming, wild-animal suffering and the far future. Retrieved from: *https://sentience-politics.org/files/Dello-Iacovo-On-terraforming-wild-animal-suffering-and-the-far-future.pdf*

Deseret News. (1996). Online Document: How the Public Views Animal Rights. Retrieved from: *https://www.deseret.com/1996/8/20/19261207/online-document-how-the-public-views-animal-rights*

Deudney, D. [Colgate University] (2010). Daniel Deudney: The Sky is the Limit. Retrieved from: *https://www.youtube.com/watch?v=neBJEaGdVYQ*

Deudney, D. [World Government Research Network] (2016). Daniel Deudney on the Practical Politics of Global Integration. Retrieved from: *https://www.youtube.com/watch?v=6D09e6igS4o*

Deudney, D. (2020). *Dark Skies: Space Expansionism, Planetary Geopolitics, and the Ends of Humanity*. Oxford: Oxford University Press.

Diener, E. & Emmons, R. (1984). The Independence of Positive and Negative Affect. *Journal of Personality and Social Psychology*, 47(5), pp. 1105-1117.

Dockterman, E. (2013). Nearly One Million Chickens and Turkeys Unintentionally Boiled Alive Each Year in U.S. Time Magazine. Retrieved from: *http://nation.time.com/2013/10/29/nearly-one-million-chickens-and-turkeys-unintentionally-boiled-alive-each-year-in-u-s/*

Donaldson, S. & Kymlicka, W. (2011). *Zoopolis: A Political Theory of Animal Rights*. Oxford England New York: Oxford University Press.

Donnely, R. [Centre for Effective Altruism] (2017). Moral Trade - Ruairí Donnelly. Retrieved from: *https://www.youtube.com/watch?v=RoomSp0THJs*

Dostoevsky, F. (1879/1950). *The Brothers Karamazov*. New York: Vintage.

Dunn, E. et al. (2008). Spending Money on Others Promotes Happiness. *Science*, 319(5870), pp. 1687-1688.

Dunn, E. et al. (2011). If money doesn't make you happy, then you probably aren't spending it right. *Journal of Consumer Psychology*, 21(2), pp. 115-125.

Dworkin, R. (1981). What Is Equality?, Part II: Equality of Resources. *Philosophy and Public Affairs*, 10, pp. 283-345.

Effective Altruism Foundation. (2016/2017). The Importance of the Far Future. Retrieved from: *https://ea-foundation.org/blog/the-importance-of-the-far-future/*

Eidelman, S. et al. (2009). The existence bias. *J Pers Soc Psychol*, 97(5), pp. 765-775.

Eigenbrod, O. et al. (2019). Rapid molecular evolution of pain insensitivity in multiple African rodents. *Science*, 364(6443), pp. 852-859.

Elwood, R. (2011). Pain and Suffering in Invertebrates? *ILAR Journal*, 52(2), pp. 175-184.

Emilsson, A. G. (2019). Logarithmic Scales of Pleasure and Pain: Rating, Ranking, and Comparing Peak Experiences Suggest the Existence of Long Tails for Bliss and Suffering. Retrieved from: *https://qualiacomputing.com/2019/08/10/logarithmic-scales-of-pleasure-and-pain-rating-ranking-and-comparing-peak-experiences-suggest-the-existence-of-long-tails-for-bliss-and-suffering/*

Engel, M. (1983). A Happy Life Afterward Doesn't Make Up for Torture. *The Washington Post*. Retrieved from: *https://www.washingtonpost.com/archive/opinions/1983/06/26/ a-happy-life-afterward-doesnt-make-up-for-torture/ ab680b30-237b-4b7a-b6da-1f7ab3da9208/*

Epperson, G. (1997). *The Mind of Edmund Gurney*. Madison London: Fairleigh Dickinson University Press Associated University Presses.

Evans, E. (1898). *Evolutional Ethics and Animal Psychology*. New York: D. Appleton and Company.

Everett, J. et al. (2016). Inference of trustworthiness from intuitive moral judgments. *J Exp Psychol Gen*, 145(6), pp. 772-87.

Everett, J. et al. (2018). The costs of being consequentialist: Social inference from instrumental harm and impartial beneficence. *Journal of Experimental Social Psychology*, 79, pp. 200-216.

Faria, C. (2014). Equality, priority and nonhuman animals. *Dilemata: International Journal of Applied Ethics*, 14, pp. 225-236,

Faria, C. (2016). Animal ethics goes wild: The problem of wild animal suffering and intervention in nature (PhD thesis). Pompeu Fabra University.

Faria, C. & Paez, E. (2015). Animals in need: The problem of wild animal suffering and intervention in nature. *Relations: Beyond Anthropocentrism*, 3(1), pp. 7-13.

Fehige, C. (1998). A pareto principle for possible people. In Fehige, C. & Wessels U. (eds.), *Preferences*. Berlin: Walter de Gruyter.

Felice, W. (1996). *Taking Suffering Seriously: The Importance of Collective Human Rights*. Albany: State University of New York Press.

Fernandez, J. (ed.) (2010). *Making Sense of Pain: Critical and Interdisciplinary Perspectives*. Oxford: Inter-Disciplinary Press.

Ferrara, E. & Yang, Z. (2015a). Quantifying the effect of sentiment on information diffusion in social media. *PeerJ Computer Science*, 1: e26.

Ferrara, E. & Yang, Z. (2015b). Measuring Emotional Contagion in Social Media. *PLOS ONE*, 10(11): e0142390.

Ferrell, B. (1996). *Suffering*. Sudbury, Mass: Jones and Bartlett Publishers.

Fetherstonhaugh, D. et al. (1997). Insensitivity to the Value of Human Life: A Study of Psychophysical Numbing. *Journal of Risk and Uncertainty*, 14, pp. 283-300.

Fink, S. (2011). Independence and Connections of Pain and Suffering. *Journal of Consciousness Studies*, 18(9-10), pp. 46-66.

Flanagan, O. (1991). *Varieties of Moral Personality: Ethics and Psychological Realism*. Cambridge, Mass: Harvard University Press

Fodor, J. (2014). How to get an Ought from an Is. Retrieved from: *https://thegodlesstheist.com/2014/10/02/how-to-get-an-ought-from-an-is/*

Fodor, J. (2019). A Case for Ethical Naturalism. Retrieved from: *https://thegodlesstheist.com/2019/04/11/a-case-for-ethical-naturalism/*

Foot, P. (2002). *Virtues and Vices and Other Essays in Moral Philosophy*. Oxford New York: Clarendon Press Oxford University Press.

Fordyce, W. (1988). Pain and suffering: A reappraisal. *American Psychologist*, 43(4), pp. 276-283.

Fox, M. (1996). *The Boundless Circle: Caring for Creatures and Creation*. Wheaton, IL, U.S.A: Quest Books.

Francione, G. (2000/2011). *Introduction to Animal Rights: Your Child or the Dog?* Temple University Press.

Francione, G. (2008). *Animals as Persons: Essays on the Abolition of Animal Exploitation.* New York: Columbia University Press.

Francione, G. (2013). Abolitionist Animal Rights/Abolitionist Veganism: in a Nutshell. Retrieved from:
https://www.abolitionistapproach.com/ abolitionist-animal-rights-abolitionist-veganism-in-a-nutshell/

Francione, G. (2019). New Atheism, Moral Realism, and Animal Rights. Retrieved from:
https://medium.com/@gary.francione/ new-atheism-moral-realism-and-animal-rights-e729c970dd09

Fredrickson, B. et al. (2008). Open Hearts Build Lives: Positive Emotions, Induced Through Loving-Kindness Meditation, Build Consequential Personal Resources. *J Pers Soc Psychol*, 95(5), pp. 1045-1062.

Frick, J. (2014). 'Making People Happy, Not Making Happy People': A Defense of the Asymmetry Intuition in Population Ethics (PhD thesis). Harvard University.

Fricke, F. (2002). Verschiedene Versionen des negativen Utilitarismus. *Kriterion*, 15, pp. 13-27.

Furnham, A. (2003). Belief in a just world: research progress over the past decade. *Personality and Individual Differences*, 34(5), pp. 795-817.

Future of Life Institute (2017). The Future of AI – What Do You Think? Retrieved from:
https://futureoflife.org/superintelligence-survey/

Garner, R. & O'Sullivan, S. (2016). *The Political Turn in Animal Ethics.* Lanham: Rowman & Littlefield International.

Geinster, D. (1998). Negative Utilitarianism - A Manifesto. Retrieved from:
http://web.archive.org/web/19981203093046/http://users.aol.com:80/geinster/NU.html

Geinster, D. (2012). The Amoral Logic of Anti-Hurt (Modified Negative Utilitarianism). Retrieved from:
https://web.archive.org/web/20120802034913/http://www.antihurt.com:80/

Gilbert, P. (1989). *Human Nature and Suffering.* Hove: Lawrence Erlbaum.

Giordano, J. & Boswell, M. (2009). *Pain Medicine: Philosophy, Ethics and Policy.* Yarnton, Oxon (UK) Chicago, IL: Linton Atlantic Books.

Gloor, L. (2016). Altruists Should Prioritize Artificial Intelligence. Retrieved from:
https://foundational-research.org/altruists-should-prioritize-artificial-intelligence/

Gloor, L. (2017). Tranquilism. Retrieved from:
https://foundational-research.org/tranquilism/

Gloor, L. (2018). Cause prioritization for downside-focused value systems. Retrieved from:
https://foundational-research.org/cause-prioritization-downside-focused-value-systems/

Gloor, L. & Mannino, A. (2016/2018). The Case for Suffering-Focused Ethics. Retrieved from:
https://foundational-research.org/the-case-for-suffering-focused-ethics/

Glover, J. (1977/1990). *Causing Death and Saving Lives.* London: Penguin.

Glover, J. (2000). *Humanity: A Moral History of the Twentieth Century.* New Haven, CT: Yale University Press.

Goodman, C. (2009). *Consequences of Compassion: An Interpretation and Defense of Buddhist Ethics.* Oxford: Oxford University Press.

Grace, K. (2012). Is it obvious that pain is very important? Retrieved from:
https://meteuphoric.com/2012/03/03/is-it-obvious-that-pain-is-very-important/

Greenberg, D. et al. (2018). Elevated empathy in adults following childhood trauma. *PLOS ONE*, 13(10), e0203886.

Griffin, D. & Speck, G. (2004). New evidence of animal consciousness. *Anim Cogn*, 7(1), pp. 5-18.

Griffin, J. (1979). Is Unhappiness Morally More Important Than Happiness? *The Philosophical Quarterly*, 29(114), pp. 47-55.

The Guardian. (2019). X-Woman? Gene mutation makes patient Jo Cameron feel no pain, scientists say. Retrieved from:
https://www.scmp.com/news/world/europe/article/3003585/x-woman-gene-mutation-makes-patient-jo-cameron-feel-no-pain

Habib, A. et al. (2019). Microdeletion in a FAAH pseudogene identified in a patient with high anandamide concentrations and pain insensitivity. *British Journal of Anaesthesia*, 123(2), pp. 249-253.

Halpern, C. (2002). *Suffering, Politics, Power: A Genealogy in Modern Political Theory*. Albany: State University of New York Press.

Hannah, B. (2001). *Yonder Stands Your Orphan*. New York: Grove Press.

Hanson, R. (1997). Are Beliefs Like Clothes? Retrieved from:
http://mason.gmu.edu/~rhanson/belieflikeclothes.html

Hanson, R. (2001/2006). Uncommon Priors Require Origin Disputes. Retrieved from:
http://citeseerx.ist.psu.edu/viewdoc/download?doi=10.1.1.63.4669&rep=rep1&type=pdf

Hanson, R. (2002). Why Meat is Moral, and Veggies are Immoral. Retrieved from:
http://mason.gmu.edu/~rhanson/meat.html

Hanson, R. (2007). Policy Tug-O-War. Retrieved from:
https://www.overcomingbias.com/2007/05/policy_tugowar.html

Hanson, R. (2012). Dear Young Eccentric. Retrieved from:
https://www.overcomingbias.com/2012/01/dear-young-eccentric.html

Hanson, R. (2014a). Look Hard, Then Steer Slightly. Retrieved from:
https://fqxi.org/data/essay-contest-files/Hanson_FQXI_Essay.pdf

Hanson, R. (2014b). Bias Is A Red Queen Game. Retrieved from:
http://www.overcomingbias.com/2014/06/bias-is-a-red-queen-game.html

Hanson, R. [Effective Altruism Global] (2015). Nature of Altruism Talk - Robin Hanson - EA Global 2015. Retrieved from:
https://www.youtube.com/watch?v=nIRvNxykvTQ

Hanson, R. (2019). Expand vs Fight in Social Justice, Fertility, Bioconservatism, & AI Risk. Retrieved from:
http://www.overcomingbias.com/2019/05/expand-vs-fight-social-justice-fertility-bioconservatism-and-ai-risk.html

Hanson, R. & Yudkowsky, E. (2013). The Hanson-Yudkowsky AI-Foom Debate. Machine Intelligence Research Institute. Retrieved from:
http://intelligence.org/files/AIFoomDebate.pdf

Harnad, S. (2016). My orgasms cannot be traded off against others' agony. *Animal Sentience*, 7(18).

Harris, S. (2004/2005). *The End of Faith: Religion, Terror, and the Future of Reason*. New York: W. W. Norton & Co.

Harris, S. (2010/2011). *The Moral Landscape: How Science Can Determine Human Values*. New York: Free Press.

Harris, S. (2011/2013). *Lying*. Opelousas, Louisiana: Four Elephants Press.

Harris, S. (2014a). *Waking Up: A Guide to Spirituality Without Religion*. New York: Simon & Schuster.

Harris, S. (2014b). #4 - The Path And The Goal A Conversation With Joseph Goldstein. Making Sense Podcast. Retrieved from: *https://samharris.org/podcasts/the-path-and-the-goal/*

Hawkins, K. (2013). Japanese Horror Story: The Torture of Junko Furuta. Retrieved from: *https://web.archive.org/web/20130222041410/http://www.trutv.com/library/crime/blog/article/japanese-horror-story-the-torture-of-junko-furuta/index.html*

Hedenius, I. (1964). *Livets Mening*. Stockholm: Aldus.

Hein, P. (2002). *Collected grooks*. 2 vols. Copenhagen: Borgen.

Henrich, N. & Henrich, J. (2007). *Why Humans Cooperate: A Cultural and Evolutionary Explanation*. Oxford New York: Oxford University Press.

Hewitt, S. (2008). Normative Qualia and a Robust Moral Realism (PhD thesis). New York University. Retrieved from: *http://www.stafforini.com/docs/Hewitt%20-%20Normative%20qualia%20and%20a%20robust%20moral%20realism.pdf*

Hiz, H. (1992). Praxiology, Society and Ethics. In Auspitz, J. et al. (eds.), *Praxiologies and the Philosophy of Economics*. New Brunswick, NJ: Transaction Publishers.

Hollander, E. (2006). Influence processes in leadership–followership: Inclusion and the idiosyncrasy credit model. In Hantula, D. (ed.), *Advances in Social and Organizational Psychology: A Tribute to Ralph Rosnow*. Mahwah, NJ: Lawrence Erlbaum Associates Publishers.

Holtug, N. (2004). Person-affecting Moralities. In Ryberg, J. & Tännsjö, T. (eds.), *The Repugnant Conclusion*. Dordrecht: Kluwer.

Horta, O. (2010a). Debunking the Idyllic View of Natural Processes: Population Dynamics and Suffering in the Wild. *Télos*, 17, pp. 73-88.

Horta, O. (2010b). What Is Speciesism? *Journal of Agricultural and Environmental Ethics*, 23, pp. 243-66.

Horta, O. [EffectiveAltruismCH] (2013a). Oscar Horta: Why animal suffering is overwhelmingly prevalent in nature. Retrieved from: *https://www.youtube.com/watch?v=cZ0XTofuGmY*

Horta, O. [Jean Pierre Froud] (2013b). Oscar Horta - About Strategies. Retrieved from: *https://www.youtube.com/watch?v=v_vsHlKZPFQ*

Horta, O. (2014). The Scope of the Argument from Species Overlap. *Journal of Applied Philosophy*, 31(2), pp. 142-154.

Horta, O. (2015). The Problem of Evil in Nature: Evolutionary Bases of the Prevalence of Disvalue. *Relations: Beyond Anthropocentrism*, 3(1), pp. 17-32.

Horta, O. (2016). Egalitarianism and Animals. *Between the Species*, 19(1), pp. 109-143.

Horta, O. (2017a). Population Dynamics Meets Animal Ethics: The Case for Aiding Animals in Nature. In Woodhall, A. & Garmendia da Trindade, G. (eds.), *Ethical and Political Approaches to Nonhuman Animal Issues*. Cham: Palgrave Macmillan.

Horta, O. (2017b). Animal Suffering in Nature: The Case for Intervention. *Environmental Ethics*, 39(3), pp. 261-279.

Horta, O. (2018). Discrimination Against Vegans. *Res Publica*, 24(3), pp. 359-373.

Horta, O. [Centre for Effective Altruism] (2019). Promoting Welfare Biology as the Study of Wild Animal Suffering. Retrieved from: *https://www.youtube.com/watch?v=GOuQ7gPIU7Q&*

Hume, D. (1751/2012). *An Enquiry Concerning the Principles of Morals*. Lexington, Ky: Maestro Reprints.

Hume, D. (1779/2002). *Dialogues Concerning Natural Religion*. Project Gutenberg. Retrieved from:
http://www.gutenberg.org/files/4583/4583-h/4583-h.htm

Hurford, P. (2014). You have a set amount of "weirdness points". Spend them wisely. Retrieved from:
https://www.lesswrong.com/posts/wkuDgmpxwbu2M2k3w/ you-have-a-set-amount-of-weirdness-points-spend-them-wisely

Hurka, T. (1983). Value and Population Size. *Ethics,* 93, pp. 496-507.

Hurka, T. (2010). Asymmetries in Value. *Nous,* 44(2), pp. 199-223.

Huxley, A. (1921). *Crome Yellow*. London: Chatto and Windus.

Iglesias, A. (2018). The overwhelming prevalence of suffering in Nature. *Revista de Bioética y Derecho,* 42, pp. 181-195.

Inmendham [graytaich0] (2011-2015). Best Work. YouTube playlist by graytaich0. Retrieved from:
https://www.youtube.com/watch?v=b1mJnEmjlLE&list=PLcm79oxph4sxzDfr2oH6tp Nij-YUH5dy3

Ishak, N. (2019). Meet Jo Cameron, The Woman Incapable Of Feeling Pain Or Stress. All That's Interesting. Retrieved from:
https://allthatsinteresting.com/jo-cameron

Jabr, F. (2018). It's Official: Fish Feel Pain. Smithsonian Magazine. Retrieved from:
https://www.smithsonianmag.com/science-nature/fish-feel-pain-180967764/

James, W. (1891/1958). The Moral Philosopher and the Moral Life. In Castell, A. (ed.), *Essays in Pragmatism*. New York: Hafner.

James, W. (1901). Letter on happiness to Miss Frances R. Morse. In James, H. (ed.) (1920). *Letters of William James*. Vol. 2. Boston: Atlantic Monthly Press.

Jayarava. (2012). Evil. Retrieved from:
http://jayarava.blogspot.com/2012/02/evil.html

Johnson, M. (2016). Principia Qualia. Retrieved from:
http://opentheory.net/PrincipiaQualia.pdf

Johnson, M. (2017). Why I think the Foundational Research Institute should rethink its approach. Retrieved from:
http://opentheory.net/2017/07/ why-i-think-the-foundational-research institute-should-rethink-its-approach/

Johnson, M. (2018). A Future for Neuroscience. Retrieved from:
https://opentheory.net/2018/08/a-future-for-neuroscience/

Johnson, N. & Mueller J. (2002). Updating the accounts: global mortality of the 1918-1920 "Spanish" influenza pandemic. *Bull Hist Med,* 76(1), pp. 105-115.

Johnson, S. (1774). *The patriot, addressed to the electors of Great Britain*. Dublin: E. Lynch.

Johnson, S. et al. (2019). Belief digitization: Do we treat uncertainty as probabilities or as bits? *Journal of Experimental Psychology: General*. Advance online publication. Retrieved from:
https://psycnet.apa.org/doiLanding?doi=10.1037%2Fxge0000720

Jules, M. (2019). Defending the Procreation Asymmetry with Conditional Interests. Retrieved from:
https://forum.effectivealtruism.org/posts/2RWQ4NrCEP7a4vzuW/ defending-the-procreation-asymmetry-with-conditional

Kagan, S. (1989). *The Limits of Morality*. Oxford New York: Clarendon Press Oxford University Press.
Kagan, S. (2013). Why Study Philosophy? *Frontiers of Philosophy in China*, 8(2), pp. 258-265.
Kagan, S. (2014). An Introduction to Ill-Being. *Oxford Studies in Normative Ethics*, 4, pp. 261-288.
Kahneman, D. (2011). *Thinking, Fast and Slow*. New York: Farrar, Straus and Giroux.
Kahneman, D. et al. (1993). When more pain is preferred to less: Adding a better end. *Psychological Science*, 4, pp. 401-405.
Kahneman, D. & Riis, J. (2005). Living, and thinking about it: Two perspectives on life. In Huppert, F. et al. (eds.), *The Science of Well-Being*. Oxford University Press.
Kaletsch, M. et al. (2014). Major depressive disorder alters perception of emotional body movements. *Front Psychiatry*, 5, 4.
Kant, I. (1785/2002). *Fundamental Principles of the Metaphysic of Morals*. Translated by Abbott, T. Project Gutenberg. Retrieved from:
http://www.gutenberg.org/files/5682/5682-h/5682-h.htm
Karlsen, D. (2013). Is God Our Benefactor? An Argument from Suffering. *Journal of Philosophy of Life*, 3, pp. 145-167.
Karnofsky, H. (2011). Why we can't take expected value estimates literally (even when they're unbiased). Retrieved from:
https://blog.givewell.org/2011/08/18/why-we-cant-take-expected-value-estimates-literally-even-when-theyre-unbiased/
Karnofsky, H. (2014). Sequence thinking vs. cluster thinking. Retrieved from:
https://blog.givewell.org/2014/06/10/sequence-thinking-vs-cluster-thinking/
Kaufman, S. (2018). What Would Happen If Everyone Truly Believed Everything Is One? Scientific American. Retrieved from:
https://blogs.scientificamerican.com/beautiful-minds/what-would-happen-if-everyone-truly-believed-everything-is-one/
Kelly, K. (2010). *What Technology Wants*. New York: Viking.
Kelly, P. J. (1990). *Utilitarianism and Distributive Justice: Jeremy Bentham and the Civil Law*. New York: Clarendon Press Oxford University Press.
Keown, D. (1992/2001). *The Nature of Buddhist Ethics*. Basingstoke, Hampshire, N.Y: Palgrave.
Kleinman, A. (1988). *The Illness Narratives: Suffering, Healing, and the Human Condition*. New York: Basic Books.
Kleinman, A. et al. (eds.) (1997). *Social Suffering*. Berkeley: University of California Press.
Klimecki, O. et al. (2013). Functional neural plasticity and associated changes in positive affect after compassion training. *Cereb Cortex*, 23(7), pp. 1552-1561.
Klocksiem, J. (2016). How to accept the transitivity of *better than*. *Philosophical Studies*, 173(5), pp. 1309-1334.
Knutsson, S. (2015a/2016). The 'Asymmetry' and Extinction Thought Experiments. Retrieved from:
https://foundational-research.org/the-asymmetry-and-extinction-thought-experiments/
Knutsson, S. (2015b/2020). The Seriousness of Suffering: Supplement. Retrieved from:
http://www.simonknutsson.com/the-seriousness-of-suffering-supplement
Knutsson, S. (2016a/2017). How Could an Empty World Be Better than a Populated One? Retrieved from:
https://foundational-research.org/how-could-an-empty-world-be-better-than-a-populated/

Knutsson, S. (2016b/2017). Measuring Happiness and Suffering. Retrieved from: *https://foundational-research.org/measuring-happiness-and-suffering/*

Knutsson, S. (2016c). Reducing Suffering Amongst Invertebrates Such As Insects. Retrieved from: *https://was-research.org/writing-by-others/reducing-suffering-amongst-invertebrates-insects/*

Knutsson, S. (2016d). What Is the Difference Between Weak Negative and Non-Negative Ethical Views? Retrieved from: *https://foundational-research.org/what-is-the-difference-between-weak-negative-and-non-negative-ethical-views/*

Knutsson, S. (2016e). Thoughts on Ord's "Why I'm Not a Negative Utilitarian". Retrieved from: *http://www.simonknutsson.com/thoughts-on-ords-why-im-not-a-negative-utilitarian*

Knutsson, S. (2016f). The One-Paragraph Case for Suffering-Focused Ethics. Retrieved from: *http://www.simonknutsson.com/the-one-paragraph-case-for-suffering-focused-ethics*

Knutsson, S. (2016g). Value Lexicality. Retrieved from: *https://foundational-research.org/value-lexicality/*

Knutsson, S. [Center on Long-Term Risk] (2017a). Simon Knutsson – Suffering-Focused Ethics and Effective Altruism. Retrieved from: *https://www.youtube.com/watch?v=2CfBcHii06w*

Knutsson, S. (2017b). Reply to Shulman's "Are Pain and Pleasure Equally Energy-Efficient?" Retrieved from: *http://www.simonknutsson.com/reply-to-shulmans-are-pain-and-pleasure-equally-energy-efficient/*

Knutsson, S. (2019a). The World Destruction Argument. *Inquiry*, DOI:10.1080/0020174X.2019.1658631.

Knutsson, S. (2019b). Many-valued logic and sequence arguments in value theory. Retrieved from: *https://www.simonknutsson.com/files/Many-valued_logic_sequence_arguments_value_theory.pdf*

Knutsson, S. (2019c). Lars Bergström on pessimism, ethics, consequentialism, Ingemar Hedenius, and quantifying well-being. Retrieved from: *https://www.simonknutsson.com/lars-bergstrom-pessimism-ethics-consequentialism-ingemar-hedenius*

Knutsson, S. (2019d). Epicurean ideas about pleasure, pain, good and bad. Retrieved from: *https://www.simonknutsson.com/epicurean-ideas-about-pleasure-pain-good-and-bad/*

Knutsson, S. & Munthe, C. (2017). A Virtue of Precaution Regarding the Moral Status of Animals with Uncertain Sentience. *Journal of Agricultural and Environmental Ethics*, 30(2), pp. 213-224. Draft version retrieved from: *https://foundational-research.org/virtue-precaution-regarding-moral-status-animals-uncertain-sentience/*

Kolak, D. (2004). *I Am You: The Metaphysical Foundations for Global Ethics*. Dordrecht Norwell, MA: Springer.

Korsgaard, C. (1989). Personal identity and the unity of agency: A Kantian response to Parfit. *Philosophy and Public Affairs*, 18(2), pp. 103-131.

Korsgaard, C. (2009). *Self-constitution: Agency, Identity, and Integrity*. Oxford New York: Oxford University Press.

Korsgaard, C. (2018). *Fellow Creatures: Our Obligations to the Other Animals*. New York, NY: Oxford University Press.

Kuhn, B. (2013). To stressed-out altruists. Retrieved from: *https://www.benkuhn.net/stress*

Kunda, Z. (1990). The case for motivated reasoning. *Psychological bulletin*, 108(3), pp. 480-498.

Laertius, D. (ca. 230/1925). *Lives of Eminent Philosophers, Volume II: Books 6-10*. Translated by Hicks, R. Cambrdige, MA: Harvard University Press.

Lampert, K. (2005). *Traditions of Compassion: From Religious Duty to Social Activism*. Basingstoke England New York: Palgrave Macmillan.

Lazari-Radek, K. & Singer, P. (2014). *The Point of View of the Universe: Sidgwick and Contemporary Ethics*. Oxford New York: Oxford University Press.

Le Guin, U. (1973/1993). *The Ones Who Walk Away from Omelas*. Mankato, Minn: Creative Education.

Leighton, J. (2011). *The Battle for Compassion: Ethics in an Apathetic Universe*. New York: Algora Pub.

Leighton, J. [Jonathan Leighton] (2015). The Battle for Compassion - a short film by Jonathan Leighton. Retrieved from: *https://www.youtube.com/watch?v=DBiKl_v5Mls*

Leighton, J. [Jonathan Leighton] (2017a). Guided Meditation for Activists. Retrieved from: *https://www.youtube.com/watch?v=D2YZew3Knj8*

Leighton, J. (2017b). Thriving in the Age of Factory Farming. Retrieved from: *https://medium.com/@jonleighton1/thriving-in-the-age-of-factory-farming-fbcca7121d67*

Leighton, J. (2019). OPIS, a think-and-do tank for an ethic based on the prevention of suffering. Retrieved from: *https://medium.com/@jonleighton1/opis-a-think-and-do-tank-for-an-ethic-based-on-the-prevention-of-suffering-eb2baa3d5619*

Leopardi, G. & Grennan, E. (1997). *Leopardi: Selected Poems*. Princeton, N.J: Princeton University Press.

Lerner, M. & Simmons, C. (1966). Observer's Reaction to the "Innocent Victim": Compassion or Rejection? *Journal of Personality and Social Psychology*, 4(2), pp. 203-210.

Lewis, G. (2016). Beware surprising and suspicious convergence. Retrieved from: *https://forum.effectivealtruism.org/posts/omoZDu8ScNbot6kXS/beware-surprising-and-suspicious-convergence*

Ligotti, T. (2011). *The Conspiracy against the Human Race: A Contrivance of Horror*. New York, NY: Hippocampus Press.

Lim, D. & DeSteno, D. (2016). Suffering and compassion: The links among adverse life experiences, empathy, compassion, and prosocial behavior. *Emotion*, 16(2), pp. 175-182.

Lodge, M. & Taber, C. (2013). *The Rationalizing Voter*. Cambridge: Cambridge University Press.

Loewy, E. (1991). *Suffering and the Beneficent Community: Beyond Libertarianism*. Albany: State University of New York Press.

Low, P. et al. (2012). The Cambridge Declaration on Consciousness. Retrieved from: *http://fcmconference.org/img/CambridgeDeclarationOnConsciousness.pdf*

MacAskill, W. (2015). *Doing Good Better: How Effective Altruism Can Help You Make a Difference*. New York, N.Y: Gotham Books.

MacAskill, W. (2017). Effective Altruism: Introduction. *Essays in Philosophy*, 18(1), pp. 1-5.

MacInnis, C & Hodson, G. (2017). It ain't easy eating greens: Evidence of bias toward vegetarians and vegans from both source and target. *Group Processes & Intergroup Relations*, 20(6), pp. 721-744.

Mancini, L. (1990). Riley-Day Syndrome, Brain Stimulation and the Genetic Engineering of a World Without Pain. *Medical Hypotheses*, 31, pp. 201-207.

Mandel, A. (2018). Why Nobel Prize Winner Daniel Kahneman Gave Up on Happiness. Haaretz. Retrieved from:
https://www.haaretz.com/israel-news/.premium.MAGAZINE-why-nobel-prize-winner-daniel-kahneman-gave-up-on-happiness-1.6528513

Mannino, A. [TEDx Talks] (2014). Our daily life and death decisions: Adriano Mannino at TEDxGundeldingen. Retrieved from:
https://www.youtube.com/watch?v=-4rh5L4iluw

Mannino, A. [Sentience Politics] (2015). Adriano Mannino: Effective Altruism for All Sentient Beings. Retrieved from:
https://www.youtube.com/watch?v=rFPqBJewI60

Mannino, A. [Sentience Politics] (2016). Adriano Mannino – Sentience Politics: Our Strategic Approach. Retrieved from:
https://www.youtube.com/watch?v=DBUsPgyXXm4

Mannino, A. [Talks at Google] (2017). Adriano Mannino: "Effective Altruism" | Talks at Google. Retrieved from:
https://www.youtube.com/watch?v=-lkrb20YGYw

Mannino, A. & Donnelly, R. [frei denken uni basel] (2014). Reducing Wild Animal Suffering. Retrieved from:
https://www.youtube.com/watch?v=4aa6g1y4l8I

Marino, G. & Marino, S. (2014). Paying Homage to the Silence of Suffering. In Green, R. & Palpant, N. (eds.), *Suffering and Bioethics*. Oxford New York, NY: Oxford University Press.

Markowski, K. & Roxburgh, S. (2019). "If I became a vegan, my family and friends would hate me:" Anticipating vegan stigma as a barrier to plant-based diets. *Appetite*, 135, pp. 1-9.

Marshall, C. (2018). *Compassionate Moral Realism*. New York: Oxford University Press.

Martin, M. (2007). *Albert Schweitzer's Reverence for Life: Ethical Idealism and Self-Realization*. Burlington: Ashgate Publishing Company.

Mathison, E. (2018). Asymmetries and Ill-Being (PhD thesis). University of Toronto. Retrieved from:
https://tspace.library.utoronto.ca/bitstream/1807/92027/3/Mathison_Eric_201811_PhD_thesis.pdf

Matlin, M. (2017). Pollyanna Principle. In Pohl, R. (ed.), *Cognitive Illusions: Intriguing Phenomena in Thinking, Judgment and Memory*. London New York: Routledge, Taylor & Francis Group.

Matlin, M. & Stang, D. (1978). *The Pollyanna Principle: Selectivity in Language, Memory, and Thought*. Cambridge, Mass: Schenkman Pub. Co.

Mayerfeld, J. (1996). The Moral Asymmetry of Happiness and Suffering. *Southern Journal of Philosophy*, 34, pp. 317-38.

Mayerfeld, J. (1999). *Suffering and Moral Responsibility*. New York Oxford: Oxford University Press.

Mayerfeld, J. (2008). In Defense of the Absolute Prohibition of Torture. *Public Affairs Quarterly*, 22(2), pp. 109-128.

Mayerfeld, J. (2016). *The Promise of Human Rights: Constitutional Government, Democratic Legitimacy, and International Law*. University of Pennsylvania Press.

McGonigal, K. (2012/2013). *The Willpower Instinct: How Self-Control Works, Why It Matters, and What You Can Do to Get More of It*. New York: Avery.

Meacham, C. (2012). Person-Affecting Views and Saturating Counterpart Relations. *Philosophical Studies*, 158, pp. 257-87.

Melzack, R. & Wall, P. (1982/1996). *The Challenge of Pain*. New York, USA: Penguin Books.

Mendola, J. (1990). An Ordinal Modification of Classical Utilitarianism. *Erkenntnis*, 33, pp. 73-88.

Mendola, J. (2006). *Goodness and Justice: A Consequentialist Moral Theory*. Cambridge University Press.

Mendola, J. (2014). *Human Interests: Or Ethics for Physicalists*. Oxford: Oxford University Press.

Metzinger, T. (2003). *Being No One: The Self-Model Theory of Subjectivity*. Cambridge, Mass: MIT Press.

Metzinger, T. (2009). *The Ego Tunnel: The Science of the Mind and the Myth of the Self*. New York: Basic Books.

Metzinger, T. (2016). Suffering. In Almqvist, K. & Haag, A. (eds.), *The Return of Consciousness*. Stockholm: Axel and Margaret Ax:son Johnson Foundation.

Metzinger, T. (2017). Benevolent Artificial Anti-Natalism (BAAN). Edge. Retrieved from: *https://www.edge.org/conversation/thomas_metzinger-benevolent-artificial-anti-natalism-baan*

Mill, J. S. (1859/2002). *On Liberty*. Mineola, NY: Dover Publications.

Mill, J. S. (1863/2007). *Utilitarianism*. Mineola, N.Y: Dover Publications.

Miller, G. (1996). Political peacocks. *Demos Quarterly*, 10, pp. 9-11.

Minson, J. & Monin, B. (2011). Do-Gooder Derogation: Disparaging Morally Motivated Minorities to Defuse Anticipated Reproach. *Social Psychological and Personality Science*, 3(2), pp. 200-207.

Mitchell, T. et al. (1997). Temporal Adjustments in the Evaluation of Events: The "Rosy View". *Journal of Experimental Social Psychology*, 33(4), pp. 421-448.

Moen, O. (2016a). The Ethics of Wild Animal Suffering. *Nordic Journal of Applied Ethics*, 10(1), pp. 91-104.

Moen, O. (2016b). An Argument for Hedonism. *Journal of Value Inquiry*, 50(2), pp. 267-281.

Moen, O. (2016c). An Argument for Intrinsic Value Monism. *Philosophica*, 44(4), pp.1375-1385.

Mogensen, A. (2011). Giving Without Sacrifice? The relationship between income, happiness, and giving. Giving What We Can Research. Retrieved from: *https://assets.ctfassets.net/dhpcfh1bs3p6/3jqEdXNDmg8SGAeOeC8KYo/63f9caa4de752b15c84455dc9025d537/giving-without-sacrifice.pdf*

Mood, A. & Brooke, P. (2010). Estimating the Number of Fish Caught in Global Fishing Each Year. Fishcount. Retrieved from: *http://fishcount.org.uk/published/std/fishcountstudy.pdf*

Mood, A. & Brooke, P. (2012). Estimating the Number of Farmed Fish Killed in Global Aquaculture Each Year. Fishcount. Retrieved from:
http://fishcount.org.uk/published/std/fishcountstudy2.pdf

Moor, M. [TEDx Talks] (2013). Impact through rationality. Retrieved from:
https://www.youtube.com/watch?v=PcWus1943K0

Moore, G. E. (1903/2004). *Principia Ethica*. Mineola, N.Y: Dover Publications.

Moore, J. H. (1906). *The Universal Kinship*. Chicago: Charles H. Kerr & Company.

Moore, J. H. (1907). *The New Ethics*. London: Ernest Bell, York House.

Morris, D. (1993). *The Culture of Pain*. Berkeley, Calif: University of California Press.

MOWE. (2018). #060 - The Curse of Existence (Prof. David Benatar). Retrieved from:
https://www.youtube.com/watch?v=y0Q59w8CY0ke&

Musk, E. (2018). Making Life Multi-Planetary. *New Space*, 6(1).

Nagel, T. (1986). *The View From Nowhere*. New York: Oxford University Press.

Narveson, J. (1973). Moral problems of population. *The Monist*, 57(1), pp. 62-86.

Natali, C. (2009). *Aristotle's Nicomachean Ethics, Book VII: Symposium Aristotelicum (Symposia Aristotelia) (Bk. 7)*. Oxford New York: Oxford University Press.

Neiman, S. (2002/2015). *Evil in Modern Thought: An Alternative History of Philosophy*. Princeton: Princeton University Press.

Newman, D. et al. (2020). Global reports of well-being overestimate aggregated daily states of well being. *The Journal of Positive Psychology*. Advance online publication. Retrieved from:
https://www.tandfonline.com/doi/full/10.1080/17439760.2020.1725608

Newman, G. & Cain, D. (2014). Tainted altruism: when doing some good is evaluated as worse than doing no good at all. *Psychol Sci*, 25(3), pp. 648-55.

Nietzsche, F. (1889/1997). *Twilight of the Idols*. Indianapolis, Ind: Hackett Pub.

Nisbett, R. & Wilson, T. (1977). The halo effect: Evidence for unconscious alteration of judgments. *Journal of Personality and Social Psychology*, 35(4), pp. 250-256.

Norcross, A. (2006). The Scalar Approach to Utilitarianism. In West, H. (ed.), *The Blackwell Guide to Mill's Utilitarianism*. Wiley-Blackwell.

Nordgren, L. et al. (2011). Empathy gaps for social pain: Why people underestimate the pain of social suffering. *Journal of Personality and Social Psychology*, 100(1), pp. 120-128.

Norwood B. & Murray, S. (2018). FooDS Food Demand Survey. Oklahoma State University. Retrieved from:
http://agecon.okstate.edu/files/january%202018.pdf

Nozick, R. (1974/2013). *Anarchy, State, and Utopia*. New York: Basic Books.

Nussbaum, M. (2001). *Upheavals of Thought: The Intelligence of Emotions*. Cambridge New York: Cambridge University Press.

Nyhus, P. et al. (2010). Human–tiger conflict over time. In Tilson, R. & Nyhus, P. (eds.), *Tigers of the world: The science, politics, and conservation of Panthera tigris* (2nd ed.). Burlington, Massachusetts. Academic Press.

Oesterheld, C. (2017). Multiverse-wide Cooperation via Correlated Decision Making. Retrieved from:
https://foundational-research.org/multiverse-wide-cooperation-via-correlated-decision-making/

Ohlsson, R. (1979). The Moral Import of Evil: On Counterbalancing Death, Suffering, and Degradation (PhD thesis). Stockholm University.

Ord, T. (2013). Why I'm Not a Negative Utilitarian. Retrieved from:
http://www.amirrorclear.net/academic/ideas/negative-utilitarianism/
Ord, T. (2015). Moral Trade. *Ethics*, 126, pp. 118-138.
Ortiz-Ospina, E. & Roser, M. (2019). Trust. Retrieved from:
https://ourworldindata.org/trust
Orwell, G. (1947). Lear, Tolstoy and the Fool. *Polemic*, 7.
Orwell, G. (1949). *Nineteen Eighty-Four*. London: Secker and Warburg.
Pandey, J. (ed.) (1998). *Gandhi and 21st Century*. New Delhi: Concept Pub. Co.
Panksepp, J. & Pasqualini, M. (2002). "Mindscoping" pain and suffering. *Behavioral and Brain Sciences*, 25(4), pp. 468-469.
Parfit, D. (1984/1987). *Reasons and Persons*. Oxford Oxfordshire: Clarendon Press.
Parfit, D. (1995). *Equality or Priority*. Lawrence: University of Kansas.
Parfit, D. (2011). *On What Matters*. Oxford New York: Oxford University Press.
Partington, C. (1838). *The British Cyclopedia of Biography: Containing the Lives of Distinguished Men of All Ages and Countries, with Portraits, Residences, Autographs, and Monuments, Volume 2*. London: WM. S. Orr, and Co., Amen Corner, Partenoster Row.
Pearce, D. (1995/2007). *The Hedonistic Imperative*. Retrieved from:
http://www.hedweb.com/hedab.htm
Pearce, D. (2005). The Pinprick Argument. Retrieved from:
http://utilitarianism.org/pinprick-argument.html
Pearce, D. (2007). The Abolitionist Project. Retrieved from:
https://www.abolitionist.com/
Pearce, D. (2008/2015). Quantum Ethics? Suffering in the Multiverse. Retrieved from:
https://www.abolitionist.com/multiverse.html
Pearce, D. (2009). Reprogramming Predators. Retrieved from:
http://www.hedweb.com/abolitionist-project/reprogramming-predators.html
Pearce, D. (2012). The Anti-Speciesist Revolution. Retrieved from:
https://www.hedweb.com/transhumanism/antispeciesist.html
Pearce, D. [Adam Ford] (2013). David Pearce - Effective Altruism - Phasing Out Suffering. Retrieved from:
https://www.youtube.com/watch?v=Yym0VzgXBGk
Pearce, D. (2015/2020). Some Quora Answers by David Pearce (2015-20). Retrieved from:
https://www.hedweb.com/quora/2015.html
Pearce, D. (2016). Compassionate Biology: How CRISPR-based "gene drives" could cheaply, rapidly and sustainably reduce suffering throughout the living world. Retrieved from:
https://www.gene-drives.com/
Pearce, D. (2017). *Can Biotechnology Abolish Suffering?* North Carolina: The Neuroethics Foundation.
Pearce, D. (2018). What is David Pearce's position on meta-ethics? Retrieved from:
https://www.quora.com/What-is-David-Pearces-position-on-meta-ethics
Perry, S. (2014). *Every Cradle Is a Grave: Rethinking the Ethics of Birth and Suicide*. Charleston, WV: Nine-Banded Books.
Peterson, J. (2018). *12 Rules for Life: An Antidote to Chaos*. Toronto: Random House Canada.

Peterson, J. & Benatar, D. (2018). The Renegade Report – Jordan B Peterson & David Benatar. Retrieved from:
http://cliffcentral.com/renegade-report/renegade-report-jordan-b-peterson-david-benatar/

Pinker, S. (2002). *The Blank Slate: The Modern Denial of Human Nature.* New York: Penguin.

Pinker, S. (2011). *The Better Angels of Our Nature: Why Violence Has Declined.* New York: Viking.

Pinker, S. (2018). *Enlightenment Now: The Case for Reason, Science, Humanism, and Progress.* New York: Viking, an imprint of Penguin Random House LLC.

Plato. (ca. 399 BC/2008). *The Apology.* Retrieved from:
http://www.gutenberg.org/files/1656/1656-h/1656-h.htm

Plato. (ca. 380 BC/2017). *The Republic.* Seattle: Amazon Classics.

Plous, S. (1993). *The Psychology of Judgment and Decision Making.* New York: McGraw-Hill.

Popper, K. (1945/2011). *The Open Society and Its Enemies.* London: Routledge.

Press, W. & Dyson, F. (2012a). Iterated Prisoner's Dilemma contains strategies that dominate any evolutionary opponent. *PNAS*, 109(26), pp. 10409-10413.

Press, W. & Dyson, F. (2012b). On "Iterated Prisoner's Dilemma Contains Strategies That Dominate Any Evolutionary Opponent". Edge. Retrieved from:
https://www.edge.org/conversation/william_h_press-freeman_dyson-on-iterated-prisoners-dilemma-contains-strategies-that

Pullman, D. (2002). Human dignity and the ethics and aesthetics of pain and suffering. *Theoretical Medicine and Bioethics*, 23(1), pp. 75-94.

Pummer, T. (2018). Spectrum arguments and hypersensitivity. *Philosophical Studies*, 175(7), pp. 1729-1744.

Putnam, H. (2002). *The Collapse of the Fact/Value Dichotomy and Other Essays.* Cambridge, MA: Harvard University Press.

Putnam, H. [SonytoBratsoni] (2012). The Fact/Value Dichotomy and its critics - Hilary Putnam. Retrieved from:
https://www.youtube.com/watch?v=wCTawI5hfEU

Rabinowicz, W. (2000). Kotarbinski's Early Criticism of Utilitarianism. *Utilitas*, 12, pp. 79-84.

Rabinowicz, W. (2003). Ryberg's Doubts About Higher and Lower Pleasures: Put to Rest? *Ethical Theory and Moral Practice*, 6(2), pp. 231-237.

Rai, T. & Holyoak, K. (2013). Exposure to moral relativism compromises moral behavior. *Journal of Experimental Social Psychology*, 49(6), pp. 995-1001.

Rawls, J. (1971/1999). *A Theory of Justice.* Cambridge, Massachusetts: The Belknap Press of Harvard University Press.

Rawls, J. (2001). *Justice as Fairness: A Restatement.* Cambridge, Mass: Harvard University Press.

Ray, G. (2017). How many neurons are there? Retrieved from:
https://eukaryotewritesblog.com/how-many-neurons-are-there/

Reed, A. & Carstensen, L. (2012). The theory behind the age-related positivity effect. *Front Psychol*, 3, 339.

Reese, J. (2016). The Animal-Free Food Movement Should Move Towards An Institutional Message. Retrieved from:
https://medium.com/@jacyreese/the-animal-free-food-movement-should-move-towards-an-institutional-message-534d7cd0298e

Reese, J. (2018). *The End of Animal Farming: How Scientists, Entrepreneurs, and Activists Are Building an Animal-Free Food System*. Boston: Beacon Press.
Reese, J. (2020). Institutional change and the limitations of consumer activism. *Palgrave Communications*, 6, 26.
Regan, T. (1983/2004). *The Case for Animal Rights*. Berkeley: University of California Press.
Resnik, D. (2000). Pain as a folk psychological concept: A clinical perspective. *Brain and Mind*, 1(2), pp. 193-207.
Ridley, M. (2010). *The Rational Optimist: How Prosperity Evolves*. New York: Harper.
Ritov, I. & Baron, J. (1990). Reluctance to vaccinate: omission bias and ambiguity. *Journal of Behavioral Decision Making*, 3, pp. 263-277.
Rogers, C. et al. (2008). Long-Term Effects of the Death of a Child on Parents' Adjustment in Midlife. *J Fam Psychol*, 22(2), pp. 203-211.
Rosling, H., Rosling, O. & Rönnlund, A. (2018). *Factfulness: Ten Reasons We're Wrong About the World—and Why Things Are Better Than You Think*. New York: Flatiron Books.
Rozin, P. & Royzman, E. (2001). Negativity Bias, Negativity Dominance, and Contagion. *Personality and Social Psychology Review*, 5(4), pp. 296-320.
Russell, B. (1954/2010). *Human Society in Ethics and Politics*. London: Routledge.
Ryder, R. (2001). *Painism: A Modern Morality*. London: Centaur.
Ryder, R. (2005). All beings that feel pain deserve human rights. The Guardian. Retrieved from:
https://www.theguardian.com/uk/2005/aug/06/animalwelfare
Ryder, R. (2006). *Putting Morality Back into Politics*. Exeter, UK Charlottesville, VA: Societas.
Ryder, R. (2009a). Painism Versus Utilitarianism. *Think*, 8, pp. 85-89.
Ryder, R. (2009b). Painism. In M. Bekoff (ed.), *Encyclopedia of Animal Rights and Animal Welfare*. Santa Barbara, Cal.: Greenwood Press.
Ryder, R. (2011/2017). *Speciesism, Painism and Happiness: A Morality for the 21st Century*. Exeter, UK: Andrews UK Ltd.
Saint Louis University (2008). How Poxviruses Such As Smallpox Evade The Immune System. ScienceDaily. Retrieved from:
https://www.sciencedaily.com/releases/2008/01/080131122956.htm
Salamon, A. & Rayhawk, S. (2009). Cached Selves. Retrieved from:
https://www.lesswrong.com/posts/BHYBdijDcAKQ6e45Z/cached-selves
Salt, H. (1914). *The Humanities of Diet*. Manchester: The Vegetarian Society.
Salt, H. (ed.) (1915). *Killing for Sport*. London: The Humanitarian League. London: G. Bell and Sons.
Salt, H. (1935). *The Creed of Kinship*. London: Constable & Co.
Sandberg, A. & Bostrom, N. (2008). Global Catastrophic Risks Survey. Technical Report, #2008-1, Future of Humanity Institute, Oxford University.
Scanlon, T. M. (1982). Contractualism and Utilitarianism. In Sen, A. & Williams, B. (eds.), *Utilitarianism and Beyond*. Cambridge: Cambridge University Press.
Scanlon, T. M. (1998). *What We Owe to Each Other*. Cambridge, MA: Harvard University Press.
Scarre, G. (1996). *Utilitarianism*. London New York: Routlege.
Scarry, E. (1985). *The Body in Pain: The Making and Unmaking of the World*. New York: Oxford University Press.

Schopenhauer, A. (1819/1966). *The World as Will and Representation*. 2 vols. New York: Dover.
Schopenhauer, A. (1840/2005). *The Basis of Morality*. New York: Dover Publications.
Schopenhauer, A. (1851/1970). *Essays and Aphorisms*. Harmondsworth, Eng: Penguin Books.
Schubert, S., Garfinkel, B., Cotton-Barrat, O. (2017). Considering Considerateness: Why communities of do-gooders should be exceptionally considerate. Retrieved from: *https://www.centreforeffectivealtruism.org/blog/considering-considerateness-why-communities-of-do-gooders-should-be/*
Schwarz, N. (1990). Feelings as information: Informational and motivational functions of affective states. In Higgins, E. & Sorrentino, R. (eds.), *The handbook of motivation and cognition: Foundations of social behavior*. New York: Guilford Press.
Schweitzer, A. (1933/2009). *Out of My Life and Thought: An Autobiography*. Baltimore, MD: Johns Hopkins University Press.
Sebo, J. [Centre for Effective Altruism] (2019). A utilitarian case for animal rights. Retrieved from: *https://www.youtube.com/watch?v=vELWCTgA9oA*
Sentience Institute (2017). Survey of US Attitudes Towards Animal Farming and Animal-Free Food October 2017. Retrieved from: *https://www.sentienceinstitute.org/animal-farming-attitudes-survey-2017*
Shapshay, S. (2019). *Reconstructing Schopenhauer's Ethics: Hope, Compassion, and Animal Welfare*. New York, NY: Oxford University Press.
Sharot, T. (2011). The optimism bias. *Current Biology*, 21(23), pp. 941-945.
Sharot, T. et al. (2007). Neural mechanisms mediating optimism bias. *Nature*, 450, pp. 102-105.
Sheikh, K. et al. (2011). Building the Field of Health Policy and Systems Research: Framing the Questions. *PLOS Medicine*, 8(8): e1001073.
Shiffrin, S. (1999). Wrongful Life, Procreative Responsibility, and the Significance of Harm. *Legal Theory*, 5, pp. 117-148.
Shriver, A. (2014). The Asymmetrical Contributions of Pleasure and Pain To Animal Welfare. *Cambridge Quarterly of Healthcare Ethics*, 23(2), pp. 152-162. Draft version retrieved from: *https://philarchive.org/archive/SHRTACv1*
Shulman, C. (2012). Are pain and pleasure equally energy-efficient? Retrieved from: *http://reflectivedisequilibrium.blogspot.com/2012/03/are-pain-and-pleasure-equally-energy.html*
Siderits, M. (2003/2016). *Personal Identity and Buddhist Philosophy: Empty Persons*. New York: Routledge.
Sidgwick, H. (1874/1981). *The Methods of Ethics*. Indianapolis: Hackett Pub. Co.
Sidgwick, H. (1879/2000). *Essays on Ethics and Method*. Oxford New York: Clarendon Press Oxford University Press.
Sikora, R. I. (1976). Negative Utilitarianism: Not Dead Yet. *Mind*, 85(340), pp. 587-588,
Simler, K. (2016). Crony Beliefs. Retrieved from: *https://meltingasphalt.com/crony-beliefs/*
Simler, K. & Hanson, R. (2018). *The Elephant in the Brain: Hidden Motives in Everyday Life*. New York, NY: Oxford University Press.
Singer, P. (1979/2011). *Practical Ethics*. New York: Cambridge University Press.

Singer, P. (1980). Right to Life? The New York Review of Books. Retrieved from: *http://www.nybooks.com/articles/1980/08/14/right-to-life/*

Singer, P. (1981/2011). *The Expanding Circle: Ethics, Evolution, and Moral Progress*. Princeton, NJ: Princeton University Press.

Singer, P. (2016). Are Insects Conscious? Project Syndicate. Retrieved from: *https://www.project-syndicate.org/commentary/are-insects-conscious-by-peter-singer-2016-05?barrier=accessreg*

Singer, P. [The Envision Team] (2018). Using Technology to Reduce Suffering | Peter Singer at Envision Conference 2018. Retrieved from: *https://www.youtube.com/watch?v=teGzSp5mybc&*

Singh, A. (2012). *Assessing anti-natalism: a philosophical examination of the morality of procreation*. University of Johannesburg.

Siu, R. (1988). Panetics: The Study of the Infliction of Suffering. *Journal of Humanistic Psychology*, 28(3), pp. 6-22.

Skowronski, J. et al. (2014). The Fading Affect Bias: Its History, Its Implications, and Its Future. *Advances in Experimental Social Psychology*, 49, pp. 163-218.

Slovic, P. (2007). "If I look at the mass I will never act": Psychic numbing and genocide. *Judgment and Decision Making*, 2(2), pp. 79-95.

Smart, R.N. (1958). Negative Utilitarianism. *Mind*, 67, pp. 542-543.

Smith, A. (1759/1976). *The Theory of Moral Sentiments*. Oxford: Oxford University Press.

Smolkin, M. (1989). *Understanding Pain: Interpretation & Philosophy*. Malabar, Fla: R.E. Krieger Pub. Co.

Soares, N. (2015-2016). The Replacing Guilt series. Retrieved from: *http://mindingourway.com/guilt/*

Sotala, K. & Gloor, L. (2017). Superintelligence as a Cause or Cure for Risks of Astronomical Suffering. *Informatica*, 41, pp. 501-514.

Speciesism: The Movie. (2012). Film. Directed by Mark Devries. Mark Devries Productions.

Spranca, M. et al. (1991). Omission and commission in judgment and choice. *Journal of Experimental Social Psychology*, 27, pp. 76-105.

Strodach, G. (1963). *The Philosophy of Epicurus*. Evanston, Illinois, United States: Northwestern University Press.

Sutton, J. (2009). Adaptive misbeliefs and false memories. *Behavioral and Brain Sciences*, 32(6), pp. 535-536.

Swanton, C. (2000). Compassion as a Virtue in Hume. In Jacobson, A. (ed.), *Feminist Interpretations of David Hume*. Pennsylvania State University Press.

Swanton, C. (2015). *The Virtue Ethics of Hume and Nietzsche*. Malden, MA: Wiley Blackwell.

Sözmen, B. [Sentience Politics] (2016). Beril Sözmen – Sentience and Metta Training in Buddhist Ethics. Retrieved from: *https://www.youtube.com/watch?v=YSpVKrmWcuE*

Sønderskov, K. & Dinesen, P. (2014). Danish Exceptionalism: Explaining the Unique Increase in Social Trust over the Past 30 Years. *European Sociological Review*, 30(6), pp. 782-795.

Tahir, S. (2012). Tolstoy's Ideology of Non-Violence: A Critical Appraisal. *Dialogue*, 7(4), pp. 347-363.

Taylor, S. (1989). *Positive Illusions: Creative Self-Deception and the Healthy Mind*. New York: Basic Books.

Taylor, S. (1991). Asymmetrical effects of positive and negative events: The mobilization-minimization hypothesis. *Psychological Bulletin*, 110, pp. 67-85.

Taylor, S. & Brown, J. (1988). Illusion and Well-Being: A Social Psychological Perspective on Mental Health. *Psychological Bulletin*, 103(2), pp. 193-210.

Thompson, S. (1999). Illusions of Control: How We Overestimate Our Personal Influence. *Current Directions in Psychological Science*, 8(6), pp. 187-190.

Todd, B. (2014). Tech startup founder. Retrieved from:
https://80000hours.org/career-reviews/tech-entrepreneurship/

Todd, B. (2016). *80,000 Hours: Find a fulfilling career that does good*. Oxford: Centre for Effective Altruism.

Todd, B. (2017a). Why and how to earn to give. Retrieved from:
https://80000hours.org/articles/earning-to-give/

Todd, B. (2017b). All the evidence-based advice we found on how to be successful in any job. Retrieved from:
https://80000hours.org/career-guide/how-to-be-successful/

Todd, W. (2012). A Selfless Response to an Illusory World: A Comparative Study of Śāntideva and Śaṅkara (PhD thesis). Lancaster University. Retrieved from:
http://eprints.lancs.ac.uk/61623/1/Warren_Todd.pdf

Tolstoy, L. (1894/2006). *The Kingdom of God Is Within You*. Mineola, N.Y: Dover Publications.

Tomasello, M. (2009). *Why We Cooperate*. Cambridge, Mass: MIT Press.

Tomasik, B. (2006a/2016). On the Seriousness of Suffering. Retrieved from:
http://reducing-suffering.org/on-the-seriousness-of-suffering/

Tomasik, B. (2006b/2016). Why Activists Should Consider Making Lots of Money. Retrieved from:
https://reducing-suffering.org/why-activists-should-consider-making-lots-of-money/

Tomasik, B. (2006c/2017). Lab Universes: Creating Infinite Suffering. Retrieved from:
https://reducing-suffering.org/lab-universes-creating-infinite-suffering/

Tomasik, B. (2007/2016). Why Maximize Expected Value? Retrieved from:
http://reducing-suffering.org/why-maximize-expected-value/

Tomasik, B. (2009a/2014). Do Bugs Feel Pain? Retrieved from:
http://reducing-suffering.org/do-bugs-feel-pain/

Tomasik, B. (2009b/2014). The Importance of Wild-Animal Suffering. Retrieved from:
https://foundational-research.org/the-importance-of-wild-animal-suffering/

Tomasik, B. (2009c/2014). The Predominance of Wild-Animal Suffering over Happiness: An Open Problem. Retrieved from:
http://reducing-suffering.org/wp-content/uploads/2014/10/wild-animals.pdf

Tomasik, B. (2009d/2014). How Many Wild Animals Are There? Retrieved from:
http://reducing-suffering.org/how-many-wild-animals-are-there/

Tomasik, B. (2010). Macro- vs. Micro-Optimization. Retrieved from:
https://reducing-suffering.org/macro-vs-micro-optimization/

Tomasik, B. (2011/2016). Risks of Astronomical Future Suffering. Retrieved from:
https://foundational-research.org/risks-of-astronomical-future-suffering/

Tomasik, B. (2012a/2016). Donating toward Efficient Online Veg Ads. Retrieved from:
http://reducing-suffering.org/donating-toward-efficient-online-veg-ads/

Tomasik, B. (2012b/2014). Suffering in Animals vs. Humans. Retrieved from:
https://reducing-suffering.org/suffering-in-animals-vs-humans/

Tomasik, B. (2013a/2017). How Would Catastrophic Risks Affect Prospects for Compromise? Retrieved from:
https://foundational-research.org/how-would-catastrophic-risks-affect-prospects-for-compromise/
Tomasik, B. (2013b/2018). Three Types of Negative utilitarianism. Retrieved from:
https://reducing-suffering.org/three-types-of-negative-utilitarianism/
Tomasik, B. (2013c/2015). Against Wishful Thinking. Retrieved from:
https://foundational-research.org/against-wishful-thinking/
Tomasik, B. (2013d/2014). Speculations on Population Dynamics of Bug Suffering. Retrieved from:
https://reducing-suffering.org/speculations-on-population-dynamics-of-bug-suffering/
Tomasik, B. (2013e/2014). Applied Welfare Biology and Why Wild-Animal Advocates Should Focus on Not Spreading Nature. Retrieved from:
https://reducing-suffering.org/applied-welfare-biology-wild-animal-advocates-focus-spreading-nature/
Tomasik, B. (2013f/2017). Omelas and Space Colonization. Retrieved from:
https://reducing-suffering.org/omelas-and-space-colonization/
Tomasik, B. (2013g/2016). Gains from Trade through Compromise. Retrieved from:
https://foundational-research.org/gains-from-trade-through-compromise/
Tomasik, B. (2013h/2016). The Horror of Suffering. Retrieved from:
http://reducing-suffering.org/the-horror-of-suffering/
Tomasik, B. (2013i/2017). Intention-Based Moral Reactions Distort Intuitions about Wild Animals. Retrieved from:
https://reducing-suffering.org/intention-based-moral-reactions-distort-intuitions-about-wild-animals/
Tomasik, B. (2013j/2018). Why Honesty is a Good Policy. Retrieved from:
https://reducing-suffering.org/why-honesty-is-a-good-policy/
Tomasik, B. (2013k/2019). Education Matters for Altruism. Retrieved from:
https://foundational-research.org/education-matters-for-altruism/
Tomasik, B. (2013l/2015). Differential Intellectual Progress as a Positive-Sum Project. Retrieved from:
https://foundational-research.org/differential-intellectual-progress-as-a-positive-sum-project/
Tomasik, B. (2013m/2015). Charity Cost-Effectiveness in an Uncertain World. Retrieved from:
https://foundational-research.org/charity-cost-effectiveness-in-an-uncertain-world/
Tomasik, B. (2013n/2016). Possible Ways to Promote Compromise. Retrieved from:
https://foundational-research.org/possible-ways-to-promote-compromise/
Tomasik, B. (2014a/2016). A Lower Bound on the Importance of Promoting Cooperation. Retrieved from:
https://foundational-research.org/a-lower-bound-on-the-importance-of-promoting-cooperation/
Tomasik, B. (2014b/2017). Why Charities Usually Don't Differ Astronomically in Expected Cost-Effectiveness. Retrieved from:
https://reducing-suffering.org/why-charities-dont-differ-astronomically-in-cost-effectiveness/
Tomasik, B. (2014c/2018). How Important Is Experiencing Suffering for Caring About Suffering? Retrieved from:
https://reducing-suffering.org/how-important-is-experiencing-suffering-for-caring-about-suffering/

Tomasik, B. (2014d/2017). Reasons to Be Nice to Other Value Systems. Retrieved from:
https://foundational-research.org/reasons-to-be-nice-to-other-value-systems/
Tomasik, B. (2014e/2018). Will Space Colonization Multiply Wild-Animal Suffering? Retrieved from:
https://reducing-suffering.org/will-space-colonization-multiply-wild-animal-suffering/
Tomasik, B. (2014f/2018). The Eliminativist Approach to Consciousness. Retrieved from:
https://foundational-research.org/the-eliminativist-approach-to-consciousness/
Tomasik, B. (2015a/2017). Are Happiness and Suffering Symmetric? Retrieved from:
https://reducing-suffering.org/happiness-suffering-symmetric/
Tomasik, B. (2015b/2016). The Importance of Insect Suffering. Retrieved from:
http://reducing-suffering.org/the-importance-of-insect-suffering/
Tomasik, B. (2015c). Should Altruists Focus on Reducing Short-Term or Far-Future Suffering? Retrieved from:
http://reducing-suffering.org/altruists-focus-reducing-short-term-far-future-suffering/
Tomasik, B. (2015d/2018). Reasons to Promote Suffering-Focused Ethics. Retrieved from:
http://reducing-suffering.org/the-case-for-promoting-suffering-focused-ethics/
Tomasik, B. (2015e). Is Utilitarianism Too Demanding? Retrieved from:
https://crucialconsiderations.org/ethics/demandingness/
Tomasik, B. [Brian Tomasik] (2016a). Preventing Extreme Suffering Has Moral Priority [graphic content in middle of video]. Retrieved from:
https://www.youtube.com/watch?v=RyA_eF7W02s
Tomasik, B. (2016b/2018). Strategic Considerations for Moral Antinatalists. Retrieved from:
https://reducing-suffering.org/strategic-considerations-moral-antinatalists/
Tomasik, B. [Brian Tomasik] (2016c). How Cravings Influence Happiness-vs.-Suffering Trades. Retrieved from:
https://www.youtube.com/watch?v=b44HmBLHI4w
Tomasik, B. (2016d/2017). Why I Don't Focus on the Hedonistic Imperative. Retrieved from:
https://reducing-suffering.org/dont-focus-hedonistic-imperative/
Tomasik, B. (2017a/2019). How Does Killing Animals Affect Total Suffering in a Simple, Food-Limited Population? Retrieved from:
https://reducing-suffering.org/how-does-killing-animals-affect-suffering/
Tomasik, B. (2017b). Against Setting Records. Retrieved from:
https://briantomasik.com/against-setting-records/
Tomasik, B. (2017c). How Likely Is a Far-Future Utopia? Retrieved from:
https://reducing-suffering.org/utopia/
Torres, P. (2018a). Space colonization and suffering risks: Reassessing the "maxipok rule". *Futures*, 100, pp. 74-85.
Torres, P. (2018b). Why We Should Think Twice About Colonizing Space. Nautilus. Retrieved from:
http://nautil.us/blog/why-we-should-think-twice-about-colonizing-space
Tranöy, K. (1967). Asymmetries in Ethics. *Inquiry*, 10, pp. 351-72.
Tye, M. (2016). *Tense Bees and Shell-Shocked Crabs: Are Animals Conscious?* New York, NY: Oxford University Press.
UNAIDS. (2019). Global HIV & AIDS statistics — 2019 fact sheet. Retrieved from:
https://www.unaids.org/en/resources/fact-sheet

Unger, P. (1996). *Living High and Letting Die: Our Illusion of Innocence*. New York: Oxford University Press.

VanDeVeer, A. D. (1979). On beasts, persons and the original position. *The Monist*, 62, pp. 368-377.

Vaughan, K. (2016). What the EA community can learn from the rise of the neoliberals. Retrieved from:
https://www.effectivealtruism.org/articles/ea-neoliberal/

Vermeulen, N. (2017). The choreography of a new research field: Aggregation, circulation and oscillation. *Environment and Planning A: Economy and Space*, 50(8), pp. 1764-1784.

Vinding, M. (2014a). *Why We Should Go Vegan*. Author.

Vinding, M. (2014b). *Why "Happy Meat" Is Always Wrong*. Author.

Vinding, M. (2014c). *A Copernican Revolution in Ethics*. Author.

Vinding, M. (2015a). *Speciesism: Why It Is Wrong and the Implications of Rejecting It*. Author.

Vinding, M. (2015b). *Anti-Natalism and the Future of Suffering: Why Negative Utilitarians Should not Aim for Extinction*. Author.

Vinding, M. (2015c). The Harm of Death. Retrieved from:
https://www.utilitarianism.com/magnus-vinding/harm-death.html

Vinding, M. (2016a). *The Speciesism of Leaving Nature Alone, and the Theoretical Case for "Wildlife Anti-Natalism"*. Author.

Vinding, M. (2016b). *Reflections on Intelligence*. Author.

Vinding, M. (2016c). Animal advocates should focus on antispeciesism, not veganism. Retrieved from:
https://sentience-politics.org/animal-advocates-focus-antispeciesism-not-veganism/

Vinding, M. (2017a). *What Should We Do? Essays on Cause Prioritization and Fundamental Values*. Author.

Vinding, M. (2017b). *You Are Them*. Author.

Vinding, M. (2017c). The future of growth: near-zero growth rates. Retrieved from:
https://foundational-research.org/the-future-of-growth-near-zero-growth-rates/

Vinding, M. (2017d). Notes on the Utility of Anti-Speciesist Advocacy. Retrieved from:
https://magnusvinding.com/2017/10/24/notes-on-the-utility-of-anti-speciesist-advocacy/

Vinding, M. (2017e). Short-Term vs. Long-Term EA Focus Depends on Annual Extinction Probability. Retrieved from:
https://magnusvinding.files.wordpress.com/2019/06/extinction2.pdf

Vinding, M. (2017f). Suffering, Infinity, and Universe Anti-Natalism. Retrieved from:
https://magnusvinding.com/2017/12/01/suffering-infinity-and-universe-anti-natalism/

Vinding, M. (2017g). A Contra AI FOOM Reading List. Retrieved from:
https://magnusvinding.com/2017/12/16/a-contra-ai-foom-reading-list/

Vinding, M. (2018a). *Effective Altruism: How Can We Best Help Others?* North Carolina: The Neuroethics Foundation.

Vinding, M. (2018b). "The Physical" and Consciousness: One World Conforming to Different Descriptions. Retrieved from:
https://magnusvinding.com/2018/04/25/the-physical-and-consciousness-one-world-conforming-to-different-descriptions/

Vinding, M. (2018c). *The Nature of Mathematics Given Physicalism*. Author.

Vinding, M. (2018d). The Endeavor of Reason. Retrieved from:
https://magnusvinding.com/2018/07/09/the-endeavor-of-reason/

Vinding, M. (2018e). Darwinian Intuitions and the Moral Status of Death. Retrieved from:
https://magnusvinding.com/2018/08/10/darwinian-intuitions-and-the-moral-status-of-death/

Vinding, M. (2018f). Why I Used to Consider the Absence of Sentience Tragic. Retrieved from:
https://magnusvinding.com/2018/08/19/why-i-used-to-consider-absence-tragic/

Vinding, M. (2018g). *In Defense of Nuance.* Author.

Vinding, M. (2018h). Moral Circle Expansion Might Increase Future Suffering. Retrieved from:
https://magnusvinding.com/2018/09/04/moral-circle-expansion-might-increase-future-suffering/

Vinding, M. (2018i). Why Altruists Should Perhaps Not Prioritize Artificial Intelligence: A Lengthy Critique. Retrieved from:
https://magnusvinding.com/2018/09/18/why-altruists-should-perhaps-not-prioritize-artificial-intelligence-a-lengthy-critique/

Vinding, M. (2018j). Narrative Self-Deception: The Ultimate Elephant in the Brain? Retrieved from:
https://magnusvinding.com/2018/09/27/narrative-self-deception-the-ultimate-elephant-in-the-brain/

Vinding, M. (2018k). Is AI Alignment Possible? Retrieved from:
https://magnusvinding.com/2018/12/14/is-ai-alignment-possible/

Vinding, M. (2019). Reducing Extreme Suffering for Non-Human Animals: Enhancement vs. Smaller Future Populations? *Between the Species*, 23(1), 8.

Vinding, M. (2020a). Lexical views without abrupt breaks. Center for Reducing Suffering. Retrieved from:
http://centerforreducingsuffering.org/lexical-views-without-abrupt-breaks/

Vinding, M. (2020b). Clarifying lexical thresholds. Center for Reducing Suffering. Retrieved from:
http://centerforreducingsuffering.org/clarifying-lexical-thresholds/

Vinding, M. (forthcoming). Anti-Natalism and Reducing Suffering: A Consequentialist Critique of Human Anti-Natalism.

Vrselja, Z. et al. (2019). Restoration of brain circulation and cellular functions hours post-mortem. *Nature*, 568, pp. 336-343.

Walker, A. D. M. (1974). Negative Utilitarianism. *Mind*, 83, pp. 424-28.

Walker, R. & Skowronski, J. (2009). The Fading affect bias: But what the hell is it for? *Applies Cognitive Psychology*, 23(8), pp. 1122-1136.

Weng, H. et al. (2018). Visual Attention to Suffering After Compassion Training Is Associated With Decreased Amygdala Responses. *Front Psychol*, 9, 771.

White, M. (2010). Necrometrics: Estimated Totals for the Entire 20th Century. Retrieved from:
http://necrometrics.com/all20c.htm

Wiblin, R. & Lempel, H. (2018). Ways people trying to do good accidentally make things worse, and how to avoid them. Retrieved from:
https://80000hours.org/articles/accidental-harm/

Wilkinson, I. (2005). *Suffering: A Sociological Introduction.* Cambridge, UK Malden, MA: Polity.

Wilkinson, I. & Kleinman, A. (2016). *A Passion for Society: How We Think About Human Suffering.* Oakland, California: University of California Press.

Wilkinson, R. & Pickett, K. (2009/2011). *The Spirit Level: Why Greater Equality Makes Societies Stronger.* New York: Bloomsbury Press.

Witwicki, K. & Greig, K. (2018). Animal Advocacy Strategies: Technology vs. Social Change. EA Global 2018: San Francisco. Retrieved from: *https://www.effectivealtruism.org/articles/ea-global-2018-animal-advocacy/*

Winsler, A. et al. (2015). Sleepless in Fairfax: The Difference One More Hour of Sleep Can Make for Teen Hopelessness, Suicidal Ideation, and Substance Use. *Journal of Youth and Adolescence*, 44, pp. 362-378.

Wolf, C. (1996). Social Choice and Normative Population Theory: A Person Affecting Solution to Parfit's Mere Addition Paradox. *Philosophical Studies*, 81, pp. 263-282.

Wolf, C. (1997). Person-Affecting Utilitarianism and Population Policy. In Heller, J. & Fotion, N. (eds.), *Contingent Future Persons.* Dordrecht Boston: Kluwer Academic Publishers. Retrieved from: *https://jwcwolf.public.iastate.edu/Papers/JUPE.HTM*

Wolf, U. (2015). How Schopenhauer's ethics of compassion can contribute to today's ethical debate. Translated by Tuider, J. *Quaderns de Filosofia,* 55, pp. 41-49.

World Health Organization. (2019). Children: reducing mortality. World Health Organization. Retrieved from: *https://www.who.int/news-room/fact-sheets/detail/children-reducing-mortality*

Xiao, Q. et al. (2015). Experiencing Physical Pain Leads to More Sympathetic Moral Judgments. *PLOS ONE,* 10(10): e0140580.

Young, L. & Durwin, A. (2013). Moral realism as moral motivation: The impact of meta-ethics on everyday decision-making. *Journal of Experimental Social Psychology*, 49(2), pp. 302-306.

Yudkin, D. et al. (2018). Actions speak louder than outcomes in judgments of prosocial behavior. *Emotion.* Advance online publication. *http://dx.doi.org/10.1037/emo0000514*

Zapffe, P. (1933/2004). The Last Messiah. Translated by Tangenes, G. *Philosophy Now*, 45.

Ziesche, S. & Yampolskiy, R. (2019a). Do No Harm Policy for Minds in Other Substrates. *Journal of Evolution and Technology*, 29(2), pp. 1-11.

Ziesche, S. & Yampolskiy, R. (2019b). Towards AI Welfare Science and Policies. *Big Data Cogn. Comput.*, 3(1), 2.

Printed in Great Britain
by Amazon